# RIGHT BETWEEN THE EARS

ADVANCE PRAISE FOR THE BOOK

'*Right between the Ears* offers a fascinating insight into the world of branding. After reading this book your brain will never look at brands the same way again'—Martin Lindstrom, *New York Times* bestselling author of *Buyology*, *Small Data* and *The Ministry of Common Sense*

'*Right between the Ears* should be mandatory reading for brand managers, product managers, CMOs and consumer business leaders. Easy-to-follow case examples illustrate the importance of understanding human psychology and why people behave the way they do. In a world where brands and corporations need to have a sense of purpose to build lasting businesses and motivate their employees, the ethical considerations framework (canonical, categorical, sunshine) should be on every marketer's desktop'—Titi Cole, head of Global Consumer Banking Operations, Citigroup

'This book shook the very foundations of my decades in brand management; and meanwhile the answers were always there, "Right between the Ears". Through a combination of fascinating brain science and rich real-world examples, Dayal reinvents the art and science of brand building'—Gina Boswell, former president, Unilever US Customer Development, and EVP chairman, Unilever UK and Ireland

'For decades, marketing professionals have been like Formula One drivers racing around the course with blindfolds on. We've tried to change the way consumers think without knowing how they really think. By taking us deep into brain science, Sandeep Dayal's new book lets us drive with our eyes open. *Right between the Ears* contains the most important advice given to marketing professionals in decades'—Rajan Anandan, managing director, Sequoia Capital India, and former vice president, Google India and SEA

'Brand-building is the X factor that will distinguish tomorrow's unicorns and superstars from the rest. However, the knowledge and skills underlying the development of iconic brands remains something of a mystery. Sandeep Dayal's book is a tour de force for it deftly describes how brain science—psychology, neuroscience and behavioural economics—is revolutionizing the art and science of branding and brand-building. Entrepreneurs and corporate managers would start with a distinct advantage if the ideas espoused here are reflected in their playbooks'—Ram Shivakumar, adjunct professor of economics and strategy, Booth School of Business, University of Chicago

'*Right between the Ears* makes you think, feel and see differently and provides actionable ways on how to truly unleash the power of brands in ways that marry art and science to gain a sustainable edge. This is a must-read for every marketer in the world'—Rishad Tobaccowala, author of *Restoring the Soul of Business*, and former chief growth officer, Publicis Groupe

'*Right between the Ears* is a timely road map for helping successful marketers take their work to the next level. We have always known that all brand purchases happen in the brain, sometimes in an instant and sometimes over years. Sandeep's book is a great guide on how marketers today can simplify the complex working of the brain into actionable insights and executable strategies. I would recommend the book to every marketer and consumer specialist. It will make them better professionals for sure'—Vipul Prakash, chief operating officer, MakeMyTrip, and former chief marketing officer, PepsiCo India

'In yesteryears, marketers played the game by the motivation and need-state framework. But in an age of hyper-competition, marketers need to find deeper anchors which keep their brands relevant and on top. Sandeep, in his book *Right between the Ears*, brings out what these new anchors are with vivid intensity. Simply put, they are behavioural insights, crafted from a precise understanding of the moorings of the consumer mind, which can be replicated globally to make brands surge across geographies. A new way to think for marketers to keep the zing in their brands going'—Vineet Kapila, founder, Goodcounsel, LLP, and former global head, Main Stream Spirits, Diageo

'In times when the marketing practice has grown increasingly tactical, it's heartening to read a marketing book that addresses the core issue of understanding the mind and shaping the behaviour of a consumer. As online marketers chase digital likes, shares and follows, and offline marketers optimize media and shelf space, this book offers practical advice on maximizing space where it matters most: "Right between the Ears"! Sandeep's book harvests the latest in brain sciences to help real-world practitioners unlock the conscious and subconscious keys to lure consumers to their brands. Easily, the most powerful marketing book to come out in decades!'—Lloyd Mathias, former APAC marketing head, HP, and CMO, Motorola South Asia

'Sandeep has woven a rich tapestry that takes the reader through a journey of discovery—where advances in brain sciences are interwoven with brands to provide deep insights on why people make the choices they do. This is a book rich in theory and practical illustrations, lucidly articulated to engage and enrich. It is wonderful to see the many facets of cognition come to life in this path-breaking work'—Vinita Bali, non-executive director and former global C-suite executive at Coca-Cola, Cadbury and Britannia

'Impressive depth and rigour, with excellent insights and practical lessons!'—Sanjay Khosla, senior fellow, Kellogg School of Management, Northwestern University, and former president, Mondelez International

'Sandeep has put together an amazing wealth of knowledge here—brand leaders better read this because the rest of the market is going to exactly do that and act on it to challenge them! Wish I had this book to guide me twenty years ago'—Raghav Prasad, division president, Sub-Saharan Africa, Mastercard

'*Right between the Ears* is a true practitioner's guide. It artfully unravels the process of building epic brands by combining the knowledge of psychology, neuroscience and human behaviour with real-world testing to present an entirely fresh and practical approach!'—Hemant Malik, divisional chief executive, Foods, ITC Limited

'A treasure trove of new insights into how to build a brand. Wish I had this knowledge early in my career'—Micky Pant, former CEO, Yum Restaurants International

'An important work that throws light on hidden mental processes. Behind intuition and witchcraft, there lurks a method in brand-building. Gripping stuff'—Sanjeev Aga, former MD, Idea Cellular

'Undoubtedly, a down-to-earth eye-opener! Highly recommended for business executives who want to compete more effectively for the demanding consumer of today. Dayal's insights, when applied across the board, well beyond the marketing enclave, can have a clear impact on not only the brand but also the customer's experience of the company and its products'—Jorge Alfaro Lara, former head, Consumer Bank, Banco Santander Mexico

'This brand marketer's guide to the consumers' mind is chock-full of vivid anecdotes that will help you build brands that glide into consumers' minds, that stick and that generate enduring dividends. Read it fast, then again, slowly'—Niraj Dawar, Professor Emeritus Marketing, Ivey Business School, Western University, Canada, and author of *TILT: Shifting Your Strategy from Products to Consumers*

# RIGHT BETWEEN THE EARS

## HOW TO USE BRAIN SCIENCE TO BUILD EPIC BRANDS

SANDEEP DAYAL

PORTFOLIO
PENGUIN
An imprint of Penguin Random House

PORTFOLIO

USA | Canada | UK | Ireland | Australia
New Zealand | India | South Africa | China

Portfolio is part of the Penguin Random House group of companies whose addresses can be found at global.penguinrandomhouse.com

Published by Penguin Random House India Pvt. Ltd
4th Floor, Capital Tower 1, MG Road,
Gurugram 122 002, Haryana, India

Penguin Random House India

First published in Portfolio by Penguin Random House India 2021



10 9 8 7 6 5 4 3 2

The views and opinions expressed in this book are the author's own and the facts are as reported by him which have been verified to the extent possible, and the publishers are not in any way liable for the same.

ISBN 9780670094929

For sale in the Indian subcontinent only

Typeset in Adobe Caslon Pro by Manipal Technologies Limited, Manipal
Printed at Replika Press Pvt. Ltd, India



www.penguin.co.in

*To all my teachers,*
*for what I have become*

# Contents

# Part One

# How Brain Science
# Is Revolutionizing Branding

# Introduction: Brands That Rock

Epic brands in the marketing sphere and chartbusters in the music world have one thing in common. No one really seems to know how to make one. They seem to come out of nowhere, like sweet accidents that rock our worlds.

Or do they?

Take the recent hit, 'Dance Monkey', by Toni Watson, known professionally as the artist Tones and I.

I like its words because they have exactly the kind of effect I want my brands to have on consumers. They speak of the trance-like hold that some street dancers can have on bystanders, when neither they nor the performer can let go of the moment. Who knows what they see, hear and feel? They just don't want the music to stop.

Yet, even Watson's managers warned her not to expect too much from the song. After all, she had spent a mere thirty minutes creating the number. Maybe it could do well with live audiences but never be a big radio hit, they thought. Well, that was before it went to number one on the charts in twenty countries, was streamed 1.1 billion times on Spotify and viewed on YouTube 700 million times.

As a busker living out of her van in Byron Bay, near Brisbane, Toni had struggled for recognition of her music beyond the streets of the small coastal town. The song itself is like nothing else actually, sung in a sort of syncopated, helium-tinged voice, with a '70s synth and thumping bass. Yet, every time she sang it in the streets, no one would just walk by. They would stop, listen, tap their feet and some danced. Locals and tourists, young and old.

It is hard to tell when a song comes together like that. But when it does, everything about it is just right —the voice, the lyrics, the beat and the bass. No one knows what that secret sauce behind a number one hit is. But we know something about it makes our brains rock.

And that is what *cognitive brands* do. Like 'Dance Monkey', they stop us dead in our tracks, and we can't walk away from them. Until now, designing iconic brands was just as much of a mystery as composing a chartbusting rock anthem. Advances in brain sciences have changed all of that, and we now know a lot about shaping consumer choice and behaviour. We see that *brands that rock our worlds are those that work the way our brain does. They hold the conscious and subconscious keys that unlock the sensations of experiences and fantasies stored in our minds, to make consumers happier and lure them to the brand.* We still don't know much about creating head-bashing rock anthems, but thanks to recent advances in brain sciences, we are a lot smarter when it comes to making hit brands.

In this book, I will show you what cognitive brands are, what's in them and how you, as a practising marketer, can build them. But before I do that, let me press the rewind key and take you back to where I began my journey into the brain science behind these brands.

## From the Ashes of a Boom and Bust

In January 2000, I worked at McKinsey's Chicago office in the digital marketing practice as an associate principal, a respectably senior grunt. On one particularly unrepentant Friday evening, with skies of molten grey, most people had left the office for the day. And yet, I sat glued to my desk. Something was very wrong.

Those were heady times, and the first dot-com wave was in a drunken swell. The NASDAQ had doubled in value just in the prior year. Traditional offline businesses felt like they were on the sinking end of an existential crisis and were clamouring to be on the Web. Even at McKinsey, many of the brightest minds jumped ship to launch their own start-ups in their parents' grungy basements. Venture capital funding was available on demand to anyone with the artistry to sketch out an idea on the requisite coffee-stained napkin.

Amid this feeding frenzy, I was sweating nervously over the reports trickling in from the field. My clients, who had invested heavily into building slick websites, griped that consumers were not buying their brands as quickly as they had thought, and that their sales were nowhere near the exponential growth rates needed to justify the sky-high stock market valuations for such companies. As the anointed tech marketer at McKinsey, it fell upon me to sniff out the answer. But it was too late already. Businesses began to fall to the earth like swatted flies from their skyward perches; among them, storied brands like AOL, Webvan (online groceries), Pets.com, Wingspan (bank), eToys, Flooz.com and Esurance.com to name just a few. In the ensuing eighteen-month bloodbath, the NASDAQ would fall by more than 50 per cent, erasing any monetary trace of the first Internet bubble.

In the following months, I travelled across the United States, speaking to many different Joe-and-Jane consumers. Some were buying a lot online and others not very much. Some used to buy a lot and then just stopped and vice versa. 'Tell me why? What happened? Tell me how?' I asked them. In 2002, I co-wrote an article with David Court that presented what we believed was the answer from our autopsy of the fallen kings: *Consumers were simply not ready to go online*! It wasn't enough for brands to have a value proposition—to say that they were better, cheaper or more convenient. Brands needed a serious strategy for changing people's minds and attitudes about shopping online. The article 'Beyond Behavioral Bounds' was published in *Marketing Management*, a publication of the American Marketing Association.[1] It noted the dilemma as follows:

> A new riddle confronts multichannel marketers: Why is it that even consumers who are fully aware of the benefits of shopping online still fail to do so? Why does a person wait patiently in line while his grocery store clerk completes a price check on the mystery vegetable being bought by the person ahead in line—when he could have his groceries delivered to his home? Why does he continue to buy and write checks and buy and lick stamps to mail bills—when he could use free bill paying services from an online bank? The answer to unlocking this second wave of consumers, lies not in redesigning the online value proposition or advertising more, but in resolving the mysteries that percolate at the intersection of good marketing and consumer behavioral psychology.

In the article, we went on to outline ways to unshackle consumers from their behavioral chains through what we dubbed 'tactical accelerators'. One such tactic, christened 'Invisible Decisioners', was described as follows: 'In a world of proliferating products and features, many consumers simply feel ill-equipped to make decisions. Rather than scare them off with a lot of options, marketers should instead reduce stress by choosing invisibly for them. The real trick is knowing when to give consumers choice and control and when to take it away.' As an example, we pushed banks to automatically sign up customers for online payments to their utility companies, the identities of which could be ascertained automatically by address.

Even then, seventeen years back, this really wasn't a stretch. After all, the banks already did enrol customers for debit/ATM cards automatically. Unknown to us at the time, the University of Chicago economist Richard Thaler was working on very similar idea in the arena of public policy, which he ultimately described as 'Libertarian Paternalism'—not limiting choices available to people (preserving liberty) while invisibly engineering their environment to help them make better choices for themselves (acting a bit like big brother). Thaler's behavioural theories, published in his widely acclaimed book *Nudge*, are familiar to many managers today.

Another tactical accelerator that we uncovered in our research was called 'Viral Advocacy'. Today, peer reviews are among the biggest drivers of online sales, and viral advocacy has led to the rise of an industry of influencers who, on Instagram and YouTube, decide the fate of many online and offline brands. As a marketer, I was hooked; it was the start of my obsession with solving the mysteries of the consumer mind through behavioural sciences.

## Frozen Connections

Fast-forward ten years. In 2010, my company, Cerenti, was working in Mexico with Scotiabank on their credit card portfolio. Consumers held credit cards from many different banks, and thus we wanted to understand which ones wound up in a person's wallet. Soon enough, in one of our focus groups, we bumped into Jose Moreno, a used-car salesman, who confided that his favourite card, the one with the fattest loan balances, was *not* in his wallet at all. In fact, it was frozen into an ice cube and buried deep inside the freezer at his home. This way, he explained, whenever his wife and he were tempted to buy something impulsively, they would need to trudge back home and thaw out the card. In those intervening few hours, the urge would hopefully pass. '*En serio* (really)?' I asked, as scribes on my team struggled to take appropriate notes. 'Dead serious, amigo!' was the response. 'Wouldn't it be better to just leave the card in the wallet and count one hundred sheep or something?' I countered. 'Nope,' Jose assured me, 'I have tried that. Only the ice cube works.'

Gradually, we understood that several customers viewed their credit card as a kind of person, a 'best friend' that could become 'the fiend from hell' at the drop of a dime. They wanted to be responsible but often could not help being tempted by the monster TV or chocolate fountain on sale. The learning for us was that consumers had very different tendencies for action. Some in the exact same situation would do nothing; and others would go ahead and do something entirely irresponsible. We discuss this later in the book as the personal conative energy in each one of us.

'Conators' are a fascinating part of cognitive brands and lead consumers from indecision to purchase. The answer for Jose-like customers was to offer a card product that allowed them to regulate their own buying behaviour. Large purchases could trigger a hold, requiring the customer to call a toll-free number and speak to a service representative for its release. The process delay was as good as an ice cube melting or better.

During the call, they could also be informed about the impact on their minimum monthly payment should they proceed with the purchase. Nowadays, all that can be done automatically with a text message, but few card companies provide such a service.

If marketers have been slow to understand that these are not behavioural quirks but predictable human tendencies and reflections of how the human brain works, confidence tricksters are fully up to speed. In one common case, the play action runs as follows. Jack 'Works-All-Day-at-Starbucks-Instead-of-Office' is happily sipping his coffee and plugging away on his laptop. Peggy Steel plops herself in the adjacent couch with her best 'I'm-so-harmless' smile. After half an hour or so, she asks him for a teeny favour, 'Could you watch my laptop while I go use the little girl's room?' He obliges. Another Grande Mocha Latte later, Jack needs to run to the little boy's room for his turn at biologic relief. Of the twenty-odd customers in the house, you guessed it, he asks Peggy to keep watch on his stuff. After all, she owes him, right? Jack returns ten minutes later to find nary a whiff of Peggy or his laptop anywhere.

This tactic relies on a behavioural factor called the reciprocity bias to work. People buy the brands they trust, but trust is a funny thing. Think for a moment. Would you leave your computer with a random stranger at Starbucks? Would you leave it if they had asked you to watch theirs? If the laptop costs \$1000 to replace, would you leave ten crisp \$100 dollar bills with a stranger at Starbucks to watch for you? Yet, these are all the same scenarios. If you set your mind to studying common crooks, you would learn a lot about the little-known cracks in human behaviour and how to work them to your advantage. We will learn later how cognitive brands can use 'vibes' to forge deep bonds with consumers so that they embrace their brand propositions.

## The March of Cognitive Sciences

Even as I was searching for ways to disentangle the mysteries of consumer behaviour in my work with clients, the news, elsewhere, was really good. Brain scientists around the world were busy. Lots of work was going on in figuring out why people do the things they do. The research into the workings of the human brain has accelerated at a breathtaking pace. In 2002, a Princeton research psychologist, Daniel Kahneman, won the Nobel Prize for his work on behavioural sciences. This was shocking for two reasons. To start with, there is no Nobel Prize for psychology. It does not exist! So, instead, he had to win it in economics for his work on 'prospect theory'—which we will apply in a later chapter—without ever having completed a single course in economics. Couple that with the fact that classical economists at the time did not consider the field of behavioural economics to be a thing, let alone be awards-worthy.

Kahneman was followed by Yale's Robert Shiller, who won a Nobel Prize for his work on behavioural economics in 2013, and by University of Chicago's Richard Thaler, who won in 2017. These intellectual titans and a cadre of other brilliant behavioural scientists who followed in their footsteps have transformed the fields as diverse as economics, public policy and investment finance. In the words of Professor Thaler himself, 'Behavioral science aims to understand why we make the choices we do. It offers a more robust view of human decision-making than economics or psychology alone, and can help explain consequential phenomena from the rise and fall of markets to how a person chooses an insurance plan. Society's most pressing challenges are, at their core, behavioral.'[2]

Likewise, two decades ago, there were very few psychologists studying human emotions as a discrete scientific field. Today, there are scores of specialists devoted to researching every distinct human emotion, such as anger, humour and sadness. Yale University even offers a fascinating, full semester elective on 'Human Emotions' to its undergraduate students, taught by the highly accomplished Professor June Gruber.

Look further and you see that the science of psychotherapy has seen the birth and widespread adoption of cognitive behaviour therapy (CBT), which focuses on reshaping negative human behaviour through a deeper understanding of the patient's thought patterns. If Dr Aaron T. Beck pioneered CBT for psychologists, it was Dr David Bell who brought it to the masses with useful tools and frameworks. Across the board, researchers have brought a new level of scientific rigour to the methods for understanding human behaviour. For example, cognitive behaviour therapy has been found in controlled clinical trials to be superior to drugs like SSRIs in successfully reshaping negative behaviour to positive, in a range of mental diseases. New imaging tools, like functional magnetic resonance imaging (fMRI) and positron emission tomography (PET), are laying bare the human brain, allowing us to map the synaptic taxonomy of different emotions and behaviours.

Interestingly, former US president Barack Obama foresaw a game-changing potential in the deeper understanding of the human brain. He seeded Project BRAIN (Brain Research through Advancing Innovative Neurotechnologies) with an investment of $100 million in 2013, billing it as the next 'Space Race'.[3] The project describes its goals as accelerating 'the development and application of new technologies that will enable researchers to produce dynamic pictures of the brain that show how individual brain cells and complex neural circuits interact at the speed of thought. These technologies will open new doors to explore how the brain records, processes, uses, stores, and retrieves vast quantities of information, and shed light on the complex links between brain function and behavior.'

Something that studies the links between brain function and human behaviour as a national priority surely ought to catch the wandering eye of marketers who believe branding is about shaping choice.

Yet, in this race to apply brain sciences to different fields of study, to our very way of life, brand marketers are nowhere to be seen. The 'Directory of Academic Experts in Behavioral Science', published by Idea42 in 2015, lists these gurus in ten different domains, stretching from education and health to finance and international development. There is none for marketing and branding, the two fields that live and breathe the art of shaping consumer behaviour and choice.

Mind you, marketers have known for some time now that what people say they will do does not exactly match up with what they actually do, and a lot of time and resources have been devoted to analysing the differences. Marketers in the consumer products world know that a 'buy one and get one free' offer may work better than 'Buy two and get 50 per cent off'. Birth control pill manufacturers knew that it was better to let people take a pill a day versus for the only the requisite twenty-one days. What is new is that now we understand a lot more about the mental machinery that makes us behave the way we do. We know why we do what we do. And that opens many doors to how we think about marketing and branding.

## Take It and Go

As for me, after my moment of enlightenment at McKinsey post the dot-com crash, I knew that the path to great branding lay in embracing behavioural sciences and psychology. In 2003, I started my own consulting company, Cerenti, with a focus on helping brands grow. Given the freedom to mould my own shop to my fancy, I decided to double down on behavioural approaches. With a small band of young and irreverent marketing firebrands, we went where few others ventured, migrating from merely designing behavioural tactics to spur sales to rethinking brands. This was an important distinction.

Most marketers who turned to the new behavioural sciences devoted themselves to selling and retailing tactics, as had I in my days at McKinsey. They focused on finding clever tricks to optimize web pages and coax people into loading their virtual shopping carts. They helped retailers reorganize their shelves and re-channel traffic to increase the 'shopping basket size'. Instead, we focused on using brain sciences to reinvent brands themselves. Our efforts, along with those of a visionary clique of clients, were instrumental in the creation of two of the world's hottest brands—PediaSure in the children's nutrition market, and Humira in pharmaceuticals, both of which we discuss later.

The good news does not stop here. A lot of insightful work has already been completed by brain scientists and is ripe for the taking. At my company, Cerenti, we have been doing exactly that; devising new frameworks and applying the extant body of research to real-world brands with our clients. *Right between the Ears* is a blueprint for designing epic brands for marketers in industries as diverse as consumer products, pharma, credit cards, high-tech and auto insurance.

The book lays out an entirely new approach, which I have dubbed Cognitive Branding, based on years of development and real-world testing, for designing and building epic brands. To translate good theories to great business, you need three things: core principles, intuitive frameworks and case studies. The principles give marketers the rules by which to play the game. Frameworks allow them to apply the rules to their own brands. Case studies provide the conviction that all of it works. I provide all three in easy-to-understand terms.

This book is written to guide and inspire you to use the work of the many brilliant, modern-day brain scientists with your brands. It has a 'let's get into it mentality'. Most of my clients are business managers who don't have the time to muck around through volumes of research in neuroscience and psychology. With this book, they can rest easy, confident in the knowledge that they don't have to. And yet, for those who may feel the urge to delve into the science, it is catalogued in the endnotes.

Many books on marketing psychology make it a point to highlight the parts of the brain anatomy that relate to specific functions of the brain. While it is nice know that there is such taxonomical research taking place in labs around the world, it is not particularly helpful to throw a bunch of challenging Latin terms at the practising marketer. If you don't believe me, try this for size: 'The [brain] circuit most associated with pleasure and reward is the mesolimbic pathway . . . located in the brainstem . . . Within [it] is an area called the ventral tegmental area (VTA) . . . [that] projects to the nucleus accumbens (thought to be the reward center). The neurotransmitter most commonly linked with the mesolimbic system is dopamine. Many people consider dopamine to be the driving force behind the human pursuit of pleasure.'[4] Ouch! Just reading that hurts! But all you really need to know is that there are systems in the brain that create sensations of pleasure and happiness in response to a brand experience.

Slipping in science-laden language in your spiel can make you look creepily smart but serves no practical purpose other than to scare your audience. For the most part, in this book, I have avoided it. I have left enough scraps here and there so that if indeed you were tempted to unnerve a disagreeable colleague, you could casually slip in a little, shall we say, Latin English into the conversation. This is a book for anyone with an interest in consumer psychology and branding, by a lifelong marketer in the everyday language of non-marketers. After all, aren't we all marketers at heart?

The stuff in this book is new and different. For that reason alone, it can be a wee bit mind-bending at times. So, having a map of where we are headed in the next several chapters can help.

In this chapter, we learnt that *cognitive brands are the hits they are because they work the way the brain does and are the key for unlocking the sensations of experiences and fantasies lodged in our minds*. That was an introduction to the idea. We will learn exactly how in the remaining book in two parts. Part I covers brand strategy and Part II, brand execution.

## Part I: Brand Strategy

In Chapter 1, 'Beyond the Illusions of the Past', I cover new findings from brain sciences that are shaking the foundations of branding as we know it today.

In Chapter 2, 'Right between the Ears', I show a new model for how the brain works, so we can go on to design brands that work the way it does.

In Chapter 3, 'No Looking Back', I show that cognitive brands are special and have three elements, namely, good *Vibes, Sense and Resolve*. This model replaces the soggy old brand constructs of the past that relied on mechanically laddering functional and emotional equities.

In Chapters 4–7, I explain in depth what each of the three elements of the cognitive branding model are, with case studies from our client experiences and examples from our research.

In Chapter 8, 'For the Love of Kids', I bring the cognitive branding model to life with a case study of PediaSure, a children's nutrition brand that my company helped turn into a global blockbuster.

In Chapter 9, 'Brands with Purpose', I discuss a special case of cognitive brands that look to do good, and pursue beneficial societal goals beyond just selling more and more.

## Part II: Brand Execution

In Chapter 10, 'Tales from the Trenches', I cover considerations in executing brand strategies in the real world, applying the latest relevant discoveries from brain sciences.

In Chapter 11, 'Brand Sensations', I describe how our five senses can and must play a role in designing and executing brand experiences.

In Chapter 12, 'Minding Your Manners', I cover ethical considerations in using brain sciences to manipulate consumers and provide a framework for making good moral brand strategy and execution choices.

In Chapter 13, 'The Future is Right between Our Ears', I talk a little about the future of cognitive branding and the required mindset for designing cognitive brands.

With that, we are ready to rock.

* * *

### *Key Takeaways*

The mystery of what makes some brands so iconic and others just also-rans is the stuff of urban legends in marketing. That coding and decoding, the mantra for how to make connections in the brain that drive consumers to buy the chosen brands, is the holy grail that marketers seek. Over the last several decades, countless scholars and practitioners have uncovered invaluable clues, but none present the whole story. Recent advances in brain sciences offer us a terrific look into our mental machinery, solving the mysteries of why consumers behave the way they do and how they choose the brands they buy.

As a result, there are three new truths in marketing:

- Cognitive brands are *the keys to unlocking the sensations of experiences and fantasies in our minds*
- They do so because they *work the way our brain does*
- What's in them are three elements, namely, *good vibes, sense and resolve*

In the rest of the book, we will dive deep into what exactly these new principles mean. In doing so, we will learn to master the art and science of cognitive branding. We start our journey in the next chapter by looking at some of the holy tenets of branding that today are under siege, and sort out what's not working and needs to change.

# 1

# Beyond the Illusions of the Past: A Quick View of What's New and Different

It is not the case that everything you knew about branding from the past is wrong; but maybe half of it is. And now we are learning a lot more about that half.

John Wanamaker, if he were alive today, would be a happier man. He is the guy who, nearly a hundred years back, famously griped, 'Half the money I spend on advertising is wasted; the trouble is I don't know which half.' He is famous for saying that because, amazingly, until recently, he was mostly right. Not so much anymore. With the help of brain sciences, we are getting to be a lot smarter about what works and how. But marketers need to shed the illusions of the past and look at the new rules.

Let's start by taking a look at the widely acclaimed recent commercial by Enbrel, a drug by Amgen for patients with rheumatoid arthritis (RA), that has people reaching for their Kleenex boxes through misty eyes. RA is a degenerative disease and gets worse over time if left untreated. Thus, it is natural for patients to be very worried about the possibility of losing their ability to walk and do things for themselves later in life. As a marketer, you can't exactly say, 'Take my drug or you will end up in a wheelchair.' You might want to, but it's not nice. Enbrel cleverly threads this needle of propriety in its commercials by using a child to voice her mother's fears. It goes something like this, 'My mom's RA pain was intense. I wondered if she could keep doing what she does for us, which is kinda a lot . . . and if that pain can mean something worse?' The little girl is adorable and just the idea of her 'losing' her mom tugs at our heartstrings. But there was a problem. In my in-depth interviews with tens of patients, many could recall the adorable little girl and her poignant story, but very few could remember that the ad was about a brand called Enbrel! With arms flailing in the air, they'd say something like, 'What's that drug where the little girl talks about her mom? It's on the tip of my tongue, but now I can't remember.'

Hmm. People remember your ad but not your brand? Not good! We will return to dissecting this ad a bit more in a later chapter focusing on its good parts. For now, let's take a look at five tectonic shifts in how we have traditionally thought about brands.

## Emotional Branding Is Tricky and May Hurt Your Brand

Marketers have long believed that 'emotionalizing' brands is good. It strengthens a brand's connection with consumers who remember it better and are more loyal to it. The good news is that research shows that we indeed do remember emotional experiences better than non-emotional ones. However, when we witness emotionally charged events, we increase our focus on the central drama but decrease it on the peripheral details.[1] In the Amgen ad, patients remember the girl because she was central to the emotional storyline, but not the brand, Enbrel, because it was a secondary, non-emotional detail. This kind of trade-off is particularly true when negative emotions are on display. Thus, over-the-top emotional branding can be effective and defective. The result? Ads that make us laugh and cry but do little for the brand.

No marketer understood this trade-off better than Steve Jobs. Between 2006 and 2009, Apple shot 300 commercials around their campaign 'Get a Mac', but only sixty-six ever aired. In a number of amusing vignettes, the ads cast a cool and hip 'Apple Guy' versus the uptight and techie 'PC Guy'. So why did Jobs say no to some of the laugh-out-loud Apple vs Microsoft ads? Justin Long, the actor who played the Apple Guy, inquired why one particularly hilarious ad, which featured Zach Galifianakis playing a drunken Santa Claus, had never aired. He was informed by Apple that 'Steve Jobs preferred when (the ads) weren't super funny because he thought it would detract from the point of the commercial. He thought if people were too focused on the humor in it, they would lose sight of the product.' Jobs was probably right about that, even though I note that the research shows that with positive emotions there is less of the narrowing of focus that I described earlier. But, hey, why risk it?

As a marketer, you have to be careful that the intensity of emotions around the brand supports but does not overwhelm the main idea behind the brand itself. Research by Ellie Parker and Adrian Furnham shows that sex doesn't necessarily sell either.[2] In their studies, people who watched on TV sexually suggestive commercials had no better recall of the brands than those who watched non-sexual commercials. Further, people who watched advertisements between sexually laced shows may remember the shows better than the ads. The memory of the sexual episode itself may overshadow the recall of the brand.[3] Similarly, there has been a high concern among marketers that when super-hot models are placed in commercials, people may focus and remember the models but not the brands. I show later that to make emotional branding work, you have to embed the brand's own narrative into the overall storyline carefully.

## You Don't Think, Feel and Act; You Just Do It!

To get inside the mind of a customer, brand marketers have always needed a theory of how the brain works. The traditional version of it goes as the 'Think-Feel-Act' model or some other glorified version of it.[4] It says that given a brand stimulus, a customer thinks about what to make of it, considers how those thoughts make him feel and finally, acts on the said feelings. The 'thinking' piece is assumed to communicate the rational benefits of the brand to you, the 'feeling' slice takes the 'emotional' benefits to your gut, and the combination of the two are supposed to lead you to 'action' or the buying-the-brand part or at least triggers in you the intent to do so. As a theory, this model has been popular because it kind of makes sense. But here's the rub. Modern behavioural science shows that our brain works in this way only 5 per cent of the time.[5] That's pretty close to never!

Imagine this. You're cruising along on I-20 in Texas, and through the corner of your eye you spot a billboard for the local smokehouse in Abilene, with the picture of a big, fat and juicy brisket. You're hungry. You're tired. The next thing you know you hear a little rumble from your stomach, you feel your mouth watering and you can almost smell the charred end tips on the meat. Hmm. But wait, if the 'think-feel-act' model is true, then you would have thought about the proposition first, before feeling aroused and salivating. And wouldn't you have realized it was a bit pointless to slobber over an interstate billboard and dispensed with that and the stomach rumbling part? Think, feel and act can be sequential, but they don't have to be so in brand experiences, and usually aren't.[6]

Brand experiences are stored in our memories as cognitive bundles. Each bundle contains smart information on a curated set of your interactions with the brand—what the stimulus and context were, what you thought and felt about it, how each one of your five senses reacted, and what choices you made and the actions you took at the time. The next time you feel the same stimulus in the appropriate context, the entire cognitive bundle is released in a flush. You choose and act even as you think and feel. These bundles of experiences are unleashed only when properly triggered. In other words, the brand message has to be just so for the cognitive bundle to unleash the full glory of the stored experience. Cognitive brands are the keys to unlocking the sensations of consumer experiences or, as we shall see, even fantasies. When properly keyed, the essence of the prior experiences is relived, detonating like a liquor-filled chocolate in the mouth, magnificently releasing the captive flavours and aromas as a single explosion.

The cognitive bundles in our brain evolve constantly. As new encounters take place with the brand, more information may be appended to previously rendered cognitive bundles. This reduces the future effort necessary to decipher sensory inputs. If you happen to smell chocolate chip cookies while walking through a shopping mall, and they smell just the way they used to when your mother made them when you were a kid, all of that will immediately come back to you in a flash, even though the food court in the mall is not your house and that is not your mother behind the counter. You may not actually remember your mom's cookies vividly, but you experience what is called the 'affective residue' or sensations of those past experiences. In a twist, the mall lady may serve her cookies with a home-made mint sweet cream sauce, and now you have another memory of an elevated experience added to the 'Chocolate Chip Cookies' cognitive bundle. This continuous enrichment of the stored experiences makes you more discerning about your future brand choices and keeps raising the bar for marketers.

## Choice Is Mostly Subconscious or 'Lowly Vigilant'

Brand marketers so far have worked under the thesis that people make choices rationally or emotionally. Instead, Daniel Kahneman points out that there are two processes, which he dubbed 'System 1' and 'System 2', by which the brain works, either of which can be rational or emotional.[7] This new model creates unique opportunities for marketers to influence behaviour consciously and subconsciously. Mastering these two systems, and how they work with each other, is the path to engineering consumer choice in the future.

System 1 is a collection of processing capabilities that the brain uses to make decisions by relating things to its past learnings and experiences. For that reason, it is referred to as the 'associative' component of the brain, and because it draws on what it already knows, it is fast and instinctive. In some cases, it taps literal memories like, 'What did I do the last time when someone threw a rotten tomato at me?' In other cases, it connects the dots with similar experiences, as in, 'What do I do now, when someone is throwing a different vegetable at my face?' System 1 is adept at responding to situations by applying beliefs and cognitive biases we have developed over the years. When brands align their message to such pre-existing wisdom, they are adopted by consumers with minimal introspection. In other words, the brand choice is made with low vigilance and in some cases subconsciously, without any vigilance at all.

If you are a brand marketer, you can see how this could be exciting—and especially so when you consider the fact that humans use System 1 to make choices 95 per cent of the time. This is why, often when you come back from grocery shopping, you may find things that you hadn't noticed you were buying ('Did I really bring back another tub of the Chunky Monkey ice-cream?'). And this is why you may have more ugly Christmas sweaters in your closet than you really need.

System 2 is the vigilant and deliberative part of the brain. Unlike System 1, which is always on, System 2 kicks in only when a more complete analysis of the situation is warranted. These are the faculties of the brain that we use when faced with complex or higher-risk brand choices. In a later chapter, I discuss how marketers must awaken System 2 in their consumers when their products and services are so different from convention that people have to change their mindsets to accept them.

System 2 methods for driving choice present a steeper hill to climb and take more time than System 1 processes but are unavoidable for some brands. This is why people did not start buying groceries online immediately during the first dot-com boom of the early 2000s, but now they do. This is why people did not cut the cord on their landlines with the advent of the cell phones, but now most have.

In today's world, marketers must be smart about how they use System 1 and System 2 drivers to design their brands. The two systems work seamlessly inside a person's brain. So, while marketers can appeal to a consumer's System 1 for an instinctive choice in many cases, the more conscious and deliberate System 2 will override System 1 when it really counts. So yes, I will not come back with that tub of Chunky Monkey every time from the grocery store. Maybe only the first five times.

Conversely, when System 2 has done all the evaluation it wanted to, it is not going to waste time and energy on it in a future similar situation. It will encode the experience into System 1. This is how System 2 encodes brand loyalty. The first time you used Uber, you probably had to think a lot about it. You had to download the app and then decide to entrust your credit card to it. But now, any time you need a ride, you just Uber it. As a matter of fact, I see people call an Uber and wait ten minutes for it, even when there are taxis parked right across the road. Although, arguably, sometimes that may be due to other advantages that Uber offers—like the convenience of non-cash payments—mostly it's just the mental momentum of repeating a choice that had been investigated and made earlier.

## The 'What' and 'How' of Branding Live as One

Traditionally, marketers work on their brand execution strategies only after they have finished developing their brand positioning. Yet, behavioural science tells us that it matters not just what you say but also how you say it.

Let's go back and take a look at what happened in the highly charged US presidential election of 2016. Border control, gun violence and access to health care were important issues to swing voters. In the traditional branding lingo, you would call these 'preference driving equities'. While both Donald Trump and Hillary Clinton were addressing these issues, they were doing so very differently. Trump warned Americans about everything they stood to lose: You'll lose your jobs to a flood of immigrants. You'll lose your guns to the government. And, you'll lose your doctor to Obamacare. In contrast, Hillary Clinton was trying to build a vision of the shining city on the hill. She talked about how open immigration would attract the best talent from across the world, how gun control would make the streets safer for children and how an expanded Obamacare would mean better health for all. So why did so many swing voters respond favourably to Trump?

Well, because of how he said it! There is a cognitive bias known as *loss aversion* that says that all else being equal, people are more sensitive to what they stand to lose versus what they could gain, even when the amount of loss or gain is the same. Trump, in massive rallies across the country, honed his message of losses to perfection as made evident in the 'Make America Great Again' chant of his followers. In psychology, there is also something called the *framing effect*.[8] It says that our choices are influenced by the way they are framed through different wordings, settings and situations. Given two equally attractive choices, you will have a preference (and pay more) for the one that is framed better. For brand marketers, the lesson is that the 'what' of branding cannot be separated from the 'how' of branding. Brand positioning and activation live and breathe as one.

In 2005, I was working with Keli Bennett, who was then a hotshot consumer marketer working on Humira, Abbott's wonder drug for treating rheumatoid arthritis. Keli was among the few marketers to have seen the potential for cognitive branding far ahead of her industry peers in the pharma world. Research from the market showed that patients felt like they needed a weapon against their disease, a smart bomb that could go kill the disease. Yet, as we debated the topic further, it also became evident that the 'Perfect Weapon' positioning that tested well in surveys and focus groups was actually hard to activate. How do you turn a patient's body into a battleground? After all, in which war does the battleground win anything? Would you do commercials with bombs exploding inside the patient's body? A deadly warrior hacking at the innards? In-depth discussions with patients slowly uncovered concerns that led Keli to pursue other more feasible avenues. In this case, the *what* of the branding was pretty solid, but the *how* was inexecutable.

## There's Something to the Brands of Our Dreams

In conventional branding, there is a fear that consumer attention spans are short. Thus, marketers dumb down the brand message in hopes of getting it across within that fleeting moment of attention. They look for magic phrases like Alibaba's 'open sesame' that could help marketers wondrously open the mouth of the treasure caves inside consumers' minds. Research shows that this happens only when the customer is already inclined to buy your product. But then, what do you need marketing for? In real life, we make choices quite differently. What we learn about a brand lingers in our minds, at some point begins to make sense and leads us to go buy it. It may be fast or slow. Think about those delayed 'aha' moments that we all experience from time to time.

In 2004, I had a team working on Humira, a year or so after its launch.* At the time it was struggling to gain traction in the market. Its nemesis was Enbrel, a drug from Amgen, that worked equally well and in pretty much the same way. There were two differences between the drugs and neither seemed to matter much to physicians prescribing the products. Humira would have to be self-injected by patients once every two weeks, and Enbrel twice a week. However, biologics were relatively new to the market and doctors were very worried about their long-term effects. Since Enbrel had entered the market three years earlier, there were thousands of patients already on it and it was a known quantity. As a result, while Humira was obviously a more convenient drug for the patient, the doctors didn't care a whit about that. The second difference was that Humira was manufactured from fully human cells, as opposed to Enbrel, which was made using part-animal cells. Again, there was no clinical data to suggest one was better or worse than the other.

* The events described in the following passages about Humira have been fictionalized to hide any non-publicly available information and preserve the privacy of the mentioned individuals. The narrative is thus designed to be instructive rather than accurately biographical or historical.

Thus, Humira was struggling to break through the bias for the tried-and-true favouring Enbrel.

To figure out how to put some wind in the sails of Humira, we crunched our databases to look for physicians who had changed their behaviour, from prescribing very little of Humira to prescribing a lot. There were only a handful across the country and one of them was a Dr Katz. I decided to jump on plane and go meet him.

There I was sitting with Dr Katz in his busy practice outside a retiree town in sunny Florida. I didn't wait long to pop the question, 'So what gives, doc? How come you went from prescribing Humira to only 6 per cent of your new patients to 83 per cent?'

'So, you understand I don't like switching patients willy-nilly from one drug to another once I start them, right?' he asked. I nodded. It was common knowledge that switching patients was inadvisable. Any biologic drug we take, triggers in our system the production of antibodies that resist the drug. Hence, once a drug settles in and is working, you don't want to muck around with it. If you try a new drug, these antibodies may block it from working, and the new antibodies that the new drug gives rise to may stop the old drug from working, leaving you flat out of options. You get the idea; switching is bad.

'You know, for the first year that your drug was in the market, I really saw no upside to trying your drug for my new patients. Humira was the last resort for patients for whom Enbrel failed to work,' he said. I nodded again. That is exactly what most other rheumatologists were doing. 'And then, one day it hit me,' he continued, suddenly energized. 'If I used Humira first on new patients, I would have to risk fewer switchovers!' I was confused, 'But you said earlier both drugs work equally well.'

'Well, what happens is that some 10–15 per cent of the patients have a form of the disease that for unknown reasons requires a higher dose. With Enbrel, since it is already twice a week, I can't double it. With Humira I can always go to once a week versus every other week and not have to switch.'

'But then you would only be writing prescriptions for those few patients that needed the higher dose? Why the 80 per cent of all new patients,' I persisted.

'Simple. I don't know which patients will require a double dose until I actually start them on the drug. So, if I always start them on Humira, I know I won't have to switch them as often because I can always step up the dose first! That was a big "Aha" moment for me. I can't believe it took me a whole year to figure it out,' he said, beaming proudly at his own discovery.

As marketers, it was an epiphany for us too. We had always thought that Humira's main advantage was its less frequent, more convenient dosing for the patient. Instead, it was the flexibility to increase the dose if needed. When we tried the latter argument with other rheumatologists, we got the same reaction, 'I hadn't quite thought of it that way, but now that you mention it, it makes a whole lot of sense.' With the help of a new brand message and a host of other innovative marketing programmes, Humira would go on to become one of the world's largest global brands, with over $20 billion in annual sales today.

Unlike System 2, System 1 processes in our brain are 'always on', scouring past experiences and making finer and finer connections. And then one day, the light bulb goes on; a flash of lightening, out of the blue. If you have emerged from your morning shower with a sudden epiphany, you know now what I'm talking about.

When the brain encounters stimuli that are too overwhelming to fully resolve, it records the information and tags it for subsequent processing. It took our Dr Katz a whole year, and us longer. In other words, marketers need not be afraid to overload the consumer with useful brand information. Don't dumb it down.

Marketers can make 'aha moments' easier for customers by leaving a trail of breadcrumbs for them to follow to the ultimate answer. Brand promises that connect with a customer's prior beliefs, experiences or learning can help do exactly that. This is in part due to a process that psychologists call 'processing fluency'. When we explained to physicians how Humira could give them greater treatment flexibility, they could get to their own 'aha' moments faster, because they already believed switching patients was a bad idea. Baby steps and breadcrumbs work far better in branding than tall tales and grandiose visions of nirvana with your brand.

For the sake of completion, I should mention that there is even a question around whether some epiphanies occur while we dream. A recent article in the *Wall Street Journal* posed the question, 'Can a person learn while sleeping?'[9] It cites research by Sanam Hafeez, a neuropsychologist who teaches at Columbia University, who explains that while the brain is bombarded by various stimuli all day, sleep is the time when the brain can filter, categorize and consolidate that information. 'As it tunes out all distractions, the brain encodes information and decides how important a memory or piece of information is.' There is actually a word for this, namely hypnopaedia or sleep-learning, whereby researchers have shown that during some non-dreaming cycles of sleep, the hippocampus, the area of the brain related to memory and learning, is activated.[10]

Who knew! Maybe there is something to the idea of the brands of our dreams? No? Well, sleep on it, will ya?

* * *

*Key Takeaways*

Traditional branding approaches are built on a foundation of many half-truths. That has been the case because until now, we knew no better. Today, brain science is shedding light on what's right and wrong with our brand premises. Here's what we are learning:

- Emotionalizing brands does work because consumers remember such narratives more easily and for longer. However, if you are not careful, they will remember the emotions of the story but not your brand.
- It seems logical to believe that when presented a brand choice, the brain would first think about it, then check to see if it feels good and, finally, prompt the consumer to buy it. In fact, whenever possible, the brain works mostly by comparing current brand experiences with related ones from the past, and thinking, feeling and acting similarly, not necessarily in any order.
- Marketers like to highlight the rational and emotional benefits of their brands. The brain works differently. It uses two processes, System 1 and System 2, which use association and deliberation to make choices.
- While the brain is perfectly capable of conscious and subconscious choice, most of the time it works with the latter, skipping a detailed evaluation of the brand benefits.
- Brand strategy and execution must be considered as one and the same and planned together rather than sequentially, as it normally is. The 'what' and 'how' of a brand has to be designed as one, or its message may be lost.
- Marketers assume that consumer attention spans are short and try to deliver their messages in small bites. In fact, brands can present longer and more complicated messages

> because the brain has the machinery to listen now and figure it out later.

This chapter was a sneak peek into how the foundations of branding are shifting. In the remainder of the book, we will learn exactly how to use this knowledge to design epic brands that work the way our brain does. In the next chapter, I present a new model of how the brain works when choosing among brands.

# 2

# Right between Your Ears: How the Marketing Brain Works

Psychologists sometimes like to point out that everything about sex happens not where you might think but between your ears. *The 'where' and 'how' of everything about branding, too, happens right there, between your ears.* If you pause for a minute, both premises should be obvious. All that we see, touch, hear, smell and taste is a sensory stimulus to the brain that triggers conscious or subconscious response. But, all of it is simply what the brain thinks it is. Even when it isn't. That is why, amputees, nearly all of them, feel the presence of a phantom limb because their brain believes it's there.[1]

It's not just limbs; it's everything. The notion that *all* reality is contrived in the mind has been around for a while, starting with Indian Vedic philosophers who lived in 1500 BCE to more recently, the Keanu Reeves character, Neo, in the movie *The Matrix*. In the latter, the wise old Morpheus gives Neo the choice of taking the red pill and facing the bitter reality, or taking the blue pill and living in a dream. He says, 'This is your last chance. After this, there is no turning back. You take the blue pill—the story ends, you wake up in your bed and believe whatever you want to believe. You take the red pill—you stay in wonderland and I show you how deep the rabbit hole goes.' Ironically, in the real world, the only reality is that of the blue pill, the one that our senses can perceive, and then what our brain constructs from those perceptions. It is all right between our ears.

Even though we cannot have reality, we do have volition. Volition is considered by philosophers to be the tiebreaker that distinguishes humans from animals.[2] And the fondness for shaping volition is what separates brand marketers from normal people. To understand how volition, or brand choice, comes about, we need to take a peek at how the brain works.

There are many mysteries and myths surrounding the human brain. Today, with what we know, hopefully there are fewer of both. So, no, humans don't just use 10 per cent of their brain capacity, leaving the remaining 90 per cent for telekinesis and other untapped feats.[3] We use all of our brain, most of the time. And no, there aren't people who are left-brained and artsy or others who are right-brained and logical. Rather, brain scans show that humans don't favour one brain hemisphere over the other and nor is one hemisphere dominant for some.[4] So sorry, you cannot segment your customer as left- and right-brained, but you could use a mix of brand strategies to appeal to their creative or logical sides. And finally, AI-based computers won't displace humans anytime soon. The brain does innumerable things better than the best supercomputers, despite being slower and having less memory, because of *how* it does them. Less is more!

The human brain consists of over 80 billion neurons, each of which, on an average, connects to 10,000 others forming a network with a hundred trillion connections.[5] While supercomputers can now beat the best human minds in games like chess and Jeopardy, even the garden-variety brain can beat a supercomputer in a multitude of everyday tasks. For example, it is difficult for computers to understand a sentence like, 'Some people think that sleeping at the wheel in their self-driving Teslas is hip, but it's just pulp-brained!' Computers would also have a hard time figuring why a movie like *Aliens* is scary given that the extraterrestrial in question is non-existent and known to you to be fictional. So how does the human brain work?

## A Working Model of the Brain

Marketers have always felt a need to have a model of how the brain works. It gives them more confidence in their assertions. Remember, we talked about the rational plus emotional model of the brain and the 'Think-Feel-Act' paradigm. Since I trashed both of those, I feel I owe you a replacement.

I am not going to discuss what part of the brain does what. If you have a thing for anatomy, you can get the basics from lessons taught to elementary-middle school kids (yes, they make them super-smart these days).[6] My goal is to give you a brand marketer's stylized version of the functions of the brain. For where we are going, that is more useful. I divide the brain into four main functional subunits:

1. Associator
2. Deliberator
3. Learner
4. Conator

It is a bit dicey to have to explain four things. So I'm going to do it fast first, and then slower, with an example.

Every stimuli or experience is evaluated either by the *Associator* using a System 1 or the *Deliberator* using a System 2 process for whether or not it makes any *sense*. In other words, the brain looks at whether what the brand says makes sense instinctively

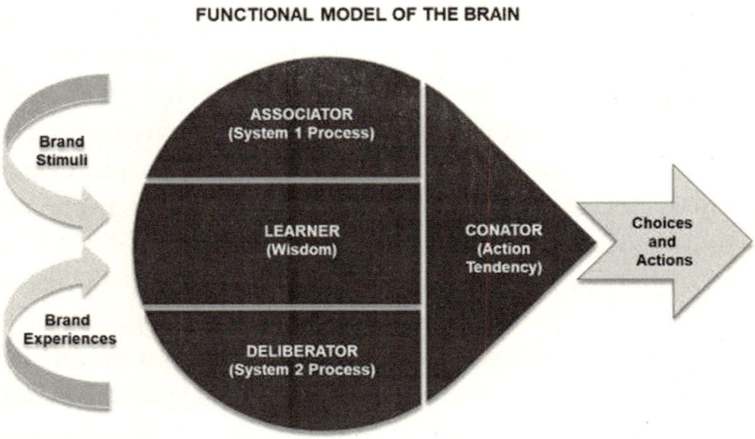


*Figure 2.1: From left to right, we see that all brand messaging and experiences are handled by four types of processes in the brain to help the consumer choose between and buy available products and services.*

or critically. If it does, then that results in a recommendation in favour of the brand. It is a good choice. The *Conator* scores how happy you would be with the proposed choice and how well it fits with your goals and then *resolves* to act or not act. The *Learner* subunit stores all of the information surrounding the event, including the recommended choice and action taken, for future reference. In this way, things that turn out well may give good subconscious *vibes* in the future if the event recurs and make us less likely to view the choice critically. Let's work through an example to understand each part of the brain in more detail.

*Oh, Look! We have some help! There's Jane at the Saks Fifth Avenue store on Michigan Avenue, eyeing a sultry mannequin swathed in an Eileen Fisher funnel neck sweater. Oh, yeah! She can totally see herself in it. She remembers how gorgeous she looks in pullovers like that and can imagine how her friends will drool over it. A smile breaks upon her lips, she feels a little warm and fuzzy, and her hand reaches out to caress the Italian cashmere.*

Ok, stop action! We are witnessing Jane's *Associator* recall past brand experiences from the *Learner* subunit. Everything she felt in that moment, from the feel of the wool on her skin to the projected gratification of envious looks from her women friends, wafts out from the cognitive bundles stored from previous encounters. Because she buys from Saks often, she also feels good vibes from the *Learner* about buying anything from there. After all, when has that ever gone wrong? Instinctively, the Eileen Fisher feels like a good idea.

We learnt in the previous chapter that the *Associator* makes choices via System 1 by comparing present experiences to past ones. It could be an identical prior event or a similar situation. It works subconsciously or with low vigilance. Jane does not actually have to force herself to imagine herself in the sweater or the reactions of her girlfriends. It happens in the blink of an eye all by itself.

In one sense, the *Learner* is a 'memorizer'. It records the entire experience—what the situation was (context), what choice was recommended by the *Associator* or *Deliberator*, what action was taken, how good it felt and how well it turned out—all as a single cognitive bundle. The *Learner*, of course, catalogues its own experiences in this way but is also capable of filing away brand choices of experts or endorsers it trusts.

But notice that I did not call the *Learner* subunit the 'Memorizer'. That is because while it does record experiences, it also learns from them continuously. Like the *Associator*, it is always on in the background, becoming a little smarter with each passing day. If Jane buys the sweater and is thrilled with it, until a month later when it starts pilling excessively, the *Learner* unit is going to take note, edit its memory, so that she does not make the same mistake again. The *Learner* also looks for relationships across experiences and will enhance the recorded information with hashtags like #Cashmere, #Sweaters, #LookAwesome,

#LoveYouEileenFisher and #SaksForever. The *Learner* subunit makes these connections whenever it has time to spare, possibly even while we sleep. The *Learner* is spectacular as a neural net that crunches data over time and makes us savvier shoppers. It is an evolving repository of what I call our individual 'cognitive wisdom'. It may not always be right, by the way, but it is our personal cache of knowledge, our conscious and subconscious guiding light.

*Ok. Let's get back to Jane. Lights! Camera! Action! Jane picks up the sweater and stares at it. It's her favourite colour, a lemon-zest yellow. As she drapes it over her arms, the price tag hidden deep in its folds slips open: $358. Ouch! She remembers that there are exactly zero dollars left in her monthly splurge-on-Jane budget. The unhappy face of her husband glowering at last month's Visa bill floats momentarily by an open window in her mind. Undeterred, she flips out her iPhone and googles for a better price. Wait! The Eileen Fisher is not available anywhere, but she can get a cashmere mock neck in heathered chai, a colour that is 'in', from Everlane, for a paltry $228. Not exactly an Eileen Fisher, but good, very good.*

All right. Stop action!

Even as the *Associator* in her brain reveled in the idea of donning the cashmere Eileen Fisher, there was a part of it that said, 'Hmm. Sounds good, but I am not a 100 per cent sure', and it referred the matter over to the *Deliberator*.

The *Deliberator* is the System 2 subunit of the brain, adept at resolving situations that pose risks and complications. It can frame issues, weigh the pros and cons, apply theorems, follow algorithms and perform computations in all kinds of neat ways. It takes effort to put on this kind of a show, so System 2 would rather avoid it if it can. In this case, the *Deliberator* helps Jane solve her three-dimensional shopping dilemma of $358 of 'awesomeness' versus a likely derailed husband versus a $228 consolation prize. It tells her that going for the latter would be wise.

The *Learner* unit, by the way, also appends a confidence score to any recommendation to account for the 'I'm not a 100 per cent' factor when it encodes the experience into the memory. That matters because answers with high confidence will not be questioned in the future. For marketers, that means that their brand will be repurchased reflexively without further thought.

Now, everything I have said so far could happen, and yet nothing happens. The *Associator* likes the idea of the Eileen Fisher. The *Deliberator* cautions that the cheaper Everlane is the sensible choice. Jane may buy the Eileen Fisher, or the Everlane, or simply walk away.

Brain sciences tell us that as humans we are programmed to pursue happiness. Happiness is *serious* business; not in a manner of speaking, but literally, and involves neurochemical reactions of hormones like dopamine, norepinephrine and oxytocin in our brain that give us actual warm fuzzies.[7] That dopamine rush is what makes her want the sweater in the first place and then want another one to keep the feeling going. The *Conator* subunit of the brain can forecast happiness, that is, it makes a guess as to how happy Jane will feel with each decision and calibrate it against her goals.

So, what happens next?

*Jane grabs the Eileen Fisher, marches off to the nearest sales counter, and is soon thereafter seen leaving the store with a glossy, black-ribbon Saks shopping bag and the biggest recorded smile on the planet.*

In this case, the happiness that Jane feels from the idea of looking stupendous in front of her friends proves too hard to resist. She goes for it.

'Conation' is one of the thousand most obscure words in the English language.[8] For brand marketers, it shouldn't be, because conation is defined as a person's innate tendency for action or resolve. Without it, you would create brand preferences but not brand buys. The *Conator* subunit is different in each of us and drives us to pursue different goals. Kathy Kolbe, a specialist in this field, attributes this to each individual's MO, or method by which their system operates.[9] So, the same brand stimulus can have a distinct effect on different people.

*Hold on! Did I mention that Jane was shopping at Saks with her identical twin, Joyce? Most people can't tell them apart, you know. Joyce, too, looked at the Eileen Fisher pullover. It left her unmoved. She passed quickly on it, picking up a $79 'Save the African Rhino' camouflage-green sweatshirt instead.*

Even though the identically bodied Joyce would look just as stupendous as Jane in the sweater, going around impressing friends is not her thing. She would be happier doing something good for the world with her money. That is her *conative MO.* It is that kind of happiness that matters to her goals.

The *Conator* captures what cognitive marketer Steve Genco describes as the two *universal* motivations that drive consumer behaviour.[10] The first is *aspirational,* a desire to be happier and better off tomorrow than today. And the second, related to having an *identity*, is a need to feel good about who we are and how we are perceived by others.

If all of this feels a little confusing, it really isn't. But it is different from how we have been used to thinking about consumer choice. Jane chooses to indulge her fantasies despite her own better judgement. Joyce saves a mammal on the other side of the planet. It's what our brain does; it connects consumer choice with happiness. This understanding of how the brain functions leads us to a different framework for designing brands that work the way the brain does. In the following chapter I do exactly that and present a new model for architecting what I call cognitive brands.

* * *

## *Key Takeaways*

Cognitive brands work the way the brain does. So, if we are to be successful in designing great brands, we need a solid understanding of how the brain works. This chapter provides a functional view of the marketing brain, which we see has four modules that work seamlessly together:

- The *Learner* subunit is where the brain stores its 'wisdom of the ages'. All past brand experiences lie here along with annotations on what the associated thoughts and feelings were at the time and what actions were taken.
- The *Associator* is one of the two choice modules in the brain. When presented a brand proposition, it subconsciously draws on its learnings from similar experiences in the past and tends to make similar choices for or against the brand.
- The *Deliberator* is the other choice module in the brain. It works by analysing a brand experience in detail with sophisticated tools and methods. It is mentally taxing and thus sparingly used.
- The *Conator* is a module in the brain that resolves whether or not to act on the choices proposed by the *Associator* or *Deliberator*. It is different from person to person and defines their MO for taking action. If a choice seems iffy to a particular consumer given their own MO, the *Conator* may decide to park it and not have the consumer buy the brand. The consumer may like your brand but not want it.

Now that we know how the brain is organized, we can design our brands to work the same way. That is exactly what we do in the next chapter.

Part Two

# How to Design Cognitive Brands

3

# Brands That Work the Way the Brain Does: A Four-Part Model for Building Cognitive Brands

Given everything we have learnt so far, you would think that the field of branding would be in the midst of a bloody revolution, with marketers tearing down the old walls, redrawing boundaries and building new pillars. Let's review the facts. *Fact #1*: Nobel Prize-winning pioneers like Kahneman, Schiller and Thaler have turned the world upside down in fields as disparate as economics, social anthropology, linguistics and neuro-psychology, with a consilience of discoveries on how consumers behave and make choices.[1] *Fact #2*: Branding is all about understanding consumer behaviour and shaping their choice to favour your brand. And yet, the art of branding is at a standstill. There is not a lot happening that hasn't already happened. And that is because marketers are either distracted or comfortable in their soggy old shoes.

Normally, the task of reinventing branding would fall upon the marketers at iconic consumer products companies like Kraft, Procter & Gamble and Unilever, which have been the torchbearers of all that is new and great in the field. But over the last two decades, these companies have been looking over their shoulders at a new kind of threat. Private equity (PE) firms were leading a charge on the destruction of the great consumer brands. 3G Capital, a Brazilian investment house, bought companies with strong 'momentum' brands and milked them. In what was proudly celebrated as a 'margin expansion strategy', 3G would cut the power, stop investing in the brands and look around for ways to prop the profits by remaking the products with cheaper stuff.

With more cash flowing in, a PE firm, like 3G, could add debt and reward itself with a handsome dividend. For some years, the brands would continue to cruise along, and reporters would dutifully barrage the company for pearls of wisdom. Carlos Sicupira, a 3G founding partner, obliged, 'Costs are like fingernails: they always have to be cut.'[2] By 2018, the wheels had come off the bus, the share price of Kraft, one of 3G's crown jewels, crashed, and the party ended. Yet, it takes time to get new religion. By then, the PE firms had cultivated a cadre of marketers who treated gilded brands like dirty, overgrown nails. And worse, other consumer products companies committed their own hara-kiri proactively, starving brands and launching margin expansion strategies to pre-empt the possibility of a takeover by a 3G-like PE cousin.

If consumer marketers were distracted and impoverished, those in other industries, like pharmaceuticals, consumer finance, insurance and automotive, suffered from an embarrassment of riches and yet, are stuck in the ways of the past. For example, in the pharma world, where money flows like water on blockbuster drugs, often the companies are married too mechanically to borrowed processes and old formulas. And they are not working. In one study after another, we found that the brands were lost in a 'sea of sameness'. Consumers often struggle to tell one brand apart from another. This is truly astonishing because I am talking about markets in which the companies as a group may spend $200–500 million per year on television and online advertising.

According to Nielsen, in 2018, pharma marketers smacked down $5 billion on television ads in the US market alone. Pfizer, all by itself, spent $1 billion, including about $200 million on Chantix, a smoking cessation drug, and $160 million on Xeljanz, a rheumatoid arthritis drug. It is true that with that much exposure to advertising, consumers are generally more aware of their options and motivated to ask their doctors about new drugs. Yet, the differential benefit to individual brands is questionable. The sea of sameness problem is not limited to the pharma world; other industries, including automotive, insurance and telecom, find themselves in a similar predicament, feeling the pressure to differentiate their brands.

The good news is that there is the proverbial light at the end of the tunnel. Consumer marketers have seen the folly of the '3G' ways and are slowly returning to a focus on brands. Forward-looking managers, from pharma to consumer insurance, are questioning the wisdom of their tired old approaches to branding and opening the doors to new ideas.

My company's work with clients across several industries is showing that the problem with branding lies not in the amount spent on commercials, the packaging, brand cues or the creative strategy. Rather, it has to do with the *way* brands are being positioned. Their message fails to rise above the clutter, not because it is not being repeated enough but because it is not sinking in. *And, it is not sinking in because it does not work the way the brain does.*

To understand why we are stuck, it helps to take a look at the approaches in use and what's wrong with them.

## Brand Ladders Don't Quite Work

One of the most common ways to design brands is to 'ladder' rational and emotional equities into a point of difference. What does that mean? Well, you go ask people what is important to them in a product. Make a note of the top three benefits that consumers get from how the product works. These are called the 'functional or rational brand equities'. Then, you ask consumers how they feel about having those benefits from the product. Make a list of those too because they will come in handy as 'emotional brand equities'. Next, mix the two lists together and knit together a brand message. This is an exercise akin to the children's game of 'I'll give you two words (or phrases) and you make a sentence with them'. Once you have done that, and this is the most important part, say a little prayer! Figure 3.1 shows you a version of the brand ladder framework.

Let's say that you sell ice cream. You may find that creaminess, a rational/functional benefit of ice-cream, is important. You also observe that people eating ice-cream seem happy, an emotional benefit. 'Voila!' You connect those two pieces of information into a tag line saying something like 'Sheer Creaminess! Sheer Happiness!' Sounds pretty solid, doesn't it? However, the whole idea that creaminess makes you happy is contrived. It may not stir a single neuron in your brain to make it care a whit. It is like a song with all the right elements, a great bass line and outstanding vocals, and yet, it doesn't rock!

The idea of brands as a bundle of rational and emotional benefits has not changed much in the last thirty or so years. Yet, its seeds were sown centuries back. Rationalism grew out of the seventeenth century, as a reaction to the stifling faith-based dictates of the times, through the works of philosophers like Descartes, Spinoza and Leibniz in the Age of Reason. If people had stopped there, all we would have today is brands with functional benefits. But thanks to David Hume, and let's just give him the title of the father of emotional branding, we learnt that humans also behave emotionally. Hume said, 'Reason is, and ought only to be, the slave of the passions and can never pretend to any other office than to serve and obey them.'[3] Pretty strong stuff! In Book Two of *A Treatise of Human Nature,* he even published a taxonomy of human emotions. Imagine that! But wait, it's 2020 now. Hume did his thing over 200 years back. Now, we know a lot more about how the brain works. Isn't it time to put that knowledge into play?

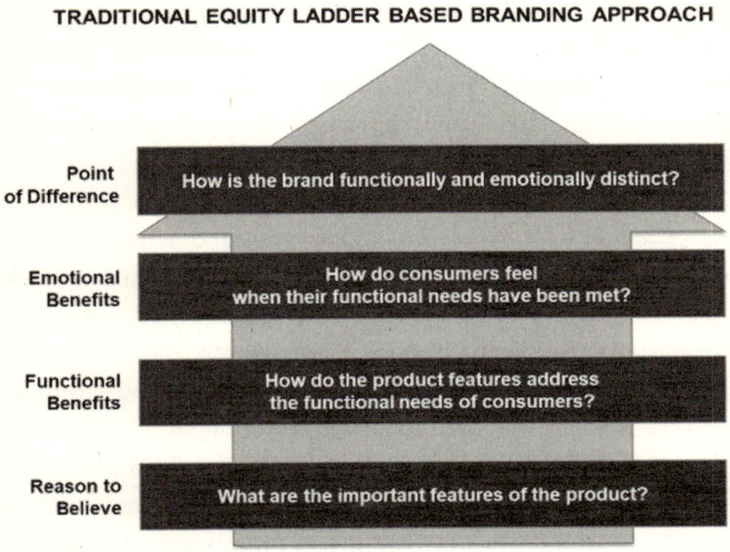


*Figure 3.1: From the bottom to the top, in the commonly used brand equity ladder, a marketer starts with features that are different about his product and adds what their rational benefits are and what the associated feelings may be. The combination of the three becomes the brand positioning.*

This is not to say that brand ladders never work. Quite to the contrary, sometimes they work spectacularly well. Over the last century, marketers have built tons of iconic brands. But for every one of those there are a thousand more buried deep in the sea of brands you've never heard of. With that kind of a hit rate, you have to wonder whether the brands that became hits were just lucky!

## List Branding Doesn't Work Either

The other way that marketers run into trouble is when they try to brand their products as a list of benefits. It is tempting to do so. After all, if the consumer has told you the three things that are most important to them in your product category, why not just say your brand is exactly those three things?

The trouble is humans are not particularly good at processing lists of disconnected benefits. I was recently chatting with the general manager of a pharma company who was in the midst of launching an exciting new drug for the treatment of atopic dermatitis. I asked him, 'Hey, Don, so what are you saying about the brand?' 'Three things,' he responded, without missing a beat. 'First, it is a highly *effective* drug; second, it works *fast*; and third, it is, uh . . .' As he was talking, he was flipping open his fingers sequentially from a tightly wound fist in case the numeric count was lost on his audience. And then, instead of the third finger snapping out, there was a seven-second silence as he struggled to recall the third benefit on his list. And then after several shakes of his hand to jog his memory, he cried, 'And third, it is *convenient* for the dermatologist to use in his practice.' He turned to me, brandishing all three of the now released fingers in my face for effect, 'Well, what do you think?' I said, 'It's brilliant, if you can remember it. But, if you are having trouble, how will distracted physicians remember it. Especially, when the brand message is being blurted out by a nervous young sales rep on a thirty second timer.'

The challenge of list branding is that not all of its pieces connect into a real story. To understand why this does not work well, let us go into the puzzle analogy. Think of your product as a twenty-piece jigsaw puzzle, where each piece is a product feature or brand equity. Close your eyes and imagine that the puzzle depicts a Cézannesque painting of a happy-go-lucky peasant girl, riding atop a cart piled high with bales of hay, a donkey straining at its reins to pull the cart through a field with daffodils swaying gently in the breeze. Now, we pull the puzzle apart and jumble up the pieces. Then, I instruct you to rank each piece individually for attractiveness and pick the top three. You may pick one with the laughing face of the girl, one with the weary donkey and a third with a flower. Well done! Now we say, knit these very cool pieces into a brand idea. You go 'Hmm, "donkey" plus "flower" plus "girl face".' So, in a moment of displaced brilliance, you say, 'Use my brand and even a *donkey* can feel like a *happy girl* that will *flower* into her true potential.' Absurd, you say. Yet, companies all over use this approach of knitting together unrelated attractive pieces to don their brand message all the time. This is wrong because our brain does not make sense of the world—in this case, the painting—in this manner. It does pick pieces, to be sure, as research has shown, but craftily only those that help it understand the picture.

Instead of following my instructions, you may have been better off picking three pieces around the donkey to show it carrying the burden of mankind, or three pieces around the peasant girl to show her ensconced in the happiness of youth, or three pieces around the swaying daffodils to show the indifference of mother nature to the travails of humanity. Even if some of those pieces were rather plain, you would have been more successful in telling a memorable story true to the essence of the painting. That is because those pieces connect together and say something. They work better because even though some important elements of the big picture are missing, the story told is true and sensible.

And so it is for cognitive branding. The idea is to take a few cognitive threads to knit together an engaging story that the audience can remember and find compelling. Not every brand equity that pops up as important in market research, has to be a part of the story, but the equities that are in there, must relate compelling threads of the drama. In the process, you may in fact leave out some key equities but don't sweat it. When customers are drawn to your brand, they will go on to discover the other parts of your brand story.

## The Cognitive Branding Framework

In the following chapters, we will learn how to create the mental threads that weave together the fabric of iconic cognitive brands. Having invoked Cezanne into colouring our analogy, let's reflect on how the master thought about great art: 'For an impressionist to paint from nature is not to paint the subject, but to realize sensations.' With cognitive brands, we look to find the keys that can unlock the sensations of past experiences or fantasies that live consciously or subconsciously in our minds, make us feel happier and that we are drawn to.

As we go through our lives, we experience sensations at every moment. If you thought that our brains recorded a snapshot from each of the five human senses, five times per second, for as long as we lived, a seventy-five-year-old man would hold nearly sixty billion impressions. Good thing, then, that a person's brain has eighty billion neurons and one trillion interconnections among them in its neural net.[4] All of this information is neuro-chemically burnt into our brain cells or sitting in little electrical charges in the synaptic net. That collection of chemicals, charges and biologic materials represents who we are, what we know, what we hold as true and how we think the world works. More to the point of this book, it governs how we, as consumers, make sense of the brands we buy. That knowledge is inscribed like biochemical tattoos in our brains. You can try to remove the tattoos and get new ones, but if you have ever tried that trick, you know how it goes. That is why what I call cognitive brands are designed to work the way the brain is programmed already. And that is why they work so well.

There are three possible elements in a cognitive brand: I call them *Brand Vibes*, *Brand Sense* and *Brand Resolve* (See Figure 3.2). I say 'elements' because they are a part of the brand that says something about its nature. It could do so in words, or with its logo and appearance, or with its smell and touch, any other cue for that matter. And I say 'possible' element, because not all need to be present formulaically in every cognitive brand. The brain is very flexible in its working and can make sense of brands in a number of ways. We are going to be diving deep

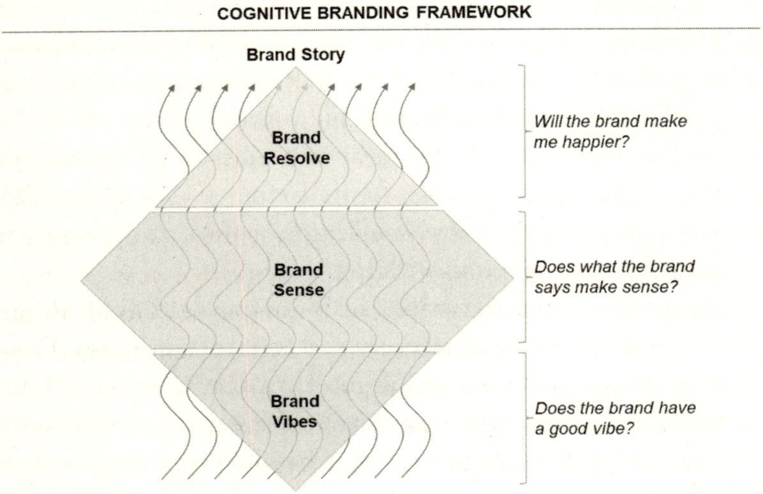


*Figure 3.2: Cognitive brands create or resonate with thought patterns in the consumer's mind that are based on a foundation of good Vibes, good Sense and good Resolve, or together, the brand Visers that lead to lasting relationships.*

into the three elements of cognitive brands, their vibes, sense and resolve, with a chapter devoted to each. But before we start on that journey, I want you to have a pocket-book summary of the concept.

I will say the following sentence over and over in this book. *Cognitive brands work the way the brain does.* Thus, it is not surprising that the cognitive branding model closely mirrors the functional subunits of the marketing brain that I described in the previous chapters. Here's what the three elements of cognitive brands do:

- **Brand Vibes:** When consumers look at brands, a question they may ask is, '*Does it give me good vibes? Can I trust it?*' Brand vibes are a way for the brand to establish a bond or shared chemistry with the consumer. They allow the brand to say to the consumer, '*I feel what you feel*' or '*I know what you are going through*'. In other cases, they look to assure the consumer that the brand is in sync with their values, beliefs or aspirations. It sees the world the way they see it. Brand vibes are *not* the product value proposition, but rather the amuse-bouche that preps the brain for the main course. When done in the right way, vibes make consumers more receptive to the core brand promise. Consumers feel like they are on the same wavelength as the brand, that they trust it and feel a bond with it.

  Brand vibes connect with the prior positive experiences in the *Learner* and *Calibrator* subunits of the brain. They sort of put the brain in a good copacetic mood. Thus, when the main brand proposition follows, the *Associator* or *Deliberator* subunits in the brain are already predisposed to accepting it. In this way, vibes condition the brain to have a favourable disposition towards the brand. For brands that have a steep hill to climb because they are new and different or are starting with a trust deficit, good vibes can be an essential tool in the arsenal.

- **Brand Sense:** The second question a consumer asks of any brand is, '*Does what it says make sense to me?*' From behavioural sciences we know that the brain works through the dual processes of System 1 and System 2 to make choices. Accordingly, cognitive brands can use what I term *System 1 Easers* or *System 2 Deliberators* to let the consumer assess whether or not the claims of a brand make good sense.

  *Easers* use System 1 processes to make consumers believe that what the brand says *makes good sense* by working with the existing wiring in their brain. They target the *Associator* subunit of the brain and just go with the flow. Easers don't like to ruffle feathers; they look for ways to align with the consumer's own cognitive biases frictionlessly. You could say that *Easers give the brand instinctive good sense.*

  Choosing is mentally taxing for the brain. If the brain can avoid that extra effort, it would much prefer to do so. Thus, as the name implies, *Easers* look for ways to make brand choice sensible by making it feel easy. They can do so in a number of ways. For example, a brand easer may make the choice feel familiar or similar to the good choices the consumer had made in the past. They can also make the brand choice easier by making it feel more true or authentic. They can make a choice simply feel good. And finally, *Easers* can make brand choice easy by finding a way to simplify it and making it non-taxing for the brain.

  In contrast, *Deliberators* use System 2 processes to make consumers believe that what the brand says makes sense by egging on the brain to scrutinize the unfamiliar or dissect its existing biases and beliefs. They are harder to pull off because they involve laying new wiring or re-inscribing tattoos in the brain. It is akin to converting someone to a new religion. As the name implies, these processes draw on the *Deliberator* subunit of the brain which, as we know, is loaded with an impressive toolkit of mental methods for comparing options and analysing needs and wants in-depth. Thus, you could say that *Deliberators give the brand reasoned good sense*. They do their thing to let the consumer know that everything about the brand 'checks out'.

*Deliberators* try to influence brand choice by highlighting the value proposition of the product and if need be by 'amping' up its benefits to make the choice feel like a no-brainer or providing hard evidence to make those benefits believable. In other cases, brand deliberators may look for ways to mitigate the risk of choice for the consumer. Finally, *Deliberators* can also change the consumer's perspective, or the lens by which they evaluate the brand, so as to shed better light on it.

- **Brand Resolve:** The final question that a consumer may ask is, '*Will I be happier if buy this brand*?' Brand resolve is responsible for pushing us off the fence of indecision and inaction. Without it, consumers would choose, but never buy. Resolve links brands with a consumer's goal of greater happiness and his conative drive to pursue it. In behavioural research, happiness is not an abstraction; it's a science. Brand resolve strategies aim to trigger the *Conator*, which is the action subunit of the brain.

  Each person's resolve or tendency for action is different and has to do with their DNA. It relates to their inborn desire to be free and in control, feel good about themselves and make the world a better place for themselves and others. That is ultimately what drives happiness. When brands enmesh themselves to this natural conative energy, they get the resolve and the brand buys they want.

I like to think that cognitive brands have great karma, what with all their good vibes, good sense (instinctive or reasoned) and good resolve. Together, I call them our *Brand Visers*. Got that? Vi-Se-R? It is a nice little acronym for remembering the three brand elements, *vi*bes, *se*nse and *re*solve, and in old French, the word *viser* means 'to aim'.[5] With cognitive brands, that is what we are doing, isn't it? Aiming for the perfect sensations right between your ears.

* * *

## *Key Takeaways*

It is time for marketers to move out of their comfort zones. Brand ladders and list branding have survived because marketers are fond of them, the same way that Grandma loves her old and decrepit rocker. With the advance of brain sciences, we have something that is way better than that languishing piece of furniture. We have cognitive brands.

Cognitive brands work the way the brain does, aiming for the sensation right between our ears. They connect with who we are and what we believe. They drive conscious and subconscious choice and make consumers happier.

Cognitive brands have three elements, namely, good vibes, sense and resolve.

- Brand vibes build a unique bond or chemistry between the consumer and the brand, and pave the way for the main proposition.
- Brand sense helps consumers make instinctive or reasoned sense of their choices with System 1 *Easers* or System 2 *Deliberators*.

- Brand resolve helps consumers consider whether it is all worth the bother and prompts them to buy the brands that would make them happier.

In the next four chapters, we discuss how to design each of these three elements of a cognitive brand, starting with brand vibes in the next.

# 4

# Brand Vibes: Tugging at the Heartstrings

## *Part 1 of Brand Architecture*

*'If you don't understand what I'm going through, how can you help me?'*

—Lisa, patient

That simple question from Lisa, a patient in one of our focus groups, left me a little unnerved. As a brand marketer, I wondered, 'Why can't I just tell you what my drug will do for you? It is what it is. You make the call. Why do you need to know if I understand how you feel?' Nothing that I had learnt in marketing by that time suggested that brands needed to have a special chemistry with their customers. Wasn't it supposed to be simply '*You've got a problem and I've got a solution*'?

Rheumatoid arthritis (RA) is an invisible disease. Everything that goes wrong, does so inside the body, at least in the earlier stages. Outwardly, Lisa looks quite normal, even when she is far from it. Her joints hurt like hell and are so stiff in the mornings that she has trouble getting out of bed and being active. As a

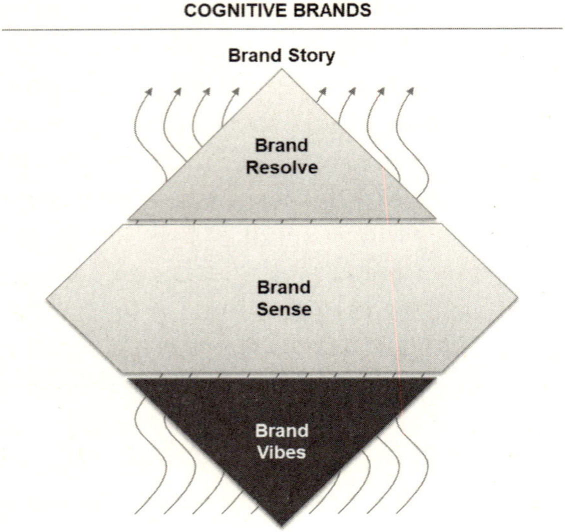


*Figure 4.1: Part 1: Using brand vibes to build empathetic connections with consumers.*

result, other people who don't know that, can be quite mean to the poor soul. In strip malls, shoppers glare at Lisa when she pulls up her cars into a handicap parking spot; she looks fine to them. Her mother-in-law, who lives nearby and often has to drop by to help around the house, often loses her patience and tells her to drag her butt out of bed like everyone else and get the house cleaned. The emotional pain can hurt as much as the physical. As she told me that day, 'You feel like you're wearing a mask for everyone else all of the time. Who wants to hear about your pain every morning? I just say I'm okay, but only my mom knows. She says, "Lisa, you're not okay."'

When my company did the branding for Humira, a drug for treating RA, we worked hard with the AbbVie managers and their agency to create print ads that let the patients know that we understood what they were going through. In one version, they showed a mother tying her daughter's hair into a ponytail. In the picture, if you looked carefully, you could see that the mother's hands were very slightly deformed from the advance of the disease. But that simple image had its own secret communication with the patients; if you have severe RA, it would be difficult for you to have the dexterity in your hands to tie hair into a knot, unless the medication was working. The picture would mean nothing special to a normal person but would resonate deeply with a woman suffering from RA. It showed that we knew that a mom with RA could not get up in the morning and do what every other mother does routinely—help her little daughter get ready for school. Reaching into that hurt was the key to connecting with the patients. They needed to know that we got it.

You don't require a textbook to tell you that people like to *connect* with people. Brand marketers don't necessarily know this, but it is true that when people think that you 'get them', they are more likely to believe in whatever else you have to say. As a matter fact, rheumatologists are known for spending a lot of time just listening to their patients. While general practitioners may see 40–60 patients per day, it is not unusual for a rheumatologist to examine just 12–15, or less than half of that. By spending more time empathizing with what their patients are going through, rheumatologists earn their trust, and their patients are much more likely to follow their advice on eating right and performing their physiotherapy regularly. Despite the hundreds of millions of dollars spent on consumer advertising by drug companies, most patients still choose the drug that their rheumatologist recommends.

For marketers, brand vibes are elements that pave the way for the main brand value proposition and make it more likely to be embraced by the consumer. It is not a necessary step for every brand, but it can ease the pain, particularly when dealing with products that have a steeper hill to climb to adoption.

When brands establish a sense of kinship with consumers, they create positive feelings and trust. That positivity then rubs off on the brand as well in related processes that psychologists refer to as 'misattribution' or 'evaluative conditioning'.[1] What happens is that when your brain processes two different signals, one of which you like a lot, together or in quick succession with one another, it can 'mistakenly' halo the feeling of positivity around both. This is because the neural circuitry in the brain for processing both signals can overlap and things get mixed up. Think of it like this. You are a woman and you pass by two attractive gents in a room. One of them is wearing a nice earthy cologne. You can't really tell which one and thus you may be primed[2] to have a generally good feeling about both. In the marketing world this happens often. When you see a brand, say, the latest perfume, J'Adore Absolu, by Dior, together with a celebrity endorser whom you like, in this case Charlize Theron, you tend to like it more.[3] That is, if you like Charlize Theron, which I do!

There are two ways for a brand to create good vibes with consumers—one is by understanding their angst or sharing their feelings, and second is by sharing their beliefs and values or getting on the same page with them. You should note that good brand vibes follow from this shared chemistry *without* necessarily any discussion about the product's attributes and benefits. If brands establish that personal connection with the consumer, all else follows more comfortably. It works for humans and it works with brands.

## Brand Vibes: I Know How You Feel

A wonderful example of a company that understood the value of creating great brand vibes and connecting with its customers is Tanishq. How Tanishq built a special bond with the emerging ranks of independent-minded Indian women in all walks of life is truly one of the great brand stories of our time.[4] From its fledgling start in the '80s to its near demise in the '90s to now, Tanishq has taken its place as the most unlikely member of the top echelon of retail brands in India. Consider what the brand had to do to get there. It had to convince women to buy jewellery from a national chain when for eons they had done so only through their local family jewellers. What it offered was jewellery that traditionally would not qualify as such in an Indian household, given that it is usually engraved in 14–18 karat gold instead of the requisite 22 karat. Top that with premium prices for a nation of thrifty-and-proud-of-it value-conscious Indians.

The Tanishq brand succeeded as it has by finding its vibe in the voice of modern Indian women, its soul in theirs. Over the last quarter century, a tsunamic gender shift has been underway in India. In a society that had been male-dominated for a long time, women were increasingly taking prominent roles in workplace and home, emerging spirited and free from the shadows of their husbands, brothers, fathers and male compatriots. They were smart, creative, charismatic and ready to show it. And in them, there was a new-found confidence to embrace all that was great in the traditions of India and to jettison all that was regressive, and to do so on their own terms. In this challenge to the ethos of the past, the clash of social norms, Tanishq wanted to be by the side of the women of India and in the face of those who may seek to pull them down.

Tanishq started with an early campaign in which a young and nubile woman is shown brushing off her parents' suggestion to meet with an eligible bachelor with unquestionably A+ credentials. That's until she enters the Tanishq store and is mesmerized by the breathtakingly beautiful jewellery. In that moment, she imagines marriage as a possibility. As she drives back again with her parents, she asks, 'So what was his name again?' Except now, it is a choice on her own terms.

As Tanishq marched on, it took on more edgy issues. With its brand theme—'For those who chose love above all'—it made its mission to celebrate love in all forms. In its print campaign, featuring two earrings—'Two of a kind always make a beautiful pair'—it gives a nod to the burning issues surrounding the rights of the closeted lesbian and gay community in India.

But it is Tanishq's 'Remarriage' commercial that is a true masterpiece.[5] In a country where it is still unusual for divorced women to remarry, Tanishq put exactly such a marriage front and center of its television campaign. It shows a bride, with her young daughter playing by her side, as she gets ready for her wedding. As the ceremonies proceed to the *pheras*, the ritual where the bride and groom walk seven times around the sacred fire and exchange their vows, the little girl too wants to follow her mother around. Even as friends and relatives try to restrain the girl, the would-be father sweeps her up in his arms and carries her around through the pheras. The ad was an unflinching signal from Tanishq to the women of India that no matter what, it was the one brand that would stand by their side, against the tide, against the odds and against the norms of a bygone era.

That was back in 2013. More recently, with its sub-brand Mia, offering jewellery for women professionals, Tanishq has launched the #BestAtWork and #MeInAction campaigns on social media that celebrate women fighting daily prejudices at work. The 'Last Thing on My Mind' commercial follows a woman as she slips on her Mia bracelet on her wrist, infusing it with a dash of perfume and heading off to take on the challenges at work.[6] The last thing on her mind, she tells us, are the people living in their little bubbles who can't imagine a woman balancing work life and home, people who think she gets ahead not because of her work but because she is a 'chick' and how she may be getting too big for her shoes. The only thing on her mind is bringing her best to work.

The Tanishq strategy wins with its brand vibes, the chemistry it establishes with Indian women on the move. The product itself, the stunning jewellery the retailer sells, is only incidental in the commercials. Yet, women have no doubt that the Tanishq brand gets them and feels what they feel. It is a friend like no other.

For those who think that opportunities for such deep brand vibes can only be seen in the odd market niche, the story of Dollar Shave Club, the unlikely David that took a punishing crack at Gillette, a sleeping Goliath, is instructive. The brainchild of Michael Dubin, a failed entrepreneur, the Dollar Shave Club disrupted a market monopoly by tapping into the deeply felt angst among men—that the money they had to spend on buying shaving blades constituted highway robbery.

The business took off when one day a desperate Dubin decided to string together a video to put on the Web. Filmed in a warehouse full of boxes of unsold blades, the one-minute-thirty-three-second film is pure angst, every drop of it.[7] Described by AdWeek as an act of 'violent comedy', the ad starts with Mike introducing himself bluntly: 'Hi, I'm Mike, founder of Dollar Shave Club. What is the Dollar Shave Club? Well, for a dollar a month, we send high quality razors right to your door.'[8] Now he gets up from his desk and starts pacing about, 'Yeah! A Dollar!' As the drama builds, you can see Mike getting all worked up, 'Are the blades any good? Nah! Our blades are f***ing great!' By now, the words are flying fast and furious, as Mike smashes through a paper divider separating his office from the main warehouse. 'Do you like spending $20 on brand name razors?' he demands to know. 'Nineteen go to Roger Federer. And do you think your razor needs a vibrating handle, a flashlight, a back scratcher and ten blades? Your handsome-ass grandfather had one blade . . . and polio.' And then finally, 'Stop paying for shave tech you don't need . . . and start deciding where you're going to stack all those dollar bills, I'm saving you.' His message hit home, despite the fact that the Dollar Club blades are not exactly the same high quality as Gillette's and don't last as long. The clip was tagged by millions to their friends. And that's exactly what happens in the Twitter and Facebook world of today. When people feel your brand vibes so deeply, they talk about you. By 2014, 50,000 people a month were being referred to the online store by fans. Mike's YouTube video has been seen by more than twenty-six million viewers.

While opportunities to find such gut-level connections with customers may be difficult to orchestrate for every brand, great vibes are a relevant consideration in each brand positioning. Showing the customer that you get them, works. As we saw in these examples, the interesting thing about brand vibes is that the angst felt by the consumer is not necessarily about the product specifically; rather, it is about how people fail to understand them. In Humira, patients feel the hurt that comes from people not understanding their physical limitations. In the Tanishq case, the angst flows from Indian social norms treating women as unequal to men. In Harry's, it comes from men feeling like they have been taken for a ride by blade manufacturers.

## Brand Vibes: I Believe What You Believe

If the first approach to good vibes is for the brand to say to the consumers 'I know how you feel', the second is to profess that 'I believe what you believe. We are on the same wavelength.' This sets the stage for the marketer to then reveal that what his brand offers is consistent with those beliefs. In other words, the brand makes an argument of the type, 'If you believe "A" is true, then you must believe that so is "B".' In this case 'A' is something that the brand marketer knows the customer will relate to, 'B' is his brand's proposition. This happens because of what Robert Cialdini identifies as the 'Consistency Principle'.[9] Once you have agreed or committed to an idea, you are inclined to agree with other related ones. Let's see how this works with an example.

Pfizer, the maker of a pain medication called Celebrex, used this strategy deftly to put value-aligned vibes into its consumer campaign. You may not know this yet, but as you grow older, the protective cartilage that cushions the ends of your bones wears down and you develop arthritis. Then, with bone rubbing against bone, it becomes painful for you to move around. However, as your doctor will strongly urge, the more you move, the more those bones will grind out the rough edges and spurs, and the less painful it will become. Bottom line, forcing yourself to be active will actually make things better. This is a belief that will be etched in your brain by the time your doctor is done with you.

In one version of Pfizer's commercial, you see a man sitting in the front porch of his winter home. [10] In the distance, his son is seen shovelling the snow. The voiceover says, 'It's simple physics. A body at rest tends to stay at rest, while a body in motion stays in motion.' Well, so far so good. Who's going to argue with simple physics? It is a shared belief. You see the man get up from his chair, a mischievous twinkle in his eye, as the voiceover continues, '. . . But if you have arthritis, staying active can be difficult. Prescription Celebrex can ease your pain so that your body can stay in motion.' The man bends down to pick up a handful of snow; he rolls it into a snowball and nails his son with it in a swift throw. The ad carefully takes any semblance of blame off you (tells you it knows what arthritis is doing to you silently) and offers Celebrex as the solution for your tendency to be inactive. It is easy to see why this ad would not have been the same thing if all it said was, 'Celebrex is great at easing your pain.' By connecting the idea of your activity and condition to simple physics, Pfizer taps into your belief biases and connects them to their brand. The connecting vibe makes an ordinary brand gambit extraordinary.

People like to be consistent with their beliefs and will align their choices and actions accordingly. This may have been news to psychologists, but not to kids who have mastered these tactics into a science. Teenaged Sophia does not start by asking dad for the car. Instead, she may say something like, "*Dad, I like the fact that you are not uptight like other dads.*" That is the connecting vibe, not the ask, in case you were not paying attention. This is soon followed by "*Dad, can I borrow the car tonight? Please?*" with a pretty favorable probability of success. When you have accepted the first premise (that you are not so uptight), you are more likely to accept the second related idea (that you should give the car). In cognitive branding too, the second idea can be the point, with the first being the connecting vibe.

A quintessential example of this strategy could be seen in Nike's decision to place the highly charged figure of Colin Kaepernick front and center on its billboard in New York's Times Square. In 2016, Colin, the star quarterback for San Francisco 49ers, lit up a firestorm of controversy when he decided to kneel during the playing of the national anthem to protest racial injustice and police brutality against blacks in the United States.[11] Donald Trump pounced on the opportunity to castigate Kaepernick as an unpatriotic liberal. In the furore that followed, Kaepernick failed to get a contract renewal with the National Football League and never played professional football again. Undaunted, Nike went ahead with making the young quarterback the star of their 'Just do it' campaign.

The black-and-white poster was almost entirely covered by Kaepernick's face, with the words 'Believe in something. Even if it means sacrificing everything' etched in stark relief across it. The idea of standing for one's rights was central to the beliefs of many in the years of divisive politics that followed Trump's election. By buying Nike branded shoes, people were expressing their solidarity with the beliefs that the brand and Kaepernick represented.

The strategy was a departure from the norm. Nike's brand is built around the idea of performance shoes. Most often, that strategy has been executed by securing endorsements from the world's top players, including Michael Jordan and LeBron James. In those instances, the brand was saying, 'These shoes are so amazing that even Jordan plays his games in them.' The Kaepernick strategy was completely different. This was a brand forging connections with its consumers, giving empathetic vibes, with an 'I believe in what you believe' strategy that had little to do with the performance aspect of the shoes. In the aftermath of the campaign, while many Trump supporters rushed to rallies in which they dutifully burnt their old Nike pairs, quarterly sales and profits for the company grew rapidly.[12]

## Words of Caution from Fallen Angels

Brand vibes can also work against you if you are not careful. If you stuck it out as an investor in L Brands since 2010, you must have had quite a ride. A stock that once quintupled on the heels of the success of its Victoria's Secret brand, had by 2020, plunged right back to earth. It's like it never went up, or worse.

The initial success of Victoria's Secret lay in forging a bond of solidarity with women. It, de facto, championed women's right to be sexy and show it. Before Victoria's Secret, bras were a comfort-and-fit purchase. The Body by Victoria line changed all of that. Its Miracle Bra was heavily padded and strapped with an underwire to accentuate cleavage. Women were looking sexier. Previously, bras and lingerie were sold in unremarkable boxes in discreet corners of big stores. Instead, Victoria's Secret not only decked their stores in racy lingerie and bras from front to end but also put them on a runway show on primetime television in 1997. It wasn't just that the brand made women feel sexier; rather that it made the new kind of sexiness a part of mainstream sensibilities. Women felt free and empowered and fell head over heels in love with the brand.

Unfortunately, somewhere along the way, Victoria's Secret betrayed that trust. It went from being a champion of women's right to be and 'show sexy', to trying to be the arbiter of who and what could be sexy. In a *Vogue* interview, its CMO dissed the idea of body positive women and transgenders modelling on its runway show. 'It's a fantasy show,' he explained.[13] It missed the trend from underwire bras to bralettes, failing to redefine sexiness in a new mould, to where modern women were headed versus where they had been. Women felt used and disrespected. It was especially painful coming from a friend they had trusted over the years—a friend that was now judging them. Women simply walked away. In March 2020, the company sold off a controlling share to the private equity firm Sycamore Partners for $1.1 billion, a pittance compared to its value in its heyday. With the COVID-19 attack of 2020, even that deal unravelled quickly.

Deep vibes with customers do wonders for brands but come with their own risks. Brand vibes are compacts, not fantasies. Brands that betray the confidence they build with their customers can find themselves deep in a hole that they cannot climb out of.

* * *

*Key Takeaways*

Cognitive brands often connect deeply with the consumer and answer their question, 'Does this brand give me good vibes? Can I trust it?'

The idea of including vibes in brands to condition consumers is new. Previously, brand strategies focused narrowly on unpacking their functional or emotional benefits. With the connective tissue of vibes, cognitive brands can do a lot more.

Brand vibe-based strategies mimic our own behaviours as humans, in how we relate to others and have social chemistry with them. When brands build that kind of kinship with consumers, choice and preference follow more easily. However, brands that connect with the customer but then betray the trust do so at their own risk. Brand vibes may be based on:

- Shared feelings, where the brand says 'I know how you feel' to the consumer, or
- Shared beliefs, where the brand says, 'I believe what you believe' to the consumer.

Now that we have learnt how to work with the first element of cognitive brands, namely brand vibes, it's time to dive into the subject of brand sense with System 1 Easers (Chapter 5) and System 2 Deliberators (Chapter 6).

# 5

# Brand Sense: Using System 1 Easers to Go with the Flow

## *Part 2A of Brand Architecture*

It has been said by some others that it is odd that my dog and I appear to behave similarly at times. That is a bit of a touchy subject with me, and so I feel obliged to call in the big guns to defend myself. Let me start with explaining what this is all about.

Take just the other week. I was taking the building elevator up to our apartment, after walking Kami, our little bichon frise, in the park. Through the corner of my eye, I noticed that the other two neighbours riding along with us in the lift were repeatedly looking at us and then looking at each other, and then chuckling. When I turned around to scowl at them with my best 'Not nice!' look, they explained, 'Oh no, it's nothing. But did you know that you and your dog were both yawning together?' I had noticed nothing of the sort but was immediately sceptical of the possibility that the smug cotton-ball puff of a dog could be exercising any level of subconscious control over my physical responses. Never!

When I related the incident to my wife, whose dog Kami really is, she didn't find it as ridiculous as I thought she would.

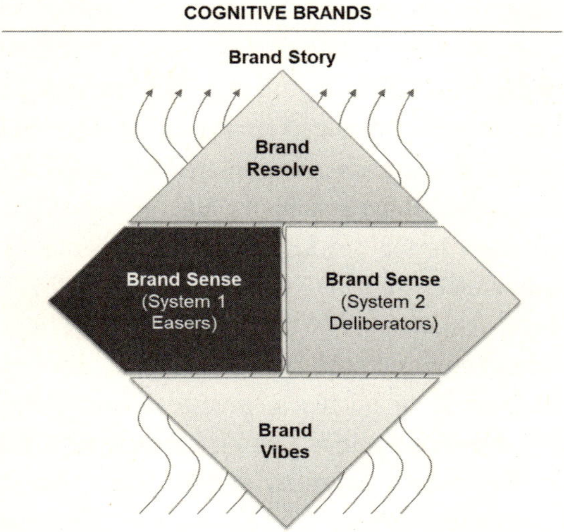


*Figure 5.1: Part 2a: Making brand sense with System 1 Easers*

And for good measure, she upped the ante, adding, 'You know, I've been meaning to tell you, but the two of you kind of look similar.' Anticipating a spate of vigorous objections from me, to settle matters pre-emptively, she produced a recent photograph of the two of us, the dog and me, in which we are in my friend Damen's boat, looking at Navy Pier at an oddly similar angle with our mouths slightly open. In the dimming light of the city, against the twinkling stars, there is admittedly a slight resemblance. Very slight, I concede, but in my mind, I am thinking I am in twilight zone.

As you may guess, this kind of mortifying event would keep me up at night. I am thinking there must be a *scientific* explanation for this, like when people imagine they have seen a UFO but it really is just a wayward weather balloon. It turns out that researchers have shown that pure-bred dogs do look like their owners, much more so than random chance would suggest.[1] This happens because we are subconsciously biased towards liking things that look and seem familiar to us. This theory implies that my wife bought Kami in the first instance because the dog looks like me and she likes the way I look. And honestly, I really prefer this explanation a lot. I'm sticking to it.

What about the yawning in sync thing? It so happens that we are also cognitively wired to fit into groups. The sense of belonging makes us feel good. To do so, we may accentuate behaviours that are common to the group, mimicking emotions, facial and body expressions of those around us. There is in fact a phenomenon known as the *chameleon effect*,[2] whereby people subconsciously imitate gestures, attitudes and behaviours of those around them in a social setting because of the activation of their so-called mirror neurons.[3] Babies in daycare centres cry when they hear other babies doing the same. Smokers light up when they see another person smoking a cigarette. It happens automatically, without much thought. There is limited research to test this hypothesis across species, but let's go with it.

There are a lot of things we do and choices we make subconsciously. As we will see shortly, familiarity and the feeling of goodness from belonging to a group trigger something called cognitive ease and drive our behaviour. In branding, what I call System 1 Easers, are elements of a brand that help the consumer make sense of the brand propositions instinctively, quickly and without much thought. As we have already discussed, 'System 1' processes of the brain govern subconscious or low-vigilance human behaviour.

## Meet the System 1 Autopilot

Daniel Kahneman and Amos Tversky identified two basic processes by which the brain works, namely System 1 and System 2. System 1 provides us the ability to react to stimuli and to do things in an automatic and instinctive manner.

Even though driving a car is an extremely complicated task, we can do it practically in our sleep. Any eighteen-month-old will inform you that walking and talking simultaneously is not that easy either, but again, once they learn it, it is no longer a problem.

System 1 processes helps us do a lot more than walking and talking effortlessly. They account for most of our daily behaviour. Some suggest that 95 per cent of the choices we make are based on System 1 processes in our brain. From the moment we are born and every minute that we are alive, we are observing and learning things consciously or subconsciously. All of it is processed and continuously encoded into our brains. The brain uses System 2 processes to create new knowledge only episodically, by applying logic and reasoning. However, System 1 creates knowledge all of the time by recognizing associations across disparate experiences and improving upon our past store of knowledge. Regardless of where it comes from, all knowledge is biochemically stencilled on to the *Learner* subunit of the brain as our personal cache of wisdom and thereafter available automatically and instinctively. We use it all the time for making sense of brands.

As consumers, we encode rules and biases about the products we buy every time we experience them. For example, over time, we may come to believe 'all organic foods are good and healthy', or 'higher horsepower engine means a faster and more expensive car', or 'branded products are better in quality than their private label clones'. Most of the time, these rules serve us well, and we apply them effortlessly and without thinking across a wide array of choices. The marketer who emblazons 'ORGANIC' on his packet of mini carrots is counting on that and wants to tap into the neural circuit in our heads that says '*Organic = Good = Buy*'. That is a classic System 1 play, whereby the marketer successfully plugs his brand into a pre-existing mental short cut that we use and positions it as an instant sensible choice.

Over time, associations become routine and habitual. Because System 1 rules and wisdom are biochemically 'burnt' into the neural network in our brain, they function as hard-to-break habits.[4] If you are used to reading your email and texting friends while walking on the street, you will find it difficult to change that behaviour, even when the consequences can be grave. Pedestrian injuries due to cell phone use are up 35 per cent since 2010.[5] Yet millions of people continue to walk and text because most of the time nothing untoward happens and the brain rules it as generally safe.

So, what other rules are wired into people's brains? What can brand marketers use? Well, researchers have documented dozens of common System 1 cognitive biases, shared learning and wisdom, whereby we have an inbuilt bias for acting in a particular way in certain situations. They are mental short cuts for choice. It is like you favouring your forehand in receiving a tennis serve, even though there are times when it is inadvisable. Yet, these mental short cuts stem from a lifetime of experiences across disparate situations. In most cases, this inlayed wisdom works well for us, but in a few, it doesn't. Just like the Ten Commandments. That is why I like to think of these biases as 'cognitive wisdom.'

The existence of these known biases presents an opportunity for marketers. When they can align their brand propositions with these universal predilections, their brands make a whole lot of sense to consumers and are preferred reflexively. Recent research by Sam Maglio and Taly Reich has shown that not only do we make choices non-deliberatively, by gut feel, with our System 1 Easers more frequently, but also that those preferences are then more resilient.[6] We believe in these choices more and don't let go of them easily.

## Brand Sense with System 1 Easers

At the heart of our System 1 processes is a 'cognitive ease' engine. When you feel that a choice is *familiar*, *true*, *good or easy*, you experience a sense of mental comfort, a 'processing fluency' that is the opposite of stress, and you tend to accept and prefer it. Thus, you experience cognitive ease and will tend to accept a brand when its choice feels either: (a) Familiar, (b) True, (c) Good or (d) Easy—four factors that were identified by Kahneman in his research.[7] You tend to embrace these brand choices without a lot of thought or vigilance. In contrast, when you feel something is foreign, false, bad for you or requires a lot of time and energy, you experience cognitive stress. You are suspicious and vigilant and will need a lot more convincing before accepting those choices.

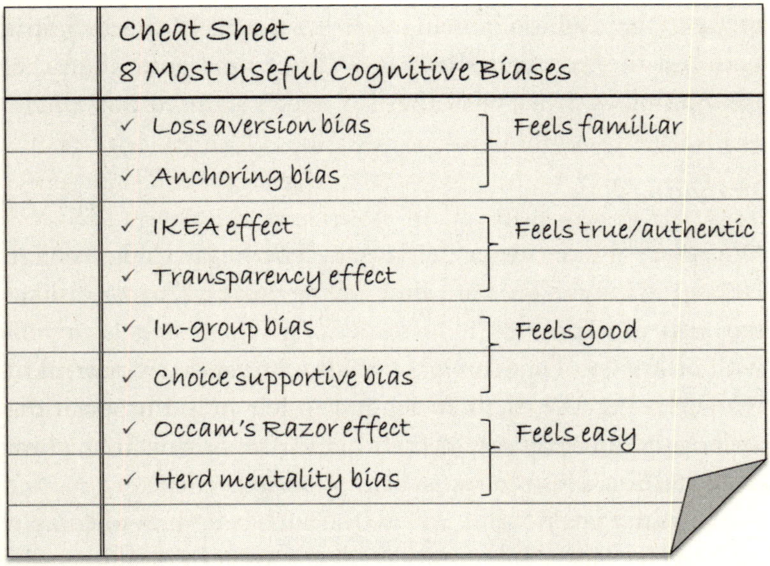


*Figure 5.2: Brands use Easers to attract consumers by appealing to the wisdom (cognitive biases) that the brain has assembled over a multitude of life experiences. The brain accepts these propositions as good sense without a lot of scrutiny. They target System 1 processes in the brain.*

Psychologists have researched and documented well over a hundred different cognitive biases that are common to most humans. A number of them are closely related to each other, and so the list of distinct biases is shorter. For our purposes in designing brands, some are more useful than others. In the following sections, I give you a cheat-sheet of eight 'System 1 Easers' that are valuable in building cognitive brands.

## 1. Brand Sense by Making Choice Feel Familiar

As consumers, we have a tendency to stick with what we have and what we know. It's like Grandpa with his old recliner. He is used to its look and feel. It's what he knows; it's what he has; it's perfect and not going anywhere, even when it is decrepit and marginally unsafe for use. There are two cognitive biases that relate to these all too human tendencies, namely, the anchoring bias and the loss aversion bias. When brands can align their positioning to these, what they say makes sense to consumers.

### *Anchoring Bias*

We all say 'I like this or that' often. The funny thing, though, is that the brain has a hard time telling what it likes or dislikes, unless it can compare it to something else that it is *familiar* with or knows. That thing is the *anchor*. This is wonderful for marketers because they can suggest to the consumer what that anchor should be as part of their brand proposition. The power of suggestion does the rest subconsciously.

In brand positioning, we use the anchoring bias to enhance the perceived value of our product by providing consumers with a strategically selected, superior anchor. Kraft's campaign for its frozen pizza, 'It's not delivery, it's DiGiorno', took the frozen pizza category by storm. Anyone who has ordered takeout pizza knows that it is hard to replicate the brick-oven aroma and charred-crust flavour of delivery pizza with a month-old, thawed-out frozen pizza at home. However, by anchoring their brand to the experience of delivery pizza, Kraft was able to plant the seed in the consumer's mind that DiGiorno was almost as good. Even if you adjusted for a slight overpromise, it was still going to feel better than any frozen pizza from the competition. Make no mistake, the brand promise cannot be an illusion; the product does have to deliver, else over time the *Learner* unit in the brain will figure out that the experience is not measuring up to the expectations and start taking points off the 'happiness scorecard' and repeat purchases will be cancelled or curtailed.

My company Cerenti's client, ConAgra, did the same kind of anchoring with its ACT II popcorn in country after country.* Almost from its inception, ACT II promised to deliver 'theatre' quality popcorn from your microwave, in the comfort of your home. The name itself came from an earlier version of the product called ACT ONE. If you look at the packaging box for ACT II, you would think the product itself is an Oscar-worthy hit release from Hollywood. It holds several visual cues highlighting the connection to movie theatres. ACT II, the brand name, is enclosed in a Hollywood-style theatre sign with incandescent bulbs around it. The name of the flavour, 'Movie Theater Butter', is splashed across a reel of film. This basic idea worked well not only in the United States, making it the top-selling popcorn in the country, but also made ACT II number one in other countries like Mexico and India.

Yet, marketers have to be careful; consumers can also anchor your brand in a manner that you fail to anticipate. Over

---

* The events described in the following passages about ConAgra have been fictionalized and the names disguised to remove any non-public information and preserve the privacy of the mentioned individuals. The narrative is thus designed to be instructive rather than accurately biographical or historical.

time, ACT II found that its link to the theatre experience was dropping like a lead anchor around its ankles, docking the brand overly to family movie-watching occasions. That was great when there was just one television that everyone in the house milled around. Now, with each household member streaming shows to their personal mobile devices, the family television watching moment is going the way of the landline phone. People snack on their own and watch movies alone. Suddenly, ACT II found itself being displaced by brands like Skinny Pop and Pirates Booty, which positioned themselves as healthy or fun snacks to eat alone. The lesson learnt is that marketers have to manage both conscious and subconscious anchors that your brand is tagged to.

Jill Ramsey, the no-nonsense, let's-grow-faster international chief for ConAgra, did not like the look of this and wanted to stop ACT II from being swallowed up by this expanding sinkhole. Together with her country heads for Mexico and India, we worked to reposition the brand around a new set of anchors. The brand was gradually reincarnated as 'the smarter choice' that could 'make any moment a special moment'. The 'smarter choice' equity *anchored against* potato chips, which by far are the fattest snack category to go after. Popcorn is smarter because it is not fried and thus healthier. With microwaves in every home and office now, and ready-to-eat packaging options, popcorn can be enjoyed anytime and anywhere. Also, microwavable popcorn is a one-of-a-kind snack. When the kernels crackle, pop and dance out of their steaming bag, there is a drama that turns any moment into a mini fiesta. Accordingly, the revised strategy in the Indian markets anchored consumers to the everyday moments instead of the rare family movie occasions. How about as a special treat when your thirteen-year-old daughter returns home from school at three in the afternoon? How about when the boyfriend steals a private moment with his girl?

ACT II was also available along with disposable containers that could make sharing easy in offices too, turning a frayed afternoon into a moment of respite. The team positioned single serving size, ready-to-eat popcorn as a healthy snack for 'hunger-pang' moments—a healthier alternative to a bag of potato chips from cross-category competitor Frito Lay.

These anchors to the use occasion are bound to be mirrored by consumers in their own lives. When you see the thirteen-year-old daughter enjoying a popcorn treat on TV, you are likely to do the same for your daughter when she returns from school. Blame it on the *chameleon effect* we discussed earlier.

### *Loss Aversion Bias*

Kahneman and Tversky are most famous for uncovering the 'Loss Aversion' bias, which developed into their Prospect Theory and earned Kahneman his Nobel Prize. (Tversky had died by then, or else would have shared in the prize.) The loss aversion bias says that people tend to view losses and gains differently. In the near term, they tend to feel losses more acutely than gains. An economist would explain this by telling you that the amount of happiness you get from being given $100 is less than the amount of sadness you feel from having $100 taken away from you. In practice, for example, researchers Tatiana Homonoff and her colleagues, showed that charging a tax of 5 cents for the use of plastic bags was more effective in curbing their use than offering a reward of 5 cents for not using them.[8] *People don't like to lose what they already have or own.* The bias towards losses goes away when the events are remote, that is, in the long term. My own theory is that this bias stems from the lessons of our childhood, forged over many generations. We are taught not to be greedy and be happy with what we have. Proverbs like 'a bird in hand is worth two in the bush', or 'the grass only seems greener on the other side', or even 'thou shalt not covet thy neighbour's wife', all say the same thing. Stick with what you have. It is sound cognitive wisdom for most real-life situations.

The loss aversion bias, when it's working well for an incumbent brand, can also help keep competitors at bay. One of Cerenti's pharma clients was able to do exactly that with their drug, which was first to market and pretty good in treating a chronic disease but eventually was facing competition from new entrants with 20–25 per cent better performance. That meant that the new drugs were able to suppress the symptoms of the patient's disease by about 75 per cent versus around 60 per cent with our client's drug. However, we were able to lock out the competition with a brand message that urged the doctors to not 'rock the boat' with their existing patients. We reminded them that they had spent a lot of time and effort in treating their patients with our drug, improving their condition, and so why would they want to take a chance on something new and unknown. In other words, we bet that the docs would be more acutely averse to losing what they had already achieved with their patients rather than experimenting with the possibility of gaining more with some other new drug! That is classic loss aversion bias in play!

For marketers, there are other slightly different but related ways of creating an aversion to a loss. Creating a sense scarcity, real or otherwise, is a common approach to increasing brand appeal. You can think of FOMO, or 'the fear of missing out', as a cousin of the loss aversion bias.[9] In this case, a person experiences a sense of anxiety at the prospect of missing out on social-interaction opportunities that others may be enjoying. The 'my product is amazing, it's yours only if you buy it now' strategy, even though we all know it for what it is, works and we fall for it all the time.

One of the more spectacular frauds committed in recent memory was the Fyre Music Festival. It was the brainchild of Billy MacFarland, now serving time in prison, who pepped up the festival with spectacular commercials on social media.[10] The spots promised 'two transformative weekends' of art, food and music in the middle of paradise ('a remote island in Exumas', previously owned by the notorious drug baron Pablo Escobar). Festival attendees would experience the 'boundaries of the impossible', replete with top bands, the hottest models, crystal-clear aquamarine waters, fast boats, private planes and luxury accommodations. There was, of course, only 'limited availability' for you to 'join this quest to push beyond those boundaries'. Thousands of people paid tens of thousands of dollars to attend what turned out to be an unmitigated disaster in a desolate parking lot on a middle-of-nowhere island, with no bands, no accommodation, no food and no nothing. Customers were so afraid of missing out on the once-in-a-lifetime extravaganza that they did not ask any questions before writing big five-figure checks. But you don't have to be crooked to use the FOMO effect. As a matter of fact, Billy wouldn't be in jail if he had delivered what he promised and not bumbled the execution of an otherwise outstanding idea.

Consumers often don't believe that it is prudent for them to lose what they own or pass on attractive opportunities. Thus, the loss aversion bias can provide many good corridors for some cognitive brands to position their propositions as the sensible choice.

## 2. Brand Sense by Making the Choice Feel True

It shouldn't be a surprise to anyone that consumers tend to favour brands that are seen as honest and authentic. Yet, in today's world of hacks, fakes and vapourware, it is harder to know what's true. Research that I led while I worked at McKinsey shows that a promising pathway for building trust with consumers is to give them either greater control over shaping the brand or transparency into what is in it.[11] As luck would have it, there are two cognitive biases, namely IKEA effect and what I call, transparency effect, that can help marketers with this approach.

## *IKEA Effect*

What better way to give consumer control than to let them build your product, or at least a part of it, themselves? That is what the IKEA effect is. [12] It says that people tend to prefer objects that they have put time and effort into building, *even when they turn out to be objectively inferior*. It's understandable. When you toil for hours to assemble an IKEA dresser, under the sceptical, 'we-should-have hired-a-professional' watch of your significant other, you are inclined to believe that your idea is immaculate. That despite the fact that you erred in the construction, as evidenced clearly by the several critical-for-structural-stability parts leftover from step 13–27 at the end of the thirty-five-step irreversible assembly. The IKEA effect is not feasible for all products, but worthy of consideration.

With the advent of innovative technology-based retailers, the IKEA effect is poised to explode with online brands. MTailor, the brainchild of Stanford computer scientists Miles Penn and Rafi Witten, uses nifty technology to deliver made-to-order, custom-fitted jeans without the need for a real tailor. However, to get the best fit, the customer too has to work at it, making seven different body measurements using their mobile phone. MTailor uses AI technology to help you pull off this feat. You don't take measurements the conventional way with a tape measure. Instead, you put your phone on the floor, leaning it against the wall and then, with the camera on, do a complete 360-degree turn in front of it. As simply as that, the app magically figures out the seven key custom tailoring measurements. This is also quite important. IKEA effect researchers caution that for it to work, the consumer must be able to finish their assigned task with reasonable comfort and success. While you want consumers to put in that labour, it cannot become an exercise in futility, or you will drive them away frustrated. Whether MTailor becomes a billion-dollar brand remains a bit iffy and is likely more dependent on their ability to get the supply chain right than on the branding.

Back in the earthy world of beverages, a Sputnik-era product called Tang has long used the IKEA effect to build a loyal fan club. Even as ready-to-drink (RTD) drinks drove away powdered beverages like Tang and Crystal Light from the US markets, the latter pair of brands are loved in the rest of the world, delivering well over a billion dollars in sales for Kraft. When we were working with Kraft's brand managers around the world, it soon became evident that a big part of Tang's appeal in these countries was that both kids and mothers could get involved in its preparation. It was more than just an affordable, fruity drink; it was a fun bonding moment between Mom and her kids. A TV commercial that plays in Pakistan shows various vignettes of a mother using her hands to braid her daughter's hair, caress her son to sleep and lock arms playfully with her children in a dance. The scenes are interspersed cleverly with shots of the same hands also preparing Tang and pouring it into glasses for the family. The voiceover reflectively concludes by observing how everything in the world is more beautiful when it is touched by a mother's hand, with the tagline 'Tang, like the love from a mother's hands'.[13] The mother–child involvement equity has put the Tang brand on steroids in many developing countries around the world.

It is not always practical to have the customer involved in the creation of the product. In such cases, it helps to acknowledge the role that customers may have played in the creation of the brand itself. For example, pharmaceutical companies, often like to say that their drug has been trialled on thousands of patients. In a slight twist, Bristol Myers Squib in its ads for Opdivo chose to thank patients, nurses and physicians who were involved with the clinical trials, indirectly reminding all three types of customers that the drug, in part, was the end result of efforts of others like them.

Additionally, marketers may do well to remember that brands today are more than the product itself. Xerox, for example, provides mailing labels to consumers, so that they return their printer cartridges and play a role in their safe disposal. Tesla's professed mission is 'to accelerate the world's transition to sustainable energy'. That is exactly what their customers passionately believe in. By buying Tesla's expensive electric cars, they are playing a role in making their own missions come true.

## *Transparency Effect or Authenticity*

People are wired to trust what they can see with their own eyes. That is why brands that are transparent or authentic make sense to them. Actually, I am hiding something here and I'd better not. There is no cognitive bias called 'transparency effect'. It is a term I coined based on prior years of research into what makes for great brands. Transparency is the idea that you are likely to trust a brand if you can feel that 'what you see is what you get'. Anyone who has been to a Criss Angel magic show at the Luxor Hotel on the strip in Las Vegas and been deceived by what their eyes thought was real, can see the problems with the 'believe your eyes' thesis.

Nonetheless, in the real world of no magic, brands that are transparent about who they are and say what they mean make perfect sense.

One fascinating newcomer to bet their brand story on transparency is the online retailer Everlane, whose fortunes have been rising like a rocket ship. When I cruise over to their website, their home page starts boldly with the assertion, 'We believe we can all make a difference.' My eyes glaze over: Isn't that only the millionth company to lay the claim to making a difference? The real head-scratcher is in the smaller letters below that statement, 'Our way: Exceptional quality. Ethical factories. Radical Transparency.' Again, ignore the first two. Who says average quality and unethical factories? But radical transparency? What is that all about? No company says that because it is not possible. I'm shocked; tell me more.

Further down that page, they explain, 'At Everlane, we want the right choice to be as easy as putting on a great T-shirt. That's why we partner with the best, ethical factories around the world. Source only the finest materials. And share those stories with you—down to the true cost of every product we make. It's a new way of doing things. We call it Radical Transparency.' That is crazy. No retailer does that. But Everlane does. I look up their slim-fit jeans in black and they are priced at $68. Below the price is the comparative retail price, which is $155. Click on their $68 price and you see an extremely easy to follow graphic that breaks down their cost: materials, $14.93; hardware, $2.15; labour, $7.50; duties, $4.06; and transport, $1.90; for a total cost of $30.54. In my consulting career of over twenty years, I have worked with or analysed the businesses of a gazillion retailers. No one shares their true costs with the customer. Does transparency do something for the Everlane brand? You be the judge. In an era of 'Amazon Kills Retail', Everlane has gone from a zero to $250 million valuation in seven years.[14]

In consumer foods, transparency has been the rage in the breakfast and energy bars category. Paul Rahal started a company called RXBAR in his mom's kitchen and sold it for $600 million to Kellogg's in just four years. The secret of his success? 'Clean Label' protein bars. Most bars they sell, offer 12 grams of protein and list just five ingredients in prominent letters, covering the entire label. Of those, four are foods and the fifth is a statement: 'No B.S.' For instance, the Chocolate Sea Salt bar contains '3 Egg Whites, 6 Almonds, 4 Cashews, 2 Dates and No B.S.'—and that's it. End of story. (Actually, I do have one gripe about their branding which I will cover later in Chapter 12 in a discussion on ethics.)

Brands are proliferating like nobody's business today. On Amazon, so many small businesses from China and other parts of the world are selling products that there are hundreds of brands birthed each day.[15] So much so that many don't even have the time to come up with a good brand name. Whom do you trust? What feels true? The transparency effect is about to go mainstream in branding.

## 3. Brand Sense by Making the Choice Feel Good

There are several things that make us feel copacetic, satisfied or at peace with the world, and sunny and warm at heart. Research has shown that being in a good mood is correlated to making choices by gut feel, that is, more intuitively, creatively, and more trustingly.[16] Brands that find ways to make consumers feel good will also find a place in their hearts (brains actually). I discuss below how you can use two cognitive biases, namely the in-group bias and the choice supportive bias, to make brand choice feel good and sensible.

### *In-Group Bias*

It feels good to belong to groups. That human beings are social creatures is not news. It is noteworthy, though, that in our anxiousness to blend we tend to be biased about our brand choices subconsciously. We do this in two ways: a) by adopting behaviours that make us more like other members in our group; or b) by doing things that make us distinct from those who are not in our group. That is the 'us-versus-them' syndrome.

One of my favourite recent examples of a brand using the in-group bias in an evocative manner is Diageo, with its Guinness beer campaign.[17] For unfortunate souls who may have lived a life deprived of the taste of this dark Irish stout, perhaps because it bears no resemblance to normal beer, it will suffice to say that Guinness is an ale like no other—with a dark plum interior, a thick and creamy head and a hard-to-define mild bitter taste. Playing to this differentiation, the Diageo marketers cleverly decided to frame Guinness as the choice of ordinary people with extraordinary attitudes.

In one of their widely acclaimed commercials, we see a team of young men playing full-intensity basketball. It could be just about any community of small-town friends playing at the local YMCA, except . . . in this game, every one of the players is in a wheelchair. Okay, so we are witnessing some version of a Special Olympics team, we think. Fine, quite admirable. But when the game ends, all of the players get up and walk away quite normally from their wheelchairs. All, except one . . . the one who is actually wheelchair-bound. The realization hits you in a tsunami of emotions. What kind of friends would play basketball in a wheelchair just to level the playing field for one person? Well, the kind who drink Guinness. In the final scene of the commercial, we see the players in a bar, enjoying their special camaraderie over pints of Guinness, with the tag line,

'Guinness. Made of More.' The beauty of the ad lies in the simple premise that Guinness is a different kind of beer, not only in what it is but also in terms of the kind of people who favour it.

Who would not want to belong to a group like that? While not everyone will climb into a wheelchair to play basketball with their disabled friend, it is the kind of thing we would all wish we would do. By drinking Guinness, you can vicariously feel a part of just such a special crew. And in making you want to belong to that group is where the genius of this ad lies, not in its poignancy. David Buchanan, creative director of the ad agency BBDO, described their brand strategy for another ad in the series in this way: 'Many years ago Arthur Guinness chose to transcend the ordinary and produce an extraordinary drink, a drink made of more . . . This campaign is about that choice: Do we settle for the way things are or do we take the bold choice to step up and be made of more? Do we settle for an ordinary drink or do we choose one that is made of more?'[18]

The challenge with aligning brands to special groups and clubs is that they can be seen as excluding others. As a marketer you have to be ready for the blowback. Augusta National, one of the most prestigious golf clubs in Georgia, United States, managed to hold out as a 'men only' zone for years. In today's world, with the risk of becoming a dinosaur looming large, it has finally relented and let more women in. The Guinness ad suffers no such problem; it creates a group within which you feel special but whose membership is open to all, with a sip of its delicious beer.

### *Choice Supportive Bias*

Steve Genco, in his book *Intuitive Marketing*, astutely notes that we don't choose what we prefer; rather, we prefer what we choose.[19] Choice supportive bias, or post-purchase rationalization, is the tendency of people to justify the choices they have already made, often ignoring or minimizing the negative information and focusing unreasonably on the positives. Even if you are not a behavioural psychologist, it makes sense that this defect in our thinking would exist. Without the 'I did good' self-congratulatory pat on the back, we would be second-guessing and beating up on ourselves and ultimately feeling depressed. We don't want to do that, do we? No! We want to feel good about our own choices, even when they are bad. Feeling good is what makes sense.

In one of our consulting engagements, my team was fielding focus groups with rheumatologists to understand how they thought about the changes that were taking place in their profession with the advent of modern biologic drugs. One of our 'ice-breaker' opening questions was around how they felt about their choice of rheumatology as a profession. At the time, the inside joke in the medical profession was that you became a rheumatologist because, well, you stood dead last in your class at med school. There is a mostly unspoken monetary hierarchy in the medical profession, and at the time rheumatologists, who generally earned under $100,000 annually, sat firmly at the bottom of the totem pole. The main diseases that they treated, namely rheumatoid arthritis, fibromyalgia and lupus, had subjective symptoms of the pain-and-stiffness variety. The available drugs to treat these symptoms were nothing to write home about, being mainly generic pain killer pills (high dose Motrin anyone?) and some old systemics, like methotrexate, with one thing in common: none worked particularly well.

Primary care physicians would question the value of referring patients to a rheumatologist, knowing that there was not much he would do that they could not do for the patients themselves. Keeping that background in mind, consider their predicament in answering our question, 'How do you like being a rheumatologist?' In detailed interviews with forty rheumatologists, thirty-nine said they loved their profession. 'Really, why?' we asked. Well, they said, in rheumatology, you could be a *true* doctor, spend meaningful time with your patients and practise medicine the way it was meant to be. The average rheumatologist would see 15–20 patients a day, spend thirty minutes or more per patient understanding their history, recommending changes in diet and lifestyle, and listening to stories about their suffering, which in all honesty did somewhat help their patients feel better. In contrast, a primary care physician would breeze through 50–60 patients in a single day, spending as little as five minutes with each and making 2–3 times more money than a rheumatologist.

But one of the forty rheumatologists burst out and said, 'I made a horrible mistake. I should have done something else.' 'What else?' we asked. 'Anything else!' was the pat reply. And that's what the choice supportive bias is. Of the forty, only one rheumatologist could bring himself to outwardly regret the choice he had made.[20]

That one man aside, for the rest we felt that it was important to discreetly account for the sense of rationalization that rheumatologists felt about their choice of careers and the way they practise medicine. Humira was a breakthrough drug which, over time, garnered more than 100 patents. It was one of the few in an entirely new-to-the-world class of drugs and worked astonishingly well compared to the older drugs that were the standard of care. The temptation therefore was to trumpet that fact and say, 'Look what Humira can do!' Instead, the marketers at AbbVie, in their early campaigns, elected to say to the doctors, 'Look what *you* can do with Humira!' That slight alteration of words was a big deal. We needed to acknowledge the fact that our wonder drug was not a wonder at all without the expert hands of the rheumatologists to guide it to the patients in a manner only they knew. It was a way to subtly support the choices they had made.

For marketers, leveraging the choice supportive bias to drive their own brand adoption can be sweet. One way to do this is to position your product as something that customers already love, but something better and more than that. In another study that we worked on, we talked to dermatologists who treated eczema. They were in a somewhat similar situation that the rheumatologists had faced before the advent of biologic drugs. There were no good drugs available for treating eczema specifically. Most of the creams available did not work particularly well, and stronger systemics, like cyclosporin, that were effective had rough side effects. When finally, Pfizer launched Dupixent, a monoclonal anti-body, it was a significant advance and worked for 65 per cent of the patients in clinical trials with fewer side effects. Having waited for this miracle for decades, dermatologists were understandably excited and prescribed the drug freely. Unfortunately, our client was coming out with a better drug, but two years later. The new drug would work in 80 per cent of the cases as compared to the 65 per cent claimed for Dupixent, but it did have exceedingly rare, but more serious, side effects.

To our surprise, when we interviewed dermatologists using Dupixent, they swore that the drug was working for 90–95 per cent of patients in their practice and not 65 per cent. This was shocking, as generally drug performance in actual practice is somewhat worse than in a clinical trial, where conditions are tightly controlled and there is persistent follow-up to ensure that the patients stay on the drug for the duration of the trial. Further, while Dupixent could cause conjunctivitis, a highly irritating eye condition, in one out of ten patients, the physicians were not concerned at all and claimed they had never seen that in their own practice. On deeper dives into their patient records and chart data, it was clear that the physicians had a rosier view of Dupixent than was the reality in their own practice. We knew we were dealing with choice supportive bias.

Physicians had been using Dupixent for a while and they were not about to call their baby ugly. After trying many different ways to position the client's drug, we found that one of the best strategies to promote our client's drug was to say it was 'Dupixent and more'. It would do everything they loved about Dupixent, but a little better and faster. In this way, we were able to affirm the choice that the dermatologists had already made, but also add to it.

Positioning your brand as an affirmation or extension of a choice that a consumer has already made can make powerful brand sense. It plays to the choice supportive bias that is wired in our brains, and make the choice feel good and the brand sensible to the consumer.

## 4. Brand Sense by Making the Choice Easy

Kahneman points out that System 2 is lazy. If it can get by with System 1 taking care of business with its instinct and intuition, it is happy to let things slide. You experience cognitive ease when the brand choices offered seem simple and effortless. Marketers can make brand choice easy in many ways and thus help brands make sense to consumers.

There is one important point about brand sense by making choice easy. You should note that this is not about providing convenience to make your life easier, as in Instacart delivering groceries to your home so you don't have to go shopping. This is about simplifying the process by which you choose a brand, so that you don't have to tax your brain painfully peeling options. There are two cognitive biases, namely Occam's razor bias and herd-mentality bias, that come in handy in making brand choice feel easy.

*Occam's Razor Bias*

As humans, we prefer simple answers rather than complicated ones that make our heads hurt. The Occam's razor principle posits that given two solutions to a problem, all else being equal, the simpler answer is better. Even in the 1300s, when friar William of Ockham noted the existence of a simplification bias, it was not a novel idea.[21] Ages ago, in 300 BC, Aristotle had declared that 'We may assume the superiority *ceteris paribus* of the demonstration which derives from fewer postulates or hypotheses.'[22] Ironically, if only Aristotle had heeded his own advice and stated the thesis more simply, the bias might have been called 'Aristotle's needle' instead of Occam's razor. Here's the rub, though. There is absolutely no evidence that there is any truth to the Occam's razor principle. In real life, personal or business, complex situations require nuanced answers. If someone did not worry about the little details, we would have airplanes falling out of the sky and the Chicago skyline leaning aside like the Tower of Pisa. Oversimplifying problems can lead to suboptimal or incorrect outcomes. Despite that knowledge, most people are instinctively biased to KISS (Keep It Simple Stupid!). As marketers, we are not here to judge. We are here to commandeer this behavioural insight for giving sense to cognitive brands.

Staples realized that while it loved office supplies, its customers didn't. Buying them is a tedious chore for people with better things to do. There is a myriad of choices for pens, paper and pencils from office supply stores. What if you were to remind people that life was complex and the best answer could be to keep choice simple and buy everything from one place, namely Staples? The company rolled out a major campaign around an outsized 'Easy' button. The early spots showed ordinary people in difficult everyday situations. In one, a teacher chalking miles of inscrutable Greek letters on a board abruptly pivots to the clueless little Josh trapped in the front row of class and asks, 'So "n" equals what?' Another features a harried mother changing diapers simultaneously for her twin infants. In the ads, in each case, the bright red 'Easy' button from Staples appears magically on scene, and pressing it saves the day. The voiceover observes, 'Wouldn't it be nice if there was an easy button for life. Now, there's one for your business. Staples. That was easy.'

The idea of not overcomplicating the trivia in life has the hallmark appeal of Occam's razor for our lazy System 2. It knows that the alternative of setting up an Excel spreadsheet, to compare three competing bids for each office supply line item, is about as exciting as sitting by the side of an Arizona interstate, beating rocks. While the spreadsheet might save you some money or get you better products, it is neither simple nor easy.

H-E-B, the popular grocery store chain in Texas, presumably figured out that Staples was on to something. If Occam's razor could help Staples sell disinfectant wipes and hanging file folders, what could it do to help move moderately edible, store-prepared meals? Their spots feature various situations in which life is getting to be ridiculously out of hand, and then remind you that mealtime does not have to be similarly complicated. In one clip, a man driving home from work in heavy traffic looks at his GPS, which estimates the time to destination as 'Next Thursday!' The voiceover then pipes in with 'When life gets crazy, keep it simple. H-E-B give you hundreds of chef-inspired meals to choose from, all ready within minutes.' Works for me.

With the advent of AI, marketers have new opportunities to build brands that make sense with Occam's razor. That is exactly what Stitch Fix is. Since shipping its first box of clothes, Stitch Fix has garnered nearly three million customers and over $1 billion in revenues. For people who like to dress well, but have trouble figuring out what they look good in or plain hate shopping, Stich Fix provides the simple answer. Its AI engine and a cadre of remote personal human stylists use a series of simple questions and pictures of things that you may like, to figure out your style. Thereon, it's a standard online subscription service and gets easier and better by the minute, so you can enjoy your moments of cognitive ease.

### *Herd Mentality Bias*

As we discussed before, we feel cognitive ease when making choices that are effortless. What better way to do this than to let someone else do the hard work of figuring out what the right choice is and then do what they do. That is the herd mentality bias, and it makes brand choice easier for us. We follow the herd rather than work out an answer for ourselves.

Have you ever found yourself at a cross street, checking messages on your iPhone while waiting for the pedestrian signal to indicate it is safe for you to cross the street? From the corner of your eye, you catch the five other people next to you step off the curb and start to cross. Without taking your eye off the WhatsApp video from Brad, of a heartbreaking owl rescue in the tar pits of Venezuela, you too start crossing the street with them. Now, let's think about this for a second. If you crossed the street without proper inspection of the oncoming traffic, you may get run over by a dump truck and turned promptly into compost. Yet, in crossing without looking, you entrust your life to five strangers who, for all you know, may be fervent disciples of a suicidal cult. That's the wonderful System 1 working the magic of the herd effect.

Online retailers leverage news flash-type alerts to egg you on to buy their brands by informing you about what the herd is doing. These are the ever-present messages telling you to buy their brands because 'six other people are looking at it now' or 'ten others bought it today'. People are trusting nameless strangers, with whom they have little in common other than the fact that they too are online shoppers, in deciding what brands to buy. That's the power of peer-to-peer System 1 herding in steering people to brands. Chickens crossing the road. Not classy, but gets the job done.

## Accidental Strains

The opposite of cognitive ease is cognitive strain or dissonance, where you ask the consumer to do something that goes against their beliefs. When this happens, customers feel like something is wrong and that they need to focus and think carefully. They use their System 2, which we will discuss in the next chapter.

One of our clients, a manufacturer of a new type of drug for the treatment of persistent skin rash, had decided that they wanted to design their brand to have the personality of an 'outlaw' that was unafraid to rebel against conventions and take risks. While that was exciting for the marketers, it wasn't so for the dermatologists who treat the disease. For one, the drug had a black-box warning, which for those not in the industry means that, in rare cases, it has the potential for serious side effects. These side effects could include the risk of inducing a rare form of cancer or hard-to-treat infection. How do you take a drug like that and tell the doctor to prescribe it with outlaw-like abandon?

Dermatologists we interviewed would tell us, 'Look here, no one has died of a persistent rash, but they could die from your drug!' That is a textbook example of inviting a 'cognitive dissonance' problem. On the other hand, there were a number of cognitive ease levers that were available. We could use the choice supportive bias to say that the choice of our drug was no different than the other choices doctors had made in the past. We could point to a lot of other drugs that dermatologists liked and used routinely that also had black-box warnings, for instance, creams, like topical calcineurin inhibitors, and systemics, like cyclosporin. In fact, we demonstrated that to diminish concerns around such black-box warnings, the company needed to do three things: one, show that the associated adverse events were very rare as in other drugs they used frequently; two, that indeed if they did occur, the risks were what they were familiar with; and finally, three, they could be easily managed with established approaches. 'Doc, the risks are very similar to the drugs that you already use a lot. In the rare case that something happens, what you have to do is nothing different from what you already do for those other drugs you use.' In this way, we were able to ease the concerns that the dermatologists had by saying it was no different than the sensible brand choices they had already made in the past.

* * *

*Key Takeaways*

Cognitive brands can create consumer preference by answering their question, 'Does this brand make intuitive sense?'

System 1 Easers are all about leading consumers to make sense of the brand proposition instinctively, by going with the flow instead of fighting it. Everyone has their own private repository of biases and wisdom from past brand experiences, whether they were good or bad, and it is just easier to reapply that knowledge rather than make a fresh evaluation. Brands that find a way to tap into that pool of cognitive wisdom will find themselves favoured as the sensible choice automatically.

There are four ways to use System 1 Easers to imbue brand sense. You have to make the *act of choosing* your brand feel effortless by making it:

- Familiar
- More True and Authentic
- Good
- Easier

Whether you use a System 1 Easer or not, be aware of them. If your brand accidentally goes against a consumer's deep-set biases and beliefs, it will hit a brick wall.

System 1 Easers are one of the two ways in which consumers make sense of what a brand says. The other way is with System 2 Deliberators, where consumers use reasoning to make sense of brands. I cover those in the next chapter.

# 6

# Brand Sense: Using System 2 Deliberators to Give New Religion

## *Part 2B of Brand Architecture*

*'The edge of a precipice is a very merciless school; over there you either learn to be serious or you die foolishly!'*

—Mehmet Murat Ildan

The *Deliberator* subunit of the brain uses what Daniel Kahneman calls System 2 processes to prevent us from suffering foolish predicaments daily. It is activated when it perceives there is a risk from making a gut feel choice that System 1 might advocate. System 2 can analyse unfamiliar situations, make complicated calculations, solve equations, apply principles, decipher trends, and map out pros and cons of distinct options. It is just the kind of toolkit that comes in handy when shopping for a complicated product, like a home mortgage, which has a huge impact on your household finances. You would compare competitive rates from different banks and read the fine print on fees, prepayment terms, post-lock period interest escalation and other such niceties before deciding what makes the most sense. It is mentally taxing, unpleasant even, but well advised in such situations.

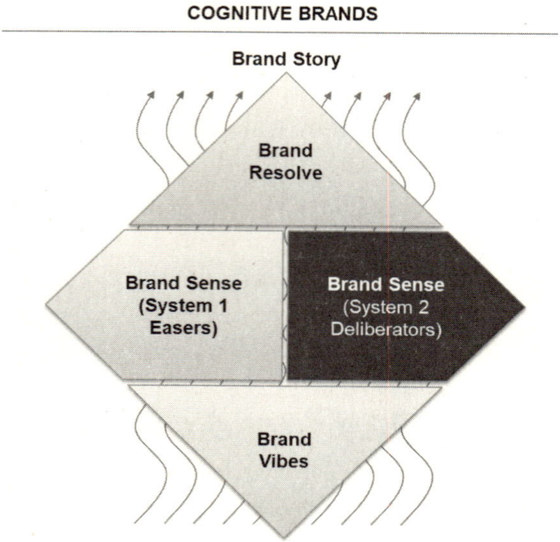


*Figure 6.1: Part 2b: Making brand sense with System 2 Deliberators.*

Some people mistakenly believe that System 2 is basically all rational thinking and System 1 all emotional thinking. Just because System 2 is built around reasoning and deliberation, it does not mean that it will not take emotions into account when making sense of brand choices. You may momentarily and logically conclude that it makes no financial sense to buy your wife $45 roses that by definition were dead leaves from the moment they were severed from the mother plant, but you may do so anyway because you figure it will be nice to see her smile on Valentine's Day. There is nothing irrational about that. It is not 'just a feeling' as the Maroon 5 song goes; it is a *calculated* feeling.

System 2 Deliberators have other peculiarities. Since they require mental effort, they do not kick in unless necessary. If you can make sense of what a brand says instinctively using the trusty old System 1 Easers, then that is what usually becomes your preference, *almost to a fault*. You may decide that instead of analysing five different mortgage products and inviting a headache, you'll just go with the one that your neighbour, a certified accountant and financial nerd, went with. All analysis is set aside, and the System 1 Easers make the call using the authority bias, a tendency to unduly defer to a so-called expert as a decision-making short cut. However, the *Conator* subunit in the brain, which is the arbiter of all actions, keeps an eye on System 1 Easers and calls for System 2 deliberation when it suspects a problem. For example, System 1 may also volunteer another useful tidbit of related information, namely, that Gordon was recently sighted flinging his green shades off into the neighbour's pool and committing several alcohol-laced indiscretions at the recent block party. That may make you hesitate in blindly following Gordon's choice of a mortgage product. If the situation warrants deliberation, and you are on the edge of 'Murat's precipice', System 2 is dragged in, even though the bar for calling for intervention remains high. Most often things are copacetic and on cruise control, and System 2 deliberation is used only 5 per cent of the time.

If your product is innovative or unusual, it may require significant scrutiny or a behavioural shift on the part of the buyer. Your brand will need to awaken the customer's System 2 Deliberators. Even though, System 2 is rarely used, there is one humbling thought about it: It is the source of all the System 1 wisdom wired into the brain. System 1 can also write rules, but they are corollaries, not new theorems. While System 2 may be the determining process in the initial evaluation period of innovative brands, repeat purchases are routinized by System 1. In other words, brand loyalty flows from the System 1 circuitry.

Oreo grew to be one of the largest cookie brands in the United States by creating a ritual around how it is partaken of. Rather than munch on it, Oreo advises consumers to 'Twist, Lick and Dunk' the cookie which involves *twisting off* the two sides of the sandwich, *licking* the cream filling inside and *dunking* the remainder in milk before placing it in your mouth. When the brand was introduced to markets like India, Pakistan and China, that method of consuming a cookie was puzzling for most. But Mondelez, the company that owns Oreo, persisted on promoting its ritual in televised campaigns. The consumers' System 2 Deliberators, which can learn by trial and error, kicked in, and Indians and Chinese alike started taking their first tentative Oreo dunks. After a few rounds of emerging unscathed and decidedly content from the experience, the ritual was in place. System 2 encoded these findings into the brain's *Learner* subunit, and even in these countries 'Twist, Lick and Dunk' has become a System 1 ritual. In India, after a shaky start, Oreo's share of the cream cookies market jumped remarkably from 1 per cent to 30 per cent in just five years.[1]

If marketers credit Kahneman for uncovering System 2, they can thank cognitive behaviour therapists, like the larger-than-life Dr David Burns, for perfecting the methods needed for applying it to change consumer behaviour. Marketers were the last of psychotherapist Dr Burns's priorities, unless their minds had wandered away from the true normal. Instead, he was obsessed with figuring out ways to help his patients, some of whom suffered desperately from depression or anxiety disorders, change their behaviour constructively. Not just on the rare occasion, but consistently and habitually. The mood-altering drugs that they were taking were just not cutting it.[2] In his book *Feeling Good*, now a bible for practitioners of cognitive behaviour therapy (CBT), Dr Burns lays out various techniques that patients can use to '*untwist their thinking*'.[3]

Dr Burns does this by helping his patients deliberate on and break the self-defeating cycle of negative thoughts, feelings and behaviours they have in response to common situations in life. It is a two-step process. First you diagnose your own problem and then solve it by 'untwisting' your negative thinking. Let's do an example. Say, one day, you find that you were not invited to an important meeting held by your boss and everyone else was. If you are the kind of person who gets anxious easily, you may feel that you are about to be fired from your job or at the minimum, demoted. Dr Burns may help you untwist your thinking by encouraging you to think of other reasons why you may not have been included. For instance, it may be the case that you are already overloaded with the two other priority projects that your boss assigned to you earlier in the week, and he does not want you to be distracted and set up for failure.

In other words, Dr Burns gets his patients to channel their System 2 Deliberators to make sense of the situation and diagnose the real issue, when the instinctive System 1 is routinely resulting in regressive thoughts and behaviours. Then the patient can take appropriate corrective action and direct his mind to thinking positively, being less anxious and not taking a reckless action like firing off an angry email to his colleagues. Behaviour changed. Problem solved.

CBT methods have been proven to change people's behaviour sustainably in controlled clinical trials.[4] Very few marketing methods go through that kind of scrutiny. In doing his thing, Dr Burns left a rich catalogue of methods for untwisting the mind. If you simply imagine that negative behaviour for our purposes is a consumer's rejection of our brand, then these methods are a trail of breadcrumbs for reshaping the consumer mindset. Surely, Dr Burns would be annoyed that I am hijacking his research for designing cognitive brands, but having acknowledged his contribution, we will not worry about him anymore. In the following, I draw inspiration from his methods to present a set of System 2 Deliberators for marketers to apply in helping consumers make sense of their brands.

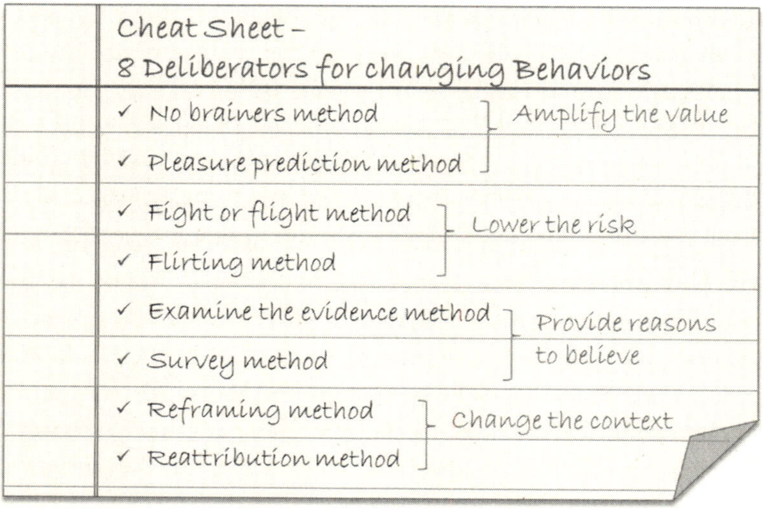


*Figure 6.2: Brands that use Deliberators to appeal to consumers, do so by providing consumers reasons for why their proposition makes good sense. They target System 2 processes in the brain.*

The good news is that System 2 Deliberators are familiar territory for marketers. In one form or another, they involve logically selling your brand's *value proposition* to the customer. Value propositions involve four types of strategies (see the 'Brand Sense' figure): (1) providing consumers a context in to think about value or risk of your brand (perception); (2) showing them how your brand adds greater (amplified) value relative to other options; (3) lowering the risk of using your brand, and finally; (4) making your proposition credible by providing reasons to believe in it. However, as I said before, *how* you do branding is just as important and inseparable from what you do with it. And that is precisely where CBT methods are invaluable. In the following, I highlight how they can be used to address the four aspects of value propositions—relative value, risk, perception, and credibility.

## 1. System 2 Deliberators: Amplify Value

In today's hypercompetitive world, to stand out from the crowd you have to offer 'extreme' value. You will catch the mind's eye of System 2, when your brand offers something that is simply too good to pass up or makes the pleasure of consuming it vivid. I discuss these next as the no-brainer method, and the pleasure amplification method.

### *No-brainer Method*

David Burns calls this the 'Cost–Benefit' method for changing behaviour. He asks his patients to catalogue the benefits they feel from their negative thoughts ('What am I getting out of thinking this way?'). Next, he tells them to evaluate the costs of engaging in the same ('What is it costing me to think this way?'). If the costs exceed the benefits, then Dr Burns asks his patients to confront and alter that unfortunate reality.

To marketers, this is the all-too-familiar value proposition method. It tries to change customer behaviour by convincing them of the opposite, namely that the value obtained from using the brand is far greater than its cost. When I was working as an associate at Booz Allen, this 'novel' concept was exciting. In the consulting world, things like that deserve their own acronym and someone came up with 'CONBO'. It stands for 'Cost of Next Best Option'. For any given products, we could catalogue all the different ways in which it delivered value for a customer. We could then spring out our Excel spreadsheets and assign a dollar value to each possible source of value. This was 'A'. Then, we would go hunting for other competing product options that could do the same thing as our brand and assign dollar values to their cost. This was 'B'. Both letters, 'A' and 'B', would entail a lot of work and keep us busy for a while. Once all this was nailed down, we could subtract the cost 'B' from the value 'A' and arrive at the consumer surplus 'C'. If the surplus were large enough, the brand had a value proposition that could rationally change the consumer's buying behaviour, post a mandatory inspection of our spreadsheets.

In the real world, consumers prefer to avoid this way of thinking, but for complex situations they can be persuaded to do so. If you sell hybrid cars it certainly makes sense to talk about the annual savings from the fifty-miles-per-gallon fuel economy and $5000 government tax credit. Still, it is not a natural thing for consumers, and they prefer mental short cuts instead. A simple way to provide a System 2 short cut is to amplify the value of the brand so much that a precise calculation is unnecessary. A quick top-down check is adequate. It still uses System 2 deliberation, but is less painful.

It took venture capitalists to really take the value proposition method to the 'no-brainer' extreme. They realized that coming up with intricate calculations of consumer surplus was not going to pass muster. Rather, brands should have smack-in-your-face value. This usually meant selling for a loss for a while and making money later.

Think about Uber. It represented a seismic shift in behaviour from how consumers were used to taking cabs. Enter the no-brainer method. Make it so that the consumer goes, 'What's there to not like about Uber?' You don't have to lean precariously into the traffic from a sidewalk to hail a cab. You can order and track it on your phone and not stand in the pouring rain until it arrives. You don't have to negotiate the rate or check if the cabbie is willing to go to your destination. You don't have to present your credit card; it will be charged, and a receipt mailed electronically. Oh, and it is often cheaper than taking a cab. That's because it is being offered to you at below-market prices by equity investors who subsidize your

Uber ride. That's smack-in-the-face value. It makes so much sense that it would be crazy to not use Uber. No spreadsheet required. Many famed unicorns (start-ups reaching $1 billion-plus valuations) like Amazon, Dropbox, Pinterest, Twitter, Facebook, Netflix, Grubhub and Spotify were born in this manner: Offer a phenomenal product, spread like wildfire and worry about making money later.

It also turns out that the brain really likes *free* stuff. There is a huge difference between offering something for nearly free versus completely free in the way the brain's reward centers in the *Conator* respond. In a now famous 'Hershey's Kiss experiment'[5] by psychologist Dan Ariely of Duke University, study participants were given the choice of buying a high-end Lindt Truffle for 26 cents or a classic Hershey's Kiss for 1 cent. Forty per cent chose the Lindt, while the other 40 per cent the Kiss (20 per cent passed). Next, participants were offered the opportunity to buy the Lindt for 25 cents and the Kiss for zero cents. While the price differential (25 cents) is the same in both cases, a surprising 90 per cent elected to take the free Kiss, suggesting the idea of free was *intrinsically* more valuable. In other versions of the experiment, the price of the Lindt was lowered from 27 cents to 26 cents and the Kiss from 2 cents to 1 cent, and the same behaviour was not observed. Ariely and company also tried this with a negative price for the Kiss: they are paying you to take the Kiss but asking you to pay for the Lindt. Again, no effect! It should then come as no surprise that one common offer with our retail clients is a BOGO, short for Buy-One-Get-One free, which often works better than the nearly identical 'half-off' offer. Thus, free offers are familiar and instinctively preferred by System 1, while System 2 takes a rest.

When you have a complex product to sell, you can make life a little easier for yourself by first finding something nice to give for free. People use WhatsApp for a lot of different things now to organize their group interactions. But WhatsApp initially gained traction in the market by offering free texting at a time when most telecom companies required you to pay for SMSes.

With the no-brainer method we also see another important aspect of System 2 deliberation, namely, that it can kick in with low vigilance if needed. When something makes a lot of sense even with a few quick calculations, a full on evaluation is unnecessary. Could your brand deliver a 'I would be crazy to say no to this' value proposition and worry about making money later? Can you give away free stuff? If not, then read on for other avenues.

### *Pleasure Amplification Method*

The second way in which Dr Burns helps his patients understand the value of positive behaviours is by making their benefits more vivid. Patients who suffer from depression often underestimate the pleasure they think they would get from engaging in social activities. This causes them to retreat into a shell. By helping them correct that error of perception, a cognitive behaviour therapist can get patients to view those activities more positively and pursue them. Similarly, in marketing, we can help consumers see the sense in our brands by letting them imagine their benefits vibrantly.

The Rainforest Alliance uses the pleasure amplification method in its 'Follow the Frog' campaign. Its mission is to help multinational companies work responsibly with farming and forest communities around the world. One of the most important tools in their arsenal is the 'Rainforest Alliance Certified' seal. When placed on products, it confirms that those brands are produced by companies in cooperation with the farmers under an audited programme which contributes to biodiversity, improved livelihoods, human well-being and natural resource conservation. However, to make this worthwhile for the companies, the Rainforest Alliance markets the seal to consumers through a consumer campaign.

The campaign is a three-minute spot viewable on YouTube.[6] It features a young family man, who could be you and at the outset is declared to be 'a good person'. Proof of the same is provided in the following narrative, 'You conserve water while showering, you drive a Prius but use your bike when you can, and you always send a card on Mother's Day.' Then, the narrator muses that 'there is a part of you that does not feel good, because rainforests are being obliterated at the rate of one football field every seventy-two seconds and all you have done is . . . yoga!' Disappointed, it continues, 'Well, this is what you are not going to do: quit your job, leave your family and take a travel to the jungle at the edge of Nicaragua.' They then show why and what would have happened if you had done that. In that imaginary voyage, they show the 'good person' suffering through a series of misadventures, finally breaking down, smoking his first cigarette in four years and accidentally starting a forest fire. He returns home to find his job gone and wife co-opted by the gym coach. They helpfully suggest that he pursue his dreams more practically in his real-life journey and 'Follow the Frog', by buying only products that carry the Rainforest Alliance seal.

In its humorous way, the spot helps you visualize how you can help rainforests around the world and be a better person by making small changes in your daily purchases. Now, all of a sudden, you are not just stuffing your face with any bananas but with purposeful Rainforest Alliance-certified Chiquita bananas. This is a clever way to amplify the pleasures from common utilitarian purchases that you may otherwise give no thought to. It drives behaviour. No one likes watching advertisements for the most part, but 5.6 million people have watched this three-minute-long commercial on YouTube alone.

Pleasure amplification is not necessarily about attaching teary-eyed emotions to brand messages. The Rainforest Alliance is telling you that there is a practical way for you to engage in sustainability initiatives, a functional benefit communicated engagingly through humour and storytelling.

The pleasure amplification method has been the go-to approach for many pharma marketers. It goes something like, 'Take my drug, and you will not only feel better, but also do all kinds of other amazing things in life that you have not been able to.' As we discussed before, this formulaic approach has resulted in a 'sea of sameness' across drug categories in how they position their brands. But sometimes you will be pleasantly surprised. Consider Opdivo[7], a drug from Bristol Myers-Squibb, for the treatment of lung cancer. In our work on terminal lung cancer, we saw that patients and physicians faced difficult choices. About half of the patients die in six to nine months, and there is no cure. We found that in many instances, patients would come to terms with the inevitable and refuse further treatment. Opdivo can extend patients' lives by about three months. If they do choose to extend their life, they also extend their suffering to some degree. Even though the drug's cost of $150,000[8] is generally covered by Medicare or private insurance, there are other costs (e.g. a home-care nurse) that suffering patients are incurring, dipping into the family's savings. Would they want to extend that life? For many, adding three months to life is neither here nor there, and so the motivation for taking a costly drug is not high. So the marketers of cancer drugs like Opdivo often have to answer the question why three months matter to an older person past their prime.

The answer is that three months can matter if they allow the patient to live long enough to bear witness to certain milestone moments—like the high school graduation day of their grandson or the birth of a granddaughter. Opdivo runs a consumer campaign around 'Who would not want to live longer?' One version of its commercials features a woman, presumably in her sixties, who is seen with her granddaughter racing towards her, arms outstretched, with the narrator posing the question, 'Who would not want another chance for . . .?' The last phrase is left unspoken, but the two are seen embracing. The scene is followed by the woman standing with her husband, who kisses her on the forehead, as the narrator asks, 'Who would say no to another . . .?'

You may think of this campaign as an emotional play, but there is nothing impulsive about the decisions a dying person has to make. They deliberate very carefully on what trade-offs they are going to make in terms of their quality of life and family obligations. The Opdivo campaign works. The drug, along with its rival Keytruda from Merck, pulled in an estimated $16 billion in annual sales (the drugs are used in other types of advanced cancers beyond lung cancer) in 2019.

## 2. System 2 Deliberators: Manage Risk

In some cases, even though the value of a brand is understood, consumers are unable to bring themselves to buy the associated products or services because of the 'what if something goes wrong' factor. The two approaches to resolving such uncertainty is either to confront it head on, the 'fight or flight method', or to take baby steps to adoption, the 'flirting training method', both of which I present next.

### *Fight or Flight Method*

In CBT, one method shown to help change behaviour is to have the patient safely face his or her fears. The patient may realize that some of their fears are unfounded or discover coping mechanisms for dealing with them. Marketers may be tempted to find a way to scare the bejesus out of the customer into buying their product. How about these example pitches: 'Put your money in my mutual fund this minute or spend your retirement living on the streets.' Or, 'Take my arthritis drug now or roll through your old age strapped to a wheelchair.' These are surely compelling arguments. They are also risky business.

Marketers jumping on the face-your-fears train may want to contain their excitement. Research into human emotion sciences has shown that fear stimulus is processed in the amygdala of the brain which is programmed to act on threats with a fight or flight response. Fear may lead the consumer to either fight your brand or run away from it. Which one do you choose? I hope you answered 'neither' because that is the right answer. While 'fight or flight' may be technically a System 1 response, confronting your fears and dealing with them thoughtfully is a System 2 comeback.

Recently, I was testing various brand concepts in a focus group with patients of rheumatoid arthritis. One of the conditioning statements opened with the phrase 'You have but one life to live, make the most of it (by taking our drug to relieve your symptoms).' From some participants, this evoked a stinging rebuke, 'I don't like it. You're making it sound like, "Take my drug or die."' You handle fight or flight methods like you would a stick of dynamite—with loving care and a little prayer!

There is debate amongst researchers around whether scare tactics work.[9] The most in-your-face example of such marketing is the anti-smoking campaign in the United States. We have all been subjected to the jarring spots of Terrie, the former chain smoker, who methodically deconstructs her face and larynx, and crackles an instructive warning against smoking through a mechanical mouthpiece.[10] It is a breathtakingly terrifying commercial. But does it work? There is some evidence to suggest that it does not. Fear ads often show extreme and uncommon situations.[11] We all have friends who smoke, and not many turn out like Terrie. People tend to believe that bad things will happen to others, but not to them. That is why people jaywalk, even though others have been killed doing the exact same thing. More importantly, people often cope with fear by tuning it out of their minds. Ironically, scare tactics may trigger the behaviour they are designed to prevent. How? Some smokers report getting so stressed out by the anti-smoking ads that they seek relief by doing what they usually do when they feel bad, namely light up!

That said, marketers can try to get away with scare tactics 'lite'. So, how about if we replaced the word 'fear' with 'concern'? How about if we made the tone less strident and rather than say 'You'd better do this', try a gentler 'Wouldn't it be wise for you to do this?'

In Chapter 1, we talked about how the ad for Enbrel, a drug for patients of rheumatoid arthritis, uses a child to voice her mother's fears of becoming disabled.[12] Instead of the brand marketers asking, 'Hey, Mom, you sure you will be able to stay Mom when you get older?' They have the cute little daughter pop that very question. After all, we are okay with children innocently asking inappropriate questions. It is clever, but it is risky as the impact on the amygdala of the brain could still be the same, namely fight or flight, or total shutdown.

Xarelto, a drug by Janssen, is a blood thinner that can treat and prevent blood clots. It helps lower the risk of stroke, deep vein thrombosis and pulmonary embolism. Unless you are actually having a stroke, you are really not going to be feeling anything in your heart or veins. Xarelto has no choice but to talk about the horrible things that could happen to you if you don't take the drug. In a slight twist, Xarelto's commercials speak instead about how wonderful it is that all kinds of awful things that could have happened did not happen, because you presciently took their drug.[13] They do this by showing a battery of emergency workers from various walks of life who profess their delight at not having had to come to your rescue. The lifeguard on the beach declares, 'I didn't have to run for help'; the waitress at the restaurant says, 'I didn't have to call 911'; the hospital helicopter pilot muses, 'I didn't have to come and get you'; and the nurse closes with, '. . . because you didn't have a heart attack, not today.' All that, because you took the advice of your cardiologist to take Xarelto to heart (yes, the pun is also in the commercial).

While we are talking about a System 2 Deliberator here, it might also be noted that there is also a System 1 play. Xarelto plays to the *loss aversion bias* by reminding you that you could lose the good life you're enjoying in a heartbeat (my pun, not Janssen's this time). Likewise, Amgen, with the Enbrel ad, whispers to the patient that she is a good mom now, but could lose the privilege in the future.

Another interesting attempt at modulating the tone of a fear message comes from down under: from the marketers at the Melbourne Metro[14] who wanted to produce a train safety message. They produced an animated mini movie and song about all the dumb ways to die.[15] The song starts perkily, enumerating all the stupid stuff you can do to kill yourself—for example, set fire to your hair, poke a stick at a grizzly bear, use your private parts as piranha bait or eat a tube of super glue (yes, it is a regular bucket of Aussie humour). Towards the end, the characters switch the catchy little ditty to list the stupid things you could do to guarantee annihilation by one of their trains: by, for instance, standing on the edge of a train station platform, driving around the barrier at a railroad crossing or running across the tracks between the platforms. Those latter few are the ones that are the point and they would rather that you avoid doing so. However, by attaching their message to a long list of dumb ways to die, they make their message seem less shrill and more commonsensical and memorable. Does it work? Who knows! However, it did generate a lot of positive press for the campaign, with the likes of Daisy Dumas of the *Sydney Morning Herald* describing the narrative as 'darkly cute – and irksomely catchy' and the chorus as 'instant earworm material'. For that free commentary alone, I'd say it is worth every penny.

So, should you frighten your customer into buying your products? Here are the words from the wise: 'Proceed at your own peril.' I showed you how marketers have done it with some success—by making grim consequences vivid, talking about calamities avoided, using friendly faces to deliver the message and finally, preceding the heavier message with lighter ones.

## *Flirting Training*

Sometimes, letting wary customers flirt a little with your brand is a great way to begin a relationship. While flirting may not be the foundation of your brand, it may be part of the scaffolding. For a number of online brands, flirting was the key to breaking out into billion-dollar brands.

Warby Parker, an online retailer of prescription glasses, disrupted the $140 billion[16] eyewear industry dominated by the industry giant EssilorLuxottica.[17] It's easy to see that shopping for prescription glasses online is risky. How do you know what the frames will look like on your face? Initially, the company tried all kinds of advanced visual simulation software that could allow people to upload pictures of their faces and superimpose the frames on them, but it just wasn't doing the trick. To get around this problem—of buying online and being stuck with the glasses you hate—Warby Parker launched its 'home try on' programme, whereby a customer receives not one but five frames by mail before buying anything at all. You can also post a picture of yourself in the frames on the #warbyhometryon hashtag and have strangers with time on their hands, and some Warby Parker staff members, give you their opinion on your spectacled mugshot. By 2019, 56,000 videos had been uploaded, and 50 per cent of the shoppers who had done so went on to make a purchase. This flirting technique has now become an essential feature of the Warby Parker brand experience.

Stitch Fix is another online apparel retailer that uses the same approach. Once you have answered a few basic questions about your preferences, their AI engine-based virtual stylist and human personal shoppers mail you a set of clothes to try. You keep what you love and send the rest back for free. Stitch Fix then sends you sets of new clothes periodically, so you can go from flirting to hooked.

Incidentally, flirting approaches also draw on a known System 1 cognitive bias called the *endowment effect*, which is closely related to the loss aversion bias we learnt about in Chapter 5.[18] It states that people are more likely to retain an object that they own rather than acquire a new identical one that they do not own. Something that you hold in your hands, even briefly, can make you feel like you own it. In India, where I come from, family jewellers understand this well.

On one of my not-so recent trips to Jaipur, the city where I grew up, my wife and I wandered unsuspectingly into exactly one such store, ostensibly just to browse the latest local trinkets. Next thing I know, my wife is seated comfortably on a chair, with one store executive dedicated to helping her try on all kinds of necklaces, each with the power to burn a hole in my wallet. Dozens of necklaces later, she had three potential candidates in the race. At this point, get this, the owner, who has vaguely known my family as long-term residents of the town, suggests, 'Why worry? Take all three home and call me at the end of the week, and I will have them picked back up.' Over the next several days, my wife flirted with all three, amassing an encyclopedia of compliments from friends and family, who were financially uninvolved in the transaction and hence, objective and unmindful of the consequences on the family finances. Amid reasoned protests from me, at the end of the week, she kept two and returned one.

Warby Parker may have hashtagged flirting now, but the old man in the jewellery store has been playing this game for years. As this example illustrates, System 1 and System 2 don't have to work at the exclusion of each other; rather, they can complement each other seamlessly. With System 2 Deliberators, the flirting technique, the crafty jeweller lowered the risk of my wife buying something that people would think didn't look good on her, and with the endowment effect he made it her own even before she had paid a penny.

## 3. System 2 Deliberators: Provide Reasons to Believe

Sometimes consumers run into a brick wall when they believe that a brand is too good to be true and promising more than it can deliver. In these cases, the marketer needs to provide pointed evidence to refute the beliefs with the 'Examine the Evidence' method, or a path for the consumer to discover the truth for themselves with the survey method.

### *Examine the Evidence Method*

In Dr Burns's handbook for cognitive behaviour therapy, he describes a method called 'Examine the Evidence', in which a patient seeking help with his condition is encouraged to assess the facts and to prove or disprove his beliefs. For example, to a patient who believes that no one likes him, Dr Burns would say 'Why don't you invite some people to go out for coffee with you and see what happens?' It is important that the facts gathered be those that 'put a lie', as he says, to the beliefs that the patient holds dear. When that happens, Dr Burns found that he could successfully change the person's behaviour. In marketing too, if people believe that your product sucks (and it doesn't), you have to hit them between the eyes with directed facts. When System 1 is faced with severe contradictions to its own deeply held beliefs, it refers the matter over to System 2 for deliberation.

In recent years, the market for frozen foods has been under pressure as consumers seek out healthy, fresh foods. Nowadays, when we think about frozen foods, our minds are flooded with unpleasant thoughts like, 'Gee! In which eon did they pick these vegetables? Is it real or synthetic? What toxic chemicals is it laced in? Is it for human consumption?' Two UK companies, one a manufacturer and the other a retailer, have taken the challenge unapologetically by promoting the healthiness of frozen foods. Birdseye, a producer of frozen vegetables, informs you that flash freezing has many advantages over fresh foods; it locks in the vitamins and minerals, unlike fresh foods, which lose them in storage; freezing uses no preservatives; many healthy vegetables are seasonal and only available frozen; and you waste less by using what you need and refreezing the rest. All of that makes sense. This battery of new facts can stir the System 2 neural net into a revaluation of the instinctive bias.

Likewise, Iceland, a British supermarket chain in Deeside, North Wales, also focuses on frozen prepared meals. Here's what they say: Buy our frozen fish and seafood, because guess what? The fresh fish you see in the supermarkets was also previously just as frozen. Eat our frozen meals, because guess what? Not only do you not have to chop and peel, but you also don't have to worry about cooking skills. This is what Dr Burns means when he reminds us to 'Examine the Evidence'.

One of the more recent brands to score with the evidence method is Chipotle. Until 2015, Chipotle was a high-flyer in the fast-casual dining market segment. In that year, Chipotle suffered a series of stumbles, starting with an outbreak of E. coli that sickened hundreds of customers across eleven states in the US. E. coli infections are serious and can kill people. Customers abandoned their beloved Mexican bites in droves. Brian Nicole, the new CEO hired to breathe life into the dying brand, knew he had an uphill task in regaining the trust of his customers.

Brian and his team came up with a strategy of rejuvenating the Chipotle brand with a campaign around 'Food with Integrity' at a time when no one believed the brand had any. Their campaign 'Behind the Foil' lifts the veil off what goes on behind the scenes at a Chipotle restaurant. And what you see there is real food and real people. In the fast-casual dining world of processed food and robot chefs, this stands in stark contrast. One commercial features a woman chef at a Chipotle location talking about the difference there as compared to the other restaurants where she had previously worked, where guacamole is squeezed out of factory packaged bags and not made by hand from real avocados as she is seen doing on camera. In another commercial, a young male employee talks about how they have no can openers at Chipotle restaurants because nothing comes out of a can. The ads close with the tag line, 'The Difference is Real. Chipotle for Real.' Their strategy of 'we're fresh and real, and they're not' is working like dynamite. If you owned their shares, you would know. Since the calamitous decline in 2015, Chipotle share price had tripled by 2019.

The 'Examine the Evidence' method works best when you can find product attributes that 'put a lie' to customers' unfounded beliefs.

### *Survey Method*

When using the survey method, Dr Burns encourages patients to go check if their (misguided) beliefs are true by asking others. For example, if Rhonda suffers from deep anxiety about public speaking, she can go ask other people if they feel similarly. In doing so, she may discover that she is not alone in feeling so and then deal with it constructively. After all, we have all had our 'Oh! I thought I was the only one doing this wrong' moments. Dr Burns does not simply tell the patient to go conduct a survey; rather, he coaches them on how to do it so that a positive outcome is assured.

The survey method is commonly used by marketers of consumer financial products. An added bonus to the approach is that the marketer can appear more objective and the customer can own the solution. A wonderful example of this approach comes from a campaign launched by Prudential Financial to encourage consumers to be more realistic in their retirement planning.

The commercials[19] feature a psychologist in real life, Harvard's Dan Gilbert, using the survey method to dispel the rosy outlook we may have about our future. Gilbert's academic research shows that people forecast future happiness very poorly and unduly optimistically. In one version of the commercials, Gilbert surveys a group of people, asking them to note down the good and bad things that had happened to them on yellow- and blue-coloured magnetic pads respectively, and to place them on a large board labelled

'The Past'. Next, he asks them to note down some of the good and bad things that could possibly happen to them on another set of yellow and blue magnetic pads and place them on a board called 'The Future'. When looked at from a distance, the board for the past has a checkered mix of yellow and blue, indicating that actual life has a pretty even share of ups and downs. The board for the future looks mainly yellow, or mostly rosy! Gilbert then turns to the participants and asks his question, 'What does this mean to you?' The sombre realization from one volunteer is that 'We all want to think about positive stuff . . . but realistically there will be downsides too.' That cues Gilbert to muse, 'It's good to think optimistically, but let's plan for whatever the future brings.' This is followed by the brand's tag line, 'Prudential, Bring Your Challenges.' And, it could just as well be added, bring us your money.

In other versions of the commercial, Gilbert poses other questions like, 'How long do you think your savings will last?' or (directed to a group of young people), 'When do you think you should start saving for your retirement?' In each case, the questions were followed by clever surveys and visuals to show how woefully inadequate most peoples' plans were. These ads are an example of the using the survey method to trigger System 2 Deliberators into correcting for the 'hakuna matata, be happy' bias of System 1.

A key piece of the puzzle is for the marketer to provide the questions to ask to ensure a desirable outcome. It is often a question that the consumer is not asking, but should be. In other cases, the consumer may be asking the question but not answering it in the way the brand would like it to be answered. In these cases, the marketer may pose the question and answer it themselves. That's not really a survey, you say. I know, but this 'pseudo-survey' technique can seem real to the brain because of the Q&A format.

De Beers is a master at telling consumers how to think about what diamonds to buy and when. However, a key question that one wrestles with is how much to spend on a diamond engagement ring. The marketers at DeBeers wanted to take no chance that people may lowball the answer. So, they went ahead and framed the survey question implicitly for the unsuspecting consumer in full-page print ads that shouted out, 'How can you make two months' salary last forever?' Below that is a picture of an engagement ring with a massive diamond. How is that for brilliance? A question with the answer embedded into the question itself.

Other tag lines for the campaign provided the same answer to the implicit question, 'Two months' salary showed the future Mrs Smith what the future is like.' The beauty of the campaign lies in the mathematical fact that it allows people with more money to part with more of it and for those with less to also not be spared the pain. As a side note, the two months' salary campaign also leverages a System 1 lever, namely the anchoring bias, whereby the consumer now subconsciously uses that as the starting point for determining their budget.

## 4. System 2 Deliberators: Change the Context

Sometimes consumers don't see the value in your brand unless you help them think about it in the right context. This may mean giving them a new way to think about your brand with the reframing method, or to clear up matters when they feel your brand is responsible for something undesirable—which it isn't really responsible for—with the reattribution method.

## *Reframing Method*

If you have ever convinced someone to come over to your point of view in a discussion and they finally relented with 'Now that you put it this way, I get it', then you know what we are talking about. The reframing method aims to change the way a customer thinks about your brand and put it in a way he or she understands it.

Patek Philippe, arguably one of the world's most expensive traditional watch brands, has been a master of this method. I want you to think about the following for a moment. Why would anyone want to buy a traditional mechanical watch in today's age? If you are like everyone else—the garden-variety non-Neanderthal—you own a smartphone, which will tell you the time more accurately than any hand-crafted Swiss watch at no additional cost. It will throw in a few extra tricks for good measure, like unlimited alarm settings, global clock, stopwatch, timer and a sleep monitor. So why would anyone shell out a whopping $40,000 to $100,000 for a conventional watch from Patek Philippe?

The challenge from smartphones is not new for this stalwart. Even when the company first introduced its watches, there were plenty of other ways to buy timekeepers for a cost that did not entail selling your front lawn.

Patek Philippe addressed this challenge with a metaphysical brand strategy. It goes something like this: Well, it is not a watch really; it is a piece of art. You are not spending any money really; you are making an investment. It is not yours really; it is a legacy for your next generation. This ontological reframing of a Patek Philippe watch—as 'what you think it is, is what it isn't'—has been the secret sauce that allowed this Stern family enterprise to rise from the ashes of the 1929 Great Depression and prosper to this day.

So where did this all start? In the 1990s, it was common for high-end watch companies to feature celebrities donning their products, in the hope that consumers would buy their products for the vicarious thrills of being seen like those celebrities. Think of Cindy Crawford on all of those 'Omega! My Choice!' advertisements. At the time, Tim Delaney, the principal at Legas Delaney, a London-based agency, was conducting focus groups with well-heeled purveyors of fine watches. And what he heard from some, made him stop and rethink the conventional wisdom of routinely selecting celebrities for jewellery commercials. The consumers were saying, 'Hey, wait a minute, I am a pretty accomplished person. Why do I have to look like someone else to feel special? Where is my story?' On the flight back to London from San Francisco, Delaney wrote four words, 'Begin your own tradition'—a line that would become an epic campaign lasting many decades.[20]

The first print ads that were launched featured photographs of people wearing no watches. The words below the photos put the brand's strategy in plain sight, 'Begin your own tradition. Each Patek Philippe watch is crafted by hand. Each one is subtly different from the next one. This is what makes it uniquely personal for each owner.' It was not any watch; it was the owner's personal story. 'The ladies' Golden Ellipse ref. 4831 has 180 carats set in 18 carat solid gold' reminded you that it was not a watch, it was jewellery. 'Any woman who owns one will treasure it. And this will be its true value to the one that wears its next' made it clear that it was a not a watch, it was a legacy. Slovenian philosopher Slavoj Žižek, who said 'Beyond the fiction of reality, there is the reality of the fiction',[21] would have happily given a nod to this campaign. In 1997, the tag line was tweaked a bit and became the iconic, 'You never truly own a Patek Philippe, you merely look after it for the next generation.'

Many observers feel that the power of the campaign lay in its emotional appeal, and they are wrong. There are plenty of ads depicting women thrilled to tears when gifted a piece of jewellery. This campaign was about reframing the issue for consumers: Spending on a Patek Phillipe was not an expense; rather it was like buying and holding a valuable asset.

The reframing method can also be a great way for brands to not just differentiate themselves but also grow by giving consumers new occasions for consumption. The grandmaster of System 2 strategies of this variety is De Beers, the diamond company that has held that crown for nearly a hundred years.[22] De Beers was conceived by British businessmen as a cartel based out of South Africa and continues to this day to be a dominant player. So how do you grow a business if you already own the whole pie? Simple, you tell everyone to eat more pies!

Diamonds are not particularly rare in nature, which is why De Beers became a cartel in the first place. Diamonds were also not considered particularly desirable in the United States and in many other parts of the world. Specifically, the concept of a diamond ring as an indispensable proof of an engagement was largely non-existent. Working with N.W. Ayer, a leading advertising agency at the time in 1938, De Beers created the 'A Diamond is Forever' campaign to change this mindset and create a mental association of diamonds with lasting matrimony. This part of the strategy was a System 1 play that subconsciously associated the diamond's well-known physical property of being one of the hardest[23] and most indestructible substances in nature to the desired property of making wedding vows long-lasting (and hard?). Over time, the solitaire ring became the unshakeable standard for commemorating engagements, with the measure of your love reflected conveniently in the size of the diamond.

But again, if you are a monopoly and you have already captured most of the addressable market for outsized rocks, what do you do next? Well, you come up with something else to celebrate 'Your Past, Present and the Future' with, of course, a three-diamond ring. And next, perhaps a life beyond this life? That would be the 'Eternity' ring, with a string of diamonds wrapped around your finger. That should cover everything, right? Yes, it certainly should. Everything, except for the right hand! Enter the 'Right Hand Is About You' campaign, serendipitously in time for the women's rights movement. Now, women can liberate their beings from the clutches (and wallets) of men by (wait for it) buying a ring for themselves. That is the picture-perfect example of the System 2 reframing method. And, nobody, does it better.

### *Reattribution Method*

Psychotherapists use reattribution techniques to help patients of depression who unduly believe that they alone are the cause of all problems. They do so by helping the patients see other reasons why things may be awry. Sometimes, brands face a similar dilemma when they are boxed into a corner due to factors beyond their control or due to the unwise choices by their marketers. The latter's job then becomes to set things right so that the brand can continue to prosper.

In pharma marketing, there is a cardinal rule of not positioning your brand as being so good that it works for even the hardest-to-treat patients. Any pharma marketer will tell you that that risks making your brand the preferred choice of 'train wrecks'—an insensitive but descriptive term, heard in the back halls of pharma companies to make the point unambiguously. It brackets your brand as the reserve choice for patients in the worst possible condition. This is the saddest thing you could do to a great drug because the most severe patients constitute a small segment of the market and treating them can be hard, dooming your drug to lots of public failures. Physicians who prescribe medications like to always have options in hand. If you position your drug as the nuclear option, you will be siloed until World War III happens.

Krystexxa, a drug for patients of gout, found itself in exactly such a predicament. It was developed by a small, financially shaky company called Savient. The US FDA rewards companies that develop drugs for neglected (orphan) diseases that impact only small populations of patients with faster approval times. Thus, Savient went ahead and positioned itself as the drug of choice for 'refractory' patients with chronic tophaceous gout, meaning those with the worst of the worst disease. This tactic succeeded in getting the drug approved in a short period of time, but for the doctors it became the brand of last resort, to be prescribed to patients who had exhausted all other options. Savient was purchased by GTCR, a private equity firm, out of bankruptcy and nursed back into health.

In 2015, Horizon Therapeutics saw a golden opportunity to buy the company from GTCR and reposition the brand. The CEO of Horizon, Tim Walbert, is a seasoned marketer and immediately recognized that there was a great opportunity to redefine Krystexxa as a drug for not just chronic refractory patients but for those whose gout was uncontrolled by other drugs. What's the difference? There are only about 40,000 or so chronic refractory gout patients. There are nearly three million gout patients treated with other drugs. Of those, at least 30 per cent or one million are not in adequate control with the treatments they use. Tim bought the drug from GTCR for $510 million, at what most thought was an outrageous premium. Working diligently with his team of crack marketers and us, over the following three years he fundamentally shifted the trajectory of the drug and tripled sales, much of this by strategically reattributing the drug as the recourse for not just patients with tophaceous gout but also the million or so whose condition was inadequately controlled by other drugs.

One word of caution for marketers eying System 2 Deliberators for growing their brands. When you trigger System 2, you need to be aware that the consumer is going to look at your brand value propositions critically. So while you may want the consumer to look at only the positives of the brand, the consumer may also consider the negatives. They will wonder 'What's the catch? What's in the fine print?' Maintaining a keen awareness of that fact can help marketers avoid nasty surprises. Be careful what you wish for.

* * *

*Key Takeaways*

Cognitive brands can create consumer preference by answering their question, 'Does this brand make reasoned sense?'

System 2 Deliberators are the second type of process by which the brain makes sense of what the brands say. In contrast to System 1 Easers, which make sense of choice by going with the flow, comparing options against prior wisdom, *Deliberators* do so by changing it and giving consumers a new religion. This must be done when the biases and beliefs that sit in the consumer's brain are unhelpful to the brand, either because they are contrary to what the brand stands for or because the brand is new and unfamiliar. Thus, we have to convince the consumer to use their System 2 Deliberators to recode their brains and lay down new wiring. They are used if Easers alone won't do the job of making good sense of the brand.

System 2 Deliberators are familiar territory for marketers used to selling brands based on their value propositions. However, instead of just listing the 'what' of the brand, namely its benefits, System 2 Deliberators also provide the 'how' of the brand. They do so in four different ways by:

- Amplifying the value of the brand
- Lowering the risk of choosing the brand
- Providing reasons to make consumers believe in the brand
- Framing the brand choice favourably

Even when a brand choice makes sense, consumers may not be motivated enough to buy its products or services. In the next chapter, we will figure out how to get the consumer off the fence of indecision or inaction, and make them go buy our brands instead of waiting. *Easers* and *Deliberators* can make the consumers like our brand and perceive it as the sensible choice. But we need brand resolve, the third component of cognitive brands, to make them really want and buy what it offers.

# 7

# Brand Resolve: A Mantra for Happiness

## *Part 3 of Brand Architecture*

If System 1 and System 2 were all there was to brand choice, we could call it a day with the previous chapter. But there is a problem. It's called 'indecision'.

Without indecision, you might have married your 'great-after-all' high-school sweetheart sooner, opened your own bacon gourmand store in the Chicago West Loop rather than stick it out as grade-thirteen shift supervisor at the piñata factory, and not eaten both the mushroom ravioli and the cheeseburger for lunch.

The consumer sitting on the fence of indecision is often a challenge for brands that require bigger purchases like a car, home mortgage or furniture. But indecision can also take the form of indifference where smaller purchases are concerned. With such detachment, you buy your morning black coffee from whatever store you happen to be near rather than making that small detour to the Starbucks on Hubbard Street for a Grande Pike.

Even when consumers trust a brand and what it says makes sense to them, they may hesitate to buy its products/

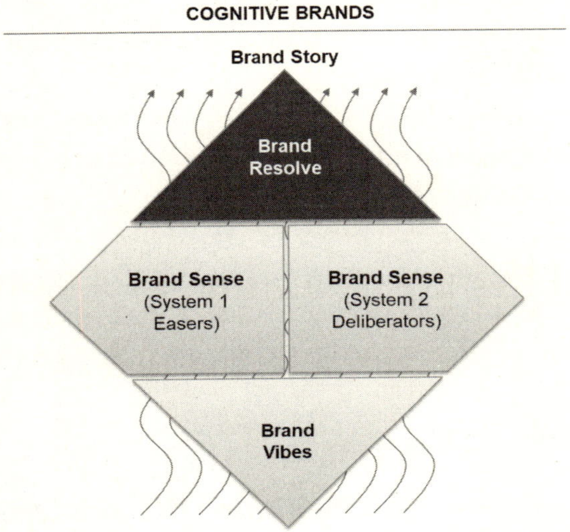


*Figure 7.1: Part 3: Using brand resolve to drive consumers to action.*

services or truly make it their own after the 'this-week-only' sales discounts are gone and the sweet sales lady who sold it to them is a wispy memory. That is where brand resolve comes into play. Marketers need to tap into the brain's conative energy to break these impasses.

The motivation to buy or attach yourself to something is a function of two things, namely how happy we expect to be with the brand choice and our inner zeal to pursue such happiness. All of this happy talk sounds a bit 'new age' at first, but it isn't. Before we delve deeper into it, let me offer a summary of the thesis:

- All consumers pursue happiness as a conscious or subconscious goal.
- It is the pursuit of happiness that gets people off the fence of indecision or indifference.
- Brands that find a way to help the consumer in this pursuit are preferred and loved by consumers.

- Brands can align with consumers' goals for happiness by addressing any of the three known universal needs or intrinsic motivations.
- The conative energy with which consumers pursue these universal needs is different from person to person and hence across customer segments.

These principles are inspired by the research of many psychologists but reflect the adaptations I have made to make their work useful in branding.[1] With that caveat out of the way, let's get started.

## The Pursuit of Happiness

The need to pursue happiness is in the DNA of all humans. This idea was so obvious to the founding fathers of the United States that they enshrined 'life, liberty and the pursuit of happiness' as the three 'unalienable rights' of all humanity in the Declaration of Independence.

If you are academically unimpressed with the founding fathers' pitch, then, for you, there are three ideas in psychology that will get you to the same place. The first is that personal goals are ubiquitous, and humans are wired for 'goal pursuit'.[2] The second is that all aspects of goal pursuit—making goals, pursuing them and making progress on them—make us happy.[3] The third is that we pursue goals consciously and subconsciously, and mostly the latter.[4] There is a truckload of research on the topic, but if you are a marketer, you will want to take my word for it: Your consumers, whether they realize it or not, are hardwired for one goal, to constantly pursue happiness and well-being.

Consequently, and ultimately, all brands are about making the consumer happier.

In brain sciences, happiness is not an abstraction; it's a science. There are specific structures in the brain, referred to as reward systems, which serve as hedonic hotspots and neuronal pleasure networks that help us calibrate which stimuli we want more or less of.[5] There are four actual chemicals in the brain that create this sensation of happiness—namely dopamine, oxytocin, serotonin and endorphins (DOSE).[6] They are triggered by everything, from the experience of sex and drugs to eating and exercising. We feel good when these chemicals are released and tend to do more of the things that trigger them.[7] When we experience brands, we feel this neurochemical-reaction-induced happiness in one shape or form.

Here's the rub. You don't have to experience the brand to feel such happiness. You can sort of feel it even when you imagine experiencing the brand. Your brain can use its circuitry to forecast roughly how happy you would feel if you were to have a certain brand experience without having it yet. For example, it can imagine how happy you would feel licking melting dollops of Ben & Jerry's Cherry Garcia ice cream off a waffle cone without requiring you to stick your face into a tub full of it.

The brain can simulate 'make-believe' happiness by recalling what it may have experienced in the past, called consummatory pleasures (if you've had Cherry Garcia before); or in other cases by dreaming about experiencing them in the future, called anticipatory pleasures (if you've never had Cherry Garcia ever).[8] A brand promise of happiness is just that—an invitation to let you relive memories of past pleasures or fantasize about possible future ones as mental sensations.

Can it be that simple? Brands are there to make people happier. Check! But wait. There's more!

## Brands as the Keys to Universal Happiness

What kind of happiness are we talking about? Two psychologists from the University of Rochester, Deci and

Ryan, gave us a pretty good answer to that question with their Self Determination Theory (SDT).[9] They found that beyond the obvious physiological needs that we all have, there are psychological needs (or wants) that we all pursue as part of our goals. They called the latter intrinsic motivations.

The wonderful news about brands that tap into intrinsic motivations is that we tend to want to stick with them of our own volition. Deci and Ryan identified three such universal needs that promote our happiness and well-being:

- *Need for autonomy*: We want to be free to make our own choices and shape our destiny. Consumers must feel like they chose their brand and were not manipulated into choosing it. In US companies, it is common to have annual charity drives with the United Way, a non-profit that raises funds through company-sanctioned campaigns, where the employer solicits contributions from their employees. Well, the employees often hate it! They feel pressured to sign up because their bosses have 'suggested' a level of giving appropriately fattened to align with their position in the company and conveniently deducted from their pay. Needless to say, most of those generous donors stop writing checks to the United Way as soon as they leave those companies. Autonomy matters.
- *Need for Competence*: We want to be better at doing stuff and feel better about ourselves for it. This can make us aspire to master the art of mixing the perfect Ramos Gin Fizz or train for excellence on the intricate path of *Nuido*, the Japanese way of embroidery. We may buy things that help us be better than our peers and revered at our work or social circles. We may experiment with the unknown to enhance our talents and learn more.
- *Need for Relatedness*: We want to be socially networked with other people and a part of something bigger than ourselves.

> We do like to make the world a better place for others because that helps us connect with them more. That is why we may favour brands that do social good and thus belong to a circle of enlightened consumers. For instance, if you live in Japan, you may ship Grandpa's old choppers to the Japan Denture Recycling Association so they can retrieve the $17 worth of silver and palladium, and donate the proceeds to UNICEF ($80,000 donated in total in 2007).[10] It takes a bit of work, but they do it to be part of a bigger social whole.

The common element here is that research has shown that these needs and wants are super motivational and resilient; we will act on and pursue them over a lifetime. In Self-Determination Theory, these three needs are not just 'nice to have' but innate, essential and universal, and lead to a psychological sense of well-being.[11]

We started with the question what is going to prompt consumers to get off the fence of indecision and go buy our brands purposefully. The answer is that *marketers must make their brands the key to unlocking happiness for the consumer by helping them in their quest to fulfil one or more of these needs.*

If you are selling a cure for headaches (and you might well have one by now), what could you do beyond saying my pill 'kills pain fast' and christening the brand 'Pronto'? Well, you could link it to the need for autonomy by talking about Pronto being the key elixir that helps a stricken consumer take back control of her day. You could link it to the need for competence by talking about Pronto as the magic eraser for her headache so she can go back to displaying her mastery of Nuido to her Japanese embroidery class. You could link it to the need for relatedness by talking about Pronto being Artemis, the Greek goddess, that slays Antaura, the migraine demon, transforming her monster mama persona into normal, lovable mom, allowing her to rejoin the human race. This making of your brand the key to, or a necessary vehicle for, happiness, is the path to engaging consumers, so they reach for Pronto over a lifetime of headaches and not the cheap generic ibuprofen proffered by your insurance company.

Pronto is not an actual brand of headache medicine. Not yet anyway. But there are real-world brands that make us happy. Let's take a look at how some marketers have made their brands the key to the three universal needs we discussed.

## Brand Resolve through Autonomy

National Car Rental's recent 'Go like a Pro'[12] campaign was a clever example of a brand that targeted frequent business travellers, tapping into their need for control. As a consultant, I was a road warrior for a long time. Every Monday morning, I was flying off to some city to work with my clients, and everywhere I went, I rented a car for the week. All I wanted was for the universe to march to my tune so I could get to work fast and easy, and do my job.

In one of National's many hilarious executions of the campaign, we see the somewhat obnoxious and overly confident protagonist, Patrick Warburton, turn to the screen and inform the world, 'I've been called a control freak, but I like to think of myself as more of a control enthusiast.'

He cuts straight to the front of the line at the coffee shop, snares the cup of coffee being served and pauses a moment to enjoy a sip of the steaming beverage, as the woman whose order it was supposed to be glares at him aghast. 'Hmmm, a perfect 177 degrees!' he murmurs unapologetically.

He turns his attention back to us and explains why he rents from National, 'Because I can skip the counter and go straight to my car, without talking to any human, unless I want to . . . and I don't! At National, I can pick any car from the aisle . . . Control! . . . Hmmm. What's the word? So Sexy!' At this point the voiceover comes on with 'National! Go like a pro!'

The campaign works like a charm with frequent business travellers. Rob Connors, the VP of brand marketing at National Car Rental, told *Marketing Daily*, 'The ads use humor to address the lack of control frequently felt by these travelers at the airport, so they relate to Warburton and overwhelmingly enjoy his portrayal of the ultimate "control enthusiast." As a result, Warburton has become a recognized brand cue for National and has helped drive home the message that National offers unparalleled autonomy over the rental experience.' The brand campaign increased communications awareness by four percentage points and grew National's airport market share by 5 per cent.[13]

With pharma brands, the promise of self-control or independence is among the more powerful ways to position drugs with patients. For many, the disease takes a life of its own, preventing patients from doing things that that they should be able to do, from unhooking their own bras to spending an hour without needing to go to the bathroom. Brand resolve for many drugs follows from the promise of delivering on this universal need for autonomy.

## Brand Resolve through Competence

In 2006, my company was working with a hot biotech start-up, NeoPharm, on launching an innovative drug code-named CB (after its biologic molecule cintredekin besudotox), for treating advanced brain cancer. CB was among the early wave of biologic smart bombs that worked by affixing itself to a cancer cell and releasing a toxin into it. However, CB was a large-molecule drug that was hard to administer as the brain is sheathed in what is called the blood–brain barrier, which prevents drugs released into the bloodstream from penetrating the brain. Hence, a new type of pump with the ability to deliver the macromolecular drug in a controlled flow over thirty-six hours was paired with the drug. Yes, the patient would be sitting in a hospital bed with a small part of his brain exposed, with the drug slowly infusing into it over a day and a half!

Selling a complicated new drug like that to doctors is hard enough. Now, we also had to convince the super-busy neurosurgeons to learn to use this newfangled pump as well. We thought it was all building up to be a royal mess. But, guess what? It wasn't. Much to our surprise, we discovered quite the opposite: the doctors were just as excited about getting their hands on the CED (convection enhanced delivery) pump as they were about having access to the groundbreaking drug. The neurosurgeons that we interviewed, from those at Duke University to the ones at the University Medical Center Hamburg-Eppendorf, confessed, 'Oh, this is the first drug that will allow us to use CED in practice. That experience will be invaluable for many other drugs in the pipeline that hold greater promise.' Without realizing it, we had stumbled upon the conative energy of the brain surgeons, namely their obsession with advancing their own mastery of their art. While CB itself, ultimately and sadly for the patients, failed to work in its Phase III clinical trials and never came to market, we learnt an important lesson: brands could influence physician resolve to buy by showing them how they could enhance their expertise.

## Brand Resolve through Relatedness

One of the best examples of this principle was Mastercard's iconic 'Priceless' campaign. In multiple vignettes on television,

Mastercard showed how you could achieve your own personal nirvana by using their card to spend your money. The first television spot, which was designed by McCann Erickson, aired in 1997. It showed a father taking his son to his first ball game.[14] In what has now become a familiar refrain, the narrator of the scene itemizes the day's expenses as two tickets for $46, hot dogs, popcorn and sodas for $27, and an autographed baseball for $50. But the 'real conversation, with your eleven-year-old son? Priceless!' The ad closes cleverly with the iconic line, 'There are some things money can't buy. For everything else, there's Mastercard.' In this way, the marketers at Mastercard shrewdly positioned their card as the key that allowed their customers to unlock a quotient of happiness well above any pain of the spend and relate or connect with the beneficiaries of their largesse. And that results in the resolve to use the Mastercard brand over and over.

This might be a good place to make a note about the idea of three universal dimensions of happiness. You could ask, 'Hey, if I won the $200 million prize on Mega-Millions lottery, wouldn't I be on seventh heaven?' How does that fit with the three dimensions of happiness? Only a moment of reflection is needed to realize that the happiness from money flows from what you imagine you will do with it. Mastercard's campaign showed exactly that: It was not about the card; it was about what you would do with it to increase your connectedness with those around you.

*I cannot emphasize enough that the brand must implicitly be the key for unlocking more happiness.* Practising marketers often forget this. They make the mistake of showing people dancing at parties or frolicking through hills in their ads without clarifying how their brand was the key to unlocking that happiness. Those ads create emotional stories for their own sake, without ever selling anything.

As a brand marketer, you have a product to sell. Show how your brand is the instrument for getting consumers from point A to point B on the happiness scale.

## Luckily, Happiness Decays

In her book *Delirium*, Lauren Oliver writes, 'You can't be happy unless you're unhappy sometimes. You know that, right?' Think of humans as hardwired to constantly pursue happiness and well-being, but without ever managing to stay perfectly happy. This unfortunate truth about the inaccessibility of lasting happiness is so much a part of the human DNA that it has plagued philosophers across generations, for as long as philosophy has been a thing.[15] What philosophers don't know, but some marketers do, is that this is a very good thing.

Let's do a little exercise here. On a scale from 1 to 10, think of the number that represents your overall happiness with life at this exact moment. A score of 10 would mean perfect happiness and fulfilment. A score of 1 would mean you are clinically depressed and need to see somebody. Ready? Close your eyes, think and trace out the number with your finger in the palm of your hand.

Okay, now here's my guess. Odds are that you wrote the number seven in your palm. Now ask yourself, 'How come he guessed my number or was pretty darn close?' After all, the readers of this book come from all walks and stages of life, make less money or more, and have different highs and lows with friends and families at this moment in their lives. The reason for this convergence is that most healthy human beings are wired for a level of happiness 20–30 per cent below the perfect score of 10. Even making a lot more money does not change the score that much.[16] The gap between perfect and actual happiness creates a healthy desire among individuals to not be satisfied with what they have and want for more. This striving for greater happiness is what gives rise to wants. And where would brands be without wants?

Happiness decays because people anticipate happiness narrowly but experience it broadly. This means that after the initial thrill of getting what you want from a brand, you go back to where you started. Consider this: Are you going to be happy eating a cup of delicious Ben & Jerry's chocolate chip cookie dough ice cream? Yeah! Make that a 9! That is anticipated happiness. As the ice cream melts and streams down your throat, you will briefly be a 10 in happiness. Then, the door swings open and in walks your wife. Does she think you made a mess of the kitchen and forgot to pick up dinner? Yeah! Bring that back to a 7! That is the diffusion of experienced happiness. But that is okay if you are the brand marketer at Ben & Jerry's, because people will want to eat your ice cream again and again to try to stay happy.[17]

## The Conative Energy to Pursue Happiness is Different across Consumers

Think of happiness as resting on three coiled springs within each of us. Each represents one of the three universal needs. When a brand promises you something that could make you incredibly happy, the spring is stretched wide apart. Now, how tightly wound that spring is depends on your genes, and everybody's spring has a different amount of tension. If yours is tightly wound and profound happiness is in sight, you are going to snap and go for it. You have a high tendency to pursue that particular need to achieve happiness.

Your friend, with a lower-tension spring, may be a lot more laid back and disinclined to pursue whatever it is that sent you marching off. That intuitively makes sense. For some people, autonomy is way more important than being a master of their craft. For others, having social bonds and relationship with others is more important than only pursuing their own will. Different people pursue different goals in the same situation.

As I write this, Chicago is burning. Two weeks back a black man, George Floyd, was choked to death by a white police officer who was suppressing him during an arrest. Protests have broken out in cities across the country. Most of us feel the deep angst, the vibes of desperation, of the people in the black community, who have been subjected to repeated injustices by the members of the police force. Most people understand why, for so many, pouring out into the streets and protesting is the only way to pressure the government into doing something. It makes total sense. And yet, not everybody rushes out to join the protestors. Some of us light candles in solidarity, others write letters of protest to newspapers, and still others do nothing more than vent our distress with neighbours. While everyone wants the world to be a happier place, our conative energies are different, and we act in different ways and sometimes, not at all. When that happens with brands, we call it brand resolve, and it is different from person to person.

Because people are different, a brand may never make everyone happy. That is why we have customer segmentation as an important tool in marketing. We only have to position our brands for resolve with the customers that we want to target. What marketers should pay attention to more is to include the right 'tendencies' or 'universal needs' as dimensions in their segmentation. At Cerenti, we dubbed this method of targeting consumers 'tendencies-based consumer segmentation'. In the following chapter, I illustrate this in an in-depth case study.

### *Key Takeaways*

This chapter introduced the final piece of the puzzle in designing great brands, namely brand resolve. If you get this right, your brand will fly. Mess it up, and you will scratch your head till it hurts trying to figure out why your brand is stuck in the mud. Remember the lessons:

- With good vibes, consumers trust your brand. With good sense, consumers believe what your brand says. With good resolve, consumers want your brand and buy its products/services.
- This happens because consumers want brands they believe will make them happier.
- Brands build resolve when they become key to helping consumers move up on the happiness scale by addressing one of the three known universal psychological needs.
- Each consumer's tendency to pursue happiness is different and based on his or her own DNA, and thus a brand must determine whom it wants to target.

If it feels like you have taken a drink from a fire hose, don't sweat it. It is not that the four parts of cognitive brands that we have discussed in this chapter, and in the previous three chapters, are complicated; it is just that they are new and different. So take your time to let it sink in. In the next chapter, we'll do a case study. We will apply all that we have learnt to a brand close to my heart, PediaSure, a children's nutritional supplement.

# 8

# For the Love of Kids: The Story of PediaSure

It was the waning end of an afternoon, in a bleak and windowless conference hall of a hotel in Florida.* There I was, giving a routine speech on branding to a sea of nodding heads. There were as many faces staring at my slides as glancing at their flight departure times on their iPhones.

All except for one man, who appeared a little restless. Barely had I ended my spiel when he jumped up and cornered me as I stepped off the podium. 'That was great! I loved it! I'm gonna hire you!' he said, by way of introduction, pressing his business card in my hands. That's how I met Tripp Chenworth, head of Abbott's sprawling international nutrition business. And minutes later, he did hire me, right on the spot.

What I couldn't tell at the time was whether he really needed help with branding or getting some monkey off his back. It turned out to be both. Tripp had a flourishing nutrition business,

* The events described in the following passages have been fictionalized and the names of individuals disguised to remove any non-public information and preserve the privacy of the mentioned individuals. The narrative is thus designed to be instructive rather than accurately biographical or historical.

selling infant formula and children's nutrition supplements. It was a well-oiled machine chugging along nicely, making plenty of money every year for Abbott and growing modestly. Despite that, two of his deputies had been haranguing him to make a push to grow the business faster. It involved making a seismic change in his business model, and Tripp was not the kind of guy to light a match in a forest without knowing what it was he was going to set on fire. He liked ideas, but he loved money more.

Later that week, I found myself seated at one end of a long conference table in Abbott's HQ on the north edge of the Chicago suburbs, across from Mel Frisker and Walt Parker, two dynamos at the helm of Tripp's marketing department. Mel Frisker was a seasoned, street-smart manager. He had been in the nutrition business for many years, knew more about it than just about anyone else in the industry and had an instinctive sense for what worked. Walt Parker was his energetic young deputy, brimming with new ideas for taking the world by storm.

What they had on their hands was PediaSure, a decades-old brand first introduced in the late 1980s as a nutritional substitute for sick, hospitalized children who were too weak to take table foods on their own. PediaSure was a milkshake-like drink, which when taken three times a day could meet all the nutritional needs of a child. This was literally true: PediaSure was medically formulated to provide balanced and complete nutrition, so that a sick child could survive for days on it with nothing else.

I'm going to tell the story of PediaSure in detail, and not just because it's a story that's close to my heart. It will show you exactly how the concepts we discussed in the previous chapters can be used as a new framework to design cognitive brands, really nice ones. With PediaSure, we'll see how good vibes, sense and resolve can work perfectly together to create stupendous brands.

It turned out that 'kids too weak to eat' constituted a tiny hospital market segment, and PediaSure was locked up in pharmacies that saw it as a medicinal product, trudging along in most countries, with low single-digit growth from one year to the next. Mel and Walt had a much bigger dream. They asked, 'Why can't all kids drink PediaSure instead of only those in hospitals?'

Taken aback a little, I looked questioningly at Walt, like, 'Really?' I asked, with more than a note of scepticism.

'I drink it all the time myself,' he responded, pulling out a can stashed in the depths of his desk drawer and helpfully proceeding with a demonstration.

'That's a sample of one, Walt,' I pointed out.

'I give it to all three of my kids, too,' he said, pointing to a picture of the three beautiful siblings in a frame teetering at the edge of a crowded corner of his desk. Great! Now, we were up to a sample of four; I had to give in.

Understand my initial scepticism. PediaSure faced an uphill battle crawling out of grungy hospitals and into peoples' homes. After all, when was the last time you saw a sick person in a hospital and said to yourself 'I want to have what she's having'?

Also, its price point of about $3 per serving was seriously high compared to the glass of milk—which is pretty much what PediaSure looked like. In developing countries, a month's worth of PediaSure could resemble the loan payment for a second-hand motorbike.

Perhaps most importantly, most mothers we knew believed that the best way for children to get nutrition was from normal table foods, not medication. Think about it: if I told you that you don't need to eat regular meals any more and that you should just take this tablet that doctors at the Cook County Hospital give to their sickest patients, would you go for it?

How in the world would we ever change anybody's mind?

'That is exactly my question,' said Tripp, who had popped into the room, adding gravely, 'Welcome to the team!' Then, he shook my hands and left the room as abruptly as he had snuck in.

Not everything was quite so grim, though. Mel noticed that sales of PediaSure in Indonesia were surging. Its price there was astronomical compared to local income levels, and yet the product was flying off the shelves. The country head, Vic Monk, was an entrepreneurial hotshot who preferred to say little. Instead, he let his numbers do the talking—and his were off the charts. PediaSure was growing at a double-digit clip year after year even as other country managers struggled.

Vic had done something very different in Indonesia. We heard that he had decided to put PediaSure on TV, where it was promoted by a hugely popular child prodigy singer called Sherina. But Walt was concerned that a sponsorship-type strategy would be hard to replicate in the thirty-plus other small and large countries where they sold PediaSure.

'Sherina is not known outside of Bahasa land. What happens in Mexico? What happens in Vietnam? Even in Indonesia, Sherina won't stay a child forever. What then?'

Mel and Walt wanted one playbook for PediaSure that could make the brand sizzle not just on the islands of Indonesia but everywhere in the world.

## Borrowing from the Shrinks

In 2004, cognitive branding was in its early days and we hadn't quite worked out everything. We needed a new framework for getting inside peoples' heads and find a door in for PediaSure. We wanted something that had proved to work. Tripp was into known quantities and firm answers, and not so much into conducting class experiments on his business.

Just then, someone on the team had an epiphany. Since it was consumer psychology we were interested in, why not peek at what the shrinks used instead of scraping the empty bottom of the marketer's toolbox? It turned out that psychotherapists had been using a recent diagnostic tool called 'cognitive schemas' to map thought patterns of their patients. They had done it with millions of patients successfully, and the evidence on how well it worked was piling up high.

Psychotherapists use cognitive schemas to decipher what they call 'automatic thought distortions' of their patients. These are sort of the first thoughts that come to your mind in reaction to an event. For people with psychological issues, these thoughts are generally negative and unhelpful. They make them feel worse and act in a manner that is unconstructive, leading to a downward spiral of mood, temperament and dysfunctionality. The therapist's goal is to break that cycle and train the patient to think positively. As we discussed in our chapter on System 2 Deliberators, over time psychotherapists have developed a library of such methods for reprogramming the thoughts of such patients and turning them around.

We figured that we could think of consumers' 'automatic thought distortions' as beliefs and behaviours that would prevent them from using PediaSure. Like a psychotherapist, our job was to *untwist* such thinking, banish these thoughts and to plant new ones with a happier disposition towards PediaSure instead. But first, we had to map out the thought distortions.

## Brand Vibes: Connecting with the Angst of the Jakarta Moms

To unravel the mystery of why PediaSure was selling like hot cakes in Indonesia, I jumped on a plane to Jakarta with my team of Cerenti consultants to search for answers.

From mornings thick with the haze of humidity to nights with unrelenting, torrential rain, we herded dozens of Jakarta moms into dark rooms for focus group research.

They all had one thing in common: they were all dishing out dollops of PediaSure instead of butternut squash to their kids. We wanted to know why it was that they would see child pop star Sherina on TV and think, 'I want what she's having for my kids.'

The following illustration shows the cognitive schema we mapped out after listening to the Jakarta mothers. It turned out that in home after home, mealtimes were traumatic primetime spectacles between moms and kids. Mum after mum told us the same story: their kids were not eating well. They didn't eat what they were supposed to, when they were supposed to or how much they were supposed to.

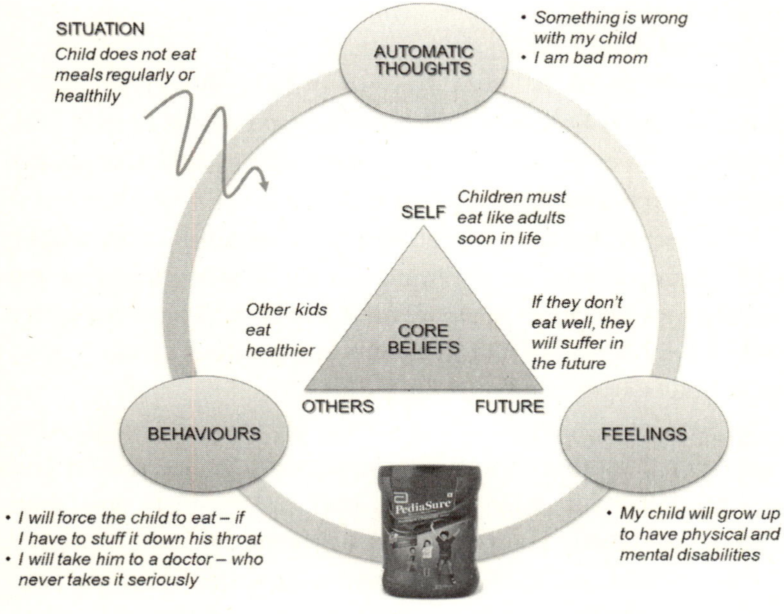


*Figure 8.1: Psychotherapists use 'cognitive schema' like the one shown here to diagnose why certain patients with depression are caught in a negative cycle of thoughts. The same framework can be useful for brand marketers to uncover consumer thought patterns.*

The mealtime stalemate would lead to several automatic mind distortions for the moms. Many thought that there was something wrong with their kids. Most would have them checked for at least the presence of stomach worms and find none. Many concluded that they themselves were the problem, 'I'm a bad mom. I'm such a klutz. I can't cook to save my life.' These thoughts would then create a swirl of emotions in them that would leave them depleted and despairing.

In cognitive schemas, you can map core belief relative to yourself, others or your expectations of the future. Moms had issues on all three fronts.

Some compared their child to Greta, the one outlier kid in the neighbourhood, who consumed a steady diet of toasted pecans and artichokes. These not-so-great mom would then feel distinctly unnerved.

Other moms believed that their kids should eat adult food, like leafy bok choy and Nantes carrots. Instead, the kids preferred gooey chocolate chip cookies with sprinkles or jumbo franks with double ketchup and no bun.

Yet other moms thought that poor nutrition now would spell certain doom in the future. Their kids would grow up with grotesque physical or mental debilities. These thoughts would bubble unchecked like a boiling goulash of worries in their brains.

Mealtimes turned into a battle of wits and will, with determined mothers shovelling kale down their kids throats, and the latter faithfully puking it back out in steely resistance with all of the attendant drama of a gagging cat.

Frustrated, many of the moms bundled their kids into the car and headed off to their paediatricians to demand on-the-spot answers, 'What's wrong with the brat? Tell me!'

At some point, the harangued paediatricians realized that they were not going to be able to fob off the moms by informing them that their kids were normal, just like millions of other kids. They had tried it and it was deemed unacceptable.

One clever old paediatrician in Surabaya came up with an idea. He started telling moms that their kids had a 'condition'—they were 'picky eaters'. To get them off his backs, he would then make a big show of drawing out his prescription pad slowly and with a flourish, write them a script for PediaSure. You didn't really need one; PediaSure was not a drug. But he did it anyway. The relief that the moms felt upon finally having an answer was palpable. Other harried paediatricians also caught on to the practice, and soon everyone was 'prescribing' PediaSure. The universe was at peace!

The wily doctors had found a way to connect with the angst that moms everywhere in Indonesia felt. No, there was nothing wrong with the mother herself; she was a good mother. She did the right thing in bringing the little tyke to their attention. Yes, there was a little something wrong with the kid. A disease called 'picky eater'. Nothing too serious, really. It was easily remedied by a glass or two of PediaSure every day.

Armed with this knowledge, we checked back with the moms in our focus groups. After several conversations with them, it became apparent that it was not so much the popular Sherina who was driving the sales, although she was surely a factor. It was more that Sherina was a beautiful and talented girl. Every parent wanted to make sure that their kid was not undernourished and won't grow up to be the diametrical opposite of a Sherina. They all nodded vigorously when we offered that maybe their kids were picky eaters.

We subsequently conducted focus groups in culturally disparate Asian countries, from Vietnam and Philippines to Malaysia and Taiwan. The cognitive schema mapped out in Indonesia played out to a T. Mel and Walt were super excited.

The fact that the Indonesian market was on fire not because of Sherina but because of this universal angst was terrific news. It meant that PediaSure could be a global brand and not just non-transmittable Indonesian aberration.

The insight that most kids are picky eaters, or rather that their moms universally believed so, gave us the 'vibes' that we needed to make moms receptive to PediaSure. Remember, in a prior chapter, I had said that one way to give a brand good vibes is by connecting with the consumer with 'I know how you feel'.

The PediaSure brand campaigns in the future would typically begin with a sentence like, 'We know that kids can be picky eaters. That's because they are kids!'

This was critical in allowing us as marketers to let moms know that we understood their anguish and that neither they nor their kids were to blame for the kids not eating nutritious food regularly. Once we had established that connection, the moms were ready to hear the rest of the PediaSure brand story.

Notice, that with this statement, we were not yet talking about what PediaSure was. We were just building an unspoken bond and common chemistry between the moms and the brand. The statement 'for picky eaters' should also not be confused with what is a framing statement in a traditional brand positioning, answering the question whom the product is for. The answer to the latter might go something like, 'For new moms between the ages of twenty-five to thirty-five, PediaSure is . . .' But nope, brand vibes are about connections not clarifications.

I should point out here that for the purposes of understanding thought patterns and mapping them in cognitive schemas, it is useful to think of a brand stimulus as triggering automatic thoughts, those sparking certain emotions, and the emotions subsequently congealing into behaviours, linearly. However, as I have shown before, the brain does not work in sequence like that. Once particular thought patterns are encoded into the brain, the right cognitive threads will directly trigger buying behaviours and attendant thoughts and emotions reflexively. Cognitive schemas are thus useful tools for understanding reality but are not reality itself.

## Brand Sense with System 1 Easers: PediaSure as Occam's Razor

Back in Chicago, when we sat down with Tripp and Mel, the verdict was that we needed to go deeper. Getting doctors to prescribe PediaSure was great and it worked, but it was very slow. Mom had to go to the doctor, who had to write a prescription, which led the mom to the pharmacist, who had to dispense PediaSure. There was simply too much scope for things to go wrong.

We needed to be on TV with our message and have moms see us and rush to the supermarket to buy PediaSure. Mel was adamant that the brand needed to be on supermarket shelves, ripe for the picking, and not hidden behind counters in pharmacies. 'Remember, the "s" at the end of the word "brands" is really a "$" sign. Make it big or go home,' offered Tripp poetically, if somewhat sombrely.

We set aside a day to lock ourselves up in a room with Mel and Walt. Now, remember I said earlier that the brain makes sense of choices using the *Associator* subunit 95 per cent of the time. We rolled up our sleeves and went through the list of cognitive biases which we had presented earlier with the intent of developing one brand concept against each. Walt wanted many different ideas to take to research. Forcing ourselves to work with one cognitive bias at a time, we generated eight distinct concepts (see the following table).

**BRAND SENSE WITH SYSTEM 1 EASERS**

| | System 1 Easers | Definition | Possible brand concept |
|---|---|---|---|
| Feels Familiar | Anchoring Bias | Tag brand to familiar anchors – showing comparability or superiority | PediaSure provides kids all the goodness of real food and more |
| | Loss Aversion Bias | Position brand as helping to avoid losses to what consumers have today | PediaSure ensures that kids don't lose their chance for proper physical and mental growth in formative years |
| Feels True | IKEA Bias | Position brand as something that consumer plays a role in making | Not viable concept |
| | Transparency Effect | Position brand as trusted because you know what goes in it | PediaSure has every one of the 26 nutrients that kids need for proper growth and development |
| Feels Easier | Occam's Razor Bias | Position your brand as the simpler and therefore correct choice | PediaSure makes any meal a perfect meal with the addition of just one glass of the nutrition kids need |
| | Herd/Expert Effect | Position your brand as the choice of the herd or expert | PediaSure is recommended by doctors for children that are picky eaters |
| Feels Good | In-Group Bias | Position brand as the way to show the special group you belong to | PediaSure puts kids in the 'Super Stars" club who have their own secret developmental advantage |
| | Choice Supportive Bias | Position brand as affirming the consumer's own choice | PediaSure comes in a taste that kids already love |

*Figure 8.2: Applying the eight cognitive biases listed here to your brand can be a great way to generate ideas on how to position it using System 1 Easers. The list can then be vetted and narrowed down through qualitative and quantitative research.*

The team bundled back into a plane and headed off to do more research in Taiwan, the Philippines, Malaysia, Indonesia and Vietnam. It was time to introduce the brand ideas to the moms.

We had thought that the concept of using the anchoring bias to tag PediaSure to 'all the goodness of' real food had promise, but Walt warned us that moms considered table foods to be an unapproachable gold standard and would be unreceptive to any suggestion that it could be replaced. He was proved right.

How about saying 'recommended by doctors' to exploit the 'expert effect'? That would get us around the problem of finding a Sherina-like child star in every country. That tested well with moms, but Mel worried that it would again limit the market by locking the product back in its medical roots as something to take only when the kid is sick.

We ended up using two System 1 Easers in our brand strategy. We used the 'Occam's razor bias' to position PediaSure as the choice simplifier. Add a glass of PediaSure to any meal and the job of 'nutrition' was done. No need to worry about finding foods with the precise quantity of vitamin E or choline or zinc and magnesium; PediaSure had them all and more.

With table foods, you virtually need a degree in nutritional science to orchestrate balanced and complete meals for the week. Compiling that is stressful for young mothers, whose cooking skills may not be quite where they need to be.

The moms in focus groups also loved the idea that PediaSure was available in flavours, like vanilla, strawberry and chocolate, that kids loved. It was the kid's choice, not mom's, and it put mealtime skirmishes at bay. That was the 'choice supportive bias' at work, the second of our two System 1 choice drivers.

Our brand concept was coming along nicely. We now had brand vibes and System 1 choice drivers working for us to make sense of the brand. PediaSure was evolving: 'For moms whose kids are picky eaters, PediaSure provides the nutrition they need, in a taste that kids love.'

## Brand Sense with System 2 Deliberators: Examining the Evidence

We knew that for many moms the idea of not worrying about what their child was eating and giving them a nutritional supplement instead was going to be a 'new religion'. We needed to break old habits and shatter beliefs around 'real food or nothing else'. That called for using System 2 choice drivers to make brand sense. So we used our frameworks to generate eight System 2 options for testing (as shown in the following table), which are the same as we discussed in Chapter 6, 'Brand Sense with System 2 Deliberators'.

**BRAND SENSE WITH SYSTEM 2 DELIBERATORS**

| | System 2 Deliberators | Definition | Possible brand concepts |
|---|---|---|---|
| Amplify Value | No Brainers | Position brand as far superior value versus its cost | PediaSure is the best of the best for the one thing that matters most in life – your kids |
| | Pleasure Prediction | Amplify ultimate impact of brand on consumer vividly | With PediaSure, you can imagine their potential – at the top of the corporate ladder or dancing with the stars |
| Lower Risk | Fight or Flight | Position brand as consumer's ally in the face of adversity | PediaSure is the nutritional shield that ensures no harm comes to your child |
| | Flirting | Make initial trial or ownership a key part the brand promise | PediaSure is so good that we guarantee that your child will love it – or your money back |
| Find RTBs | Examine the Evidence | Position brand as the right answer given the weight of the available evidence | PediaSure is balanced and complete nutrition – 100% of what my child needs, nothing less and nothing more |
| | Survey | Position brand as the preferred choice in consumer orchestrated surveys | More mothers everywhere choose PediaSure over any other brand for kids who are picky eaters |
| Change Context | Reframing | Position brand as the answer to a much bigger problem than the obvious one | PediaSure is not just nutrition; it is an investment in your child's health and future |
| | Reattribution | Position brand as the agent for getting to the real cause of the problem | It's not you Mom, its just that kids are kids. Let PediaSure help. |

*Figure 8.3: Applying the eight methods listed here to your brand can be a simple way to generate ideas on how to position it using System 2 Deliberators. The list should then be tested and narrowed down through qualitative and quantitative research.*

PediaSure's main System 2 benefit was that it was 'balanced and complete' nutrition. In fact, given its origins as a medical product, PediaSure had been proven to be exactly that in clinical trials. We didn't want to get technical with the consumers, but this was a claim that PediaSure alone could make. We leveraged the 'examine the evidence' method to string together this cognitive thread. The evidence itself appeared not only as a long list of nutrients on every PediaSure box, but also in other campaigns across various channels in stores and magazines. Ultimately, in various executions around the world, the promotions highlighted the 'twenty-five essential nutrients' or 'triple benefit' of increased immunity, accelerated growth and improved appetite, with kid-friendly images of teddy bears (suggestive of pleasant looks) and giraffes (suggestive of healthy growth).

The System 2 options used in the brand strategy were adopted after we carefully tested them using survey and focus group research to confirm that the cognitive keys we had uncovered were just the right ones for opening consumer minds. Other credible threads around 'PediaSure as best for the one that matters most in your life' and 'PediaSure as an investment in your kid's future' were tested and dropped for lack of resonance. The moms had heard it all before. With the System 2 information added, the PediaSure positioning was fortified to, 'For moms whose kids are picky eaters, PediaSure provides balanced and complete nutrition in a taste that kids love.'

## Brand Resolve: PediaSure as the Key to Bliss

Recalling Tripp's mantra that brands needed to come with a '$' sign appended to the end, we wanted to be certain that moms were not just going to prefer PediaSure but also that they would go out and resolve to buy it. Ultimately, all moms wanted their kids to grow up to be their best and turn out like Sherina in Indonesia—beautiful and talented, competent in their craft. As mothers, that was their goal.

As I explained in Chapter 7, when you tie your brands to consumers' innate goals, you set them on a path to greater happiness and spur them into action. Thus, the final PediaSure positioning morphed into, 'For moms whose kids are picky eaters, PediaSure provides balanced and complete nutrition in a taste that kids love, so they can grow up to be all they can be, physically and mentally.'

By then, Mel, Walt and my teams had done a ton of work. We felt good with where we were and headed off to Tripp with our recommendation. After reviewing our work, Tripp suddenly turned around to us and asked, 'You know what the proof of the pudding is?' As Walt and I looked on warily, he proceeded to answer his own question, 'Go make this work in Mexico and then I'll believe it.'

Without skipping a beat, Mel leant forward and countered with, 'Then give me a Blue Plan.' A Blue Plan at Abbott means you get extra money, over and above any budget you have, to invest in your idea. Remember, I told you, Mel was a street-smart cookie. This wasn't his first rodeo. We got the money. The show was on.

## A Conative Segmentation of PediaSure Moms

We never expected every mum to become a PediaSure mom. One of the first things we did in Mexico was to segment the market to find the moms most likely to become one.

It is common for marketers to start with attitudinal segmentation—grouping of people who generally think alike—for this purpose. However, marketers have long struggled with this approach, as attitudinal segmentation does not correlate well with consumer brand preferences and purchases. Even groups of people who think about, say, nutrition in the same way will have wildly different favourite foods. So we went instead for the two known psychological drivers of resolve: happiness and tendency.

We developed a simple 2x2 matrix. The horizontal axis was 'Tendency', and the vertical axis was 'Happiness'. As noted earlier, people are naturally wired to increase their happiness quotient. Yet, customers differ in their tendency to act on a given stimulus. Thus, when marketers can promise a bit of happiness to a segment of customers who have more of an inclination to act, they can carve a lucrative place for themselves.

Tendencies are not attitudes. Your attitude may be that the health-care system in America stinks, but that does not mean that you will leave the country. The latter would happen only if you had a high tendency to seek health-care happiness elsewhere. A very small number of people have left the US and moved to France, for instance, for that reason; most are unwilling to take such a dramatic step.

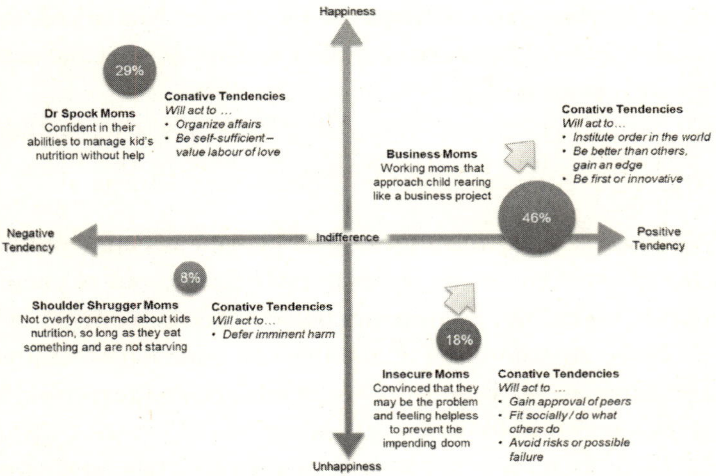


*Figure 8.4: Tendencies-based segmentation puts emphasis on including the drivers of intrinsic motivation in your research to identify sets of consumers that are likely to not simply like your brand but to really want it and buy it.*

We used a consumer segment where a tendency can be positive, inert or negative. A positive tendency will predispose you towards certain actions, and a negative tendency may incline you to do the opposite. An inert tendency would leave you indifferent to the brand stimulus, which might pique your interest, but you are unlikely to do anything about it. In the chart above, we show the output of such a conative segmentation in the children's nutrition market in Mexico. We found four kinds of moms:

1. *Business moms* who were generally working women who approached child rearing like a job-to-be-done project. They had a conative, or innate, tendency to institute order

into their lives by getting on top of problems as soon as they spotted them. If her child was a picky eater, she might gather the facts on a spreadsheet and run a regression so to speak, or at least keep track of what the kid liked and didn't like. Outsourcing nutritional needs to PediaSure was an appealing path to happiness for this mom.

2. *Shoulder shrugger moms* didn't feel like their children's nutrition was such a big deal. So long as their kids were munching on beef jerky and ice cream, they would live. Shoulder shrugger moms would have a conative or natural tendency to act only if things were getting out of hand, but not otherwise. Trying to counteract this tendency would have been hard for PediaSure. It would have been like trying to sell vitamins for Pubert, the indestructible baby from *The Addams Family*.
3. *Dr Spock moms* was another segment that was hard to crack for PediaSure. These moms—whom we named after the once-pervasive US child-rearing practices bible by the eponymous Dr Benjamin Spock—also had a conative tendency to arrange and organize their lives, but not with anyone's help. They liked to get their hands dirty and solve problems. They tended to make perfect nutritional meals for their kids and derive happiness from their own labour of love. PediaSure, if anything, would have taken away from that happiness.
4. *Insecure moms* were miserable and felt unfit for reporting to sound motherhood duty. They had a conative tendency to avoid risks, overcompensate and make attempts to not be seen as incompetent. They would take help, any help from anywhere and anyone. PediaSure was that extra help and their ticket to happiness.

Business moms and insecure moms constituted nearly two-thirds of the Mexican market. We could live with that.

In 2005, when Mel, Walt and I arrived in the haze-filled Valle de México, with the Blue Plan money burning in our pockets, PediaSure was growing at just 1 per cent per year in the country, as it had done for the preceding five years or so. We spent a year there with our teams prepping the market. We went to the *supermercados* like Walmart and Chedraui to convince merchandisers to shift PediaSure out of the in-store pharmacies and on to the shelves. We hired an army of in-store samplers to intercept moms and kids as they walked into the stores with chilled cups of chocolate PediaSure.

We went on TV, but with no Sherina-like child star to promote the product, as had been the case in Indonesia. We teamed up with a brilliant ad man, Ricardo Ferraris, who at the time led Grey's agency office in Mexico. His team developed a memorable commercial that would go on to win many awards.

It opened with a mother and son in an everyday mealtime standoff. Mom is there; the kid is staring back; the dinner plate is there; chicken and broccoli are in place. But Mom makes a fatal mistake: she looks away for one half of a second. As she turns back around, the chicken is gone, only traces of the broccoli remain, and the remaining plate is clean.

As she is about to declare victory, the overhead fan turns gently in the breeze, and the drumstick casts a long, pale shadow across the table. It is a delightful moment that captures the interplay between a caring mother and a mischievous, but obviously intelligent, child. Mom gives in and gives her son PediaSure. Both are happy. Problem solved.

In the following three years, sales of PediaSure in Mexico grew by a whopping 1000 per cent. Tripp had nailed his '$' sign to the end of the word 'brands'. Working with us, Abbott turned the PediaSure story into a 'Global Branding Playbook' for the company. The legend of Mexico was told and replicated in many other countries. Today, PediaSure is a multi-billion dollar brand in Abbott's portfolio—one of the largest and most profitable nutrition brands anywhere in the world.

The things we do for the love of kids!

* * *

*Key Takeaways*

The three-part cognitive brand model is not just a fancy theory; it has been applied and seen to work fabulously with real-world brands. PediaSure was a good proof of this concept in my work. As a matter of fact, my firm, Cerenti, has used these methods successfully, over and over, with clients in industries as disparate as consumer products, financial services and pharmaceuticals.

The eight specific System 1 Easers and System 2 Deliberators that I have described in the previous chapters are more than enough when it comes to designing brands. But for marketers feeling like they need more, there are over 100 different cognitive biases that have been documented by psychologists, and Dr David Burns offers over fifty System 2 methods to 'untwist your thinking'. With a little bit of online research, these lists are easy to find but hard to use. Using the Occam's razor principle, start simple and start first with the ones I have picked for you.

# 9

# Brands with Purpose: Branding to Make a Difference

The venture capital industry is great at finding and betting on winning formulas for building businesses. They work until they don't. The new formula of the day is adding a dash of purpose to companies targeting millennials. If you are that kind of consumer products start-up, you must tick the 'brand purpose' box.

Consider Harry's, an insurgent brand launched by Jeff Raider and Andy Katz-Mayfield in 2013. It quickly captured a 4 per cent share of the men's razorblades market and was almost acquired by Edgewell (which makes razors under the Schick brand) for $1.4 billion in 2019, until regulators scuttled that deal. How did they create this billion-dollar market cap rock star in just five years? Answer: They found a way to sell and mail decent-quality razorblades, direct to you at your home, for a cheaper price. But there's more!

Harry's worked with Mythology, a marketing studio on Lafayette Street in New York that specializes in working with 'brands of the new economy'. It works with up-and-coming companies to ensure that their brands have a memorable story and a good-for-the-world purpose.

For Harry's, the brand narrative is around how the company was born from the frustration that the founders felt at running around from store to store to find the right blades for their razors, standing in long lines at the CVS pharmacy and then overpaying for Gillette and Schick blades. Not particularly original; after all, that *is* what all online products offer; but very sensible nevertheless.

But Mythology wanted more. They believe that 'the feeling of belonging to something positive is the most influential marketing'. Thus, to give Harry's more of an edge and make it more than just cheap blades, Mythology also added a larger-than-life purpose to the brand: it would donate 1 per cent of its revenue to charities, like Crisis Text Line, that serve as a resource for men with mental health issues. That 1 per cent with every purchase could be a reason to keep buying Harry's blades.[1] Given the billion-dollar valuation milestone cracked by Harry's, every other VC-backed consumer brand of the new economy is busy replicating some version of this strategy. But does it work?

If you are going to build a brand with purpose, there is a right way and a wrong way. Harry's is the wrong way. I could argue that all they are doing is charging me 1 per cent more than they need to and donating that money to a charity. Now, remind me why I am giving Harry's money to donate to a charity when I could Zelle[2] it myself in my own name instead of theirs?

Don't get me wrong. Brands that do good add to the consumer's resolve to buy the product by appealing to their intrinsic motivation for relatedness, a desire to make the world a better place for others. But, are all 'acts of doing good' equal? As I showed earlier, in our chapter on System 2 Deliberators, the Rainforest Alliance amplifies your pleasure of buying everyday consumer products certified by them. Their seal signals that those products were manufactured by farming communities that use sustainable cultivation methods.

I have also argued that conative motivations are key to getting people off the fence of indecision. People are highly motivated to buy brands that allow them to express their identity in a way that contributes towards making the world a better place. So, you may well ask what's my beef with Harry's. Isn't Harry's making the world a better place with their mission to help 5,00,000 people with mental health-care needs?

Okay, I owe you an answer. And here it is. Brands with purpose must meet the following three criteria to be successful:

- They support causes that mesh with what the brand is.
- They do good in a way their consumers cannot on their own.
- They are seen to be authentic.

Let's check this out.

## Support What Your Brand Is About

Ask yourself this: What if Harry's gave 1 per cent of its revenues to Toys for Tots, which distributes playthings to needy families, or to the Humane Society, which works to stop animal cruelty? Would you feel better about that? There are plenty of worthy causes around the world. You can write cheques all day long. Which is the one that makes sense for your brand?

So, rule number one is to work with a charity that fits with what your brand is about. In Harry's case, yes, it is a men's grooming product and yes, it is giving money for an issue that relates to men, although not exclusively so. Yet, wouldn't Harry's be better off with some charity that helps men be better and affordably groomed? Not everyone can afford an expensive razor, but being better dressed and shaved would help such a person get a better job.

Maybe Harry's could work with young kids who can't afford to get a haircut and are made fun of at school? After all, the brand is also about affordability.

Mental health care for men is undoubtedly a great cause, but as a consumer I am hard-pressed to see its connection to grooming or cheap razors—the stuff that Harry's is about. And that's the link consumers need to see. If you do that right, the charitable organization will enrich your brand through what in psychology is known as the evaluative conditioning effect, which we discussed in Chapter 4.

In contrast, Warby Parker, another new-economy rocket that sells prescription eyeglasses, gets this exactly right. Through their 'Buy-A-Pair, Give-A-Pair' charity programme, the company makes monthly donations to their nonprofit partner, VisionSpring, which provides free eyewear to people in developing countries. The company has distributed more than four million pairs of glasses since its start in 2010.[3] From a branding lens, it is easy to see how a company that wants to be the leader in affordable, quality prescription wear would also want to bring the gift of better sight to those most in need. It is a cause that mirrors the brand itself.

This is not just for start-ups. Pfizer is one of the largest manufacturers of anti-infectives in the world. Currently, 7,00,000 people die from infections caused by drug-resistant microbes, and that number could well rise to millions by 2050.[4]

The problem is getting worse because 'superbugs' are proliferating dangerously in different parts of the world. Pfizer has launched several initiatives to educate people about the seriousness of the threat and how they can play a role in mitigating it through better daily hygiene.

In the UK, they work with organizations that educate children in schools and through public exhibitions in science museums. They have also set up surveillance programmes to allow health-care workers to rapidly report the emergence of evolving new strains across the world.

Arguably, some of these programmes will slow down the evolution of new microbes and reduce the size of the market for Pfizer. They will have fewer anti-infectives to sell than if they do nothing. But it is the right purpose for the brand. It helps Pfizer stand out as a brand for public good and not one interested in making a quick buck with its drugs. It is not all public service; some of these programmes will present opportunities for developing and introducing new anti-infectives.

## Do What Your Consumers Can't

Brands with purpose need to do more than just write a check. Tim Brown, the ex-vice captain of New Zealand's 2010 FIFA soccer team, totally gets this. After retiring from the game in 2012, he founded Allbirds, a sneakers company, out of his annoyance at all the fancy shoes from Nike and Adidas he got to play in.

All he wanted was a good, comfortable pair of sneakers made without loud colours and logos, or non-degradable, engineered plastics. As did a lot of other people. So Allbirds became a $1.4 billion sneaker company overnight.[5] But what made the brand great was not a mushy shoe to plant your feet in; it was the singular purpose that the Allbirds, the brand, pursued.

The company is committed to manufacturing and marketing shoes made entirely of planet-friendly or recycled materials. This was not easy. Allbirds invested a lot of time and money into research and engineering to make shoes from natural merino wool and eucalyptus tree fibres, and shoelaces out of recycled plastic bottles. Most of us want to recycle, but all we can do is to separate our trash into two bins, or three if we are really good. But by buying Allbirds, we can do something that otherwise is out of reach for us. It is not just another slap-on-a-dollar donation to the next green charity. That is why Allbirds is so special for many of its customers. It is a way for them to do more than they can on their own.

## Be Authentic

A few months back I was talking to a business buddy, Henrique (not his real name), who is a senior partner in a 100-plus-persons placement agency. He had seen my recent blog on 'Brands with Purpose' on LinkedIn and was commiserating about his own experience. In his company, there was a fist-pounding debate about what the company ought to do to give back to the community. If you have ever worked in a partnership-based firm, you already know that internally they are often completely dysfunctional. Because many partners have a nearly equal share in the business, there are many masters running the company. Most are highly accomplished and thus have strong opinions about all topics, even trivial ones. Not that 'giving' is a minor topic, but it is certainly one that elicits more ideas than you can sort through. Henrique felt like they were stuck. Maybe the best option was to let each partner do their own thing.

As we talked some more, Henrique shared with me his own personal story. His son, Dion, unfortunately, had got into drugs and been fired from a string of jobs. He had completely hosed his career.

After years of struggle and multiple recovery programmes, Dion finally broke the spell. With Henrique's handholding and coaching, he was finally able to return to work and keep a job. But it has not been easy, and Henrique has to keep working with Dion in his spare time, in the evenings or on weekends at home, to keep him on track.

As it turned out, Henrique was not the only one with this problem. Slowly, there were other parents, friends of friends, who wanted advice for their own children. As a professional in the placement industry, helping people with their careers was what Henrique did for a living. He advised them on how to be seen at work and handle pressure. Clients paid him big bucks for exactly that. In fact, his firm was full of professionals like him who had that skill and training.

One thing led to another, and with Henrique's strong support, the firm decided its new purpose: helping recovering drug addicts return to productive careers and counselling them on how to keep their jobs. It made the firm a brand with purpose.

You would guess that I like this story because it meets my first two criteria for successful brands with purpose. The nature of the charity, free career management advice, fits like a glove with a placement firm's DNA, and the company is providing a service that draws on its unique talents and resources. Check and check.

Actually, I like it a lot for another reason and that is, authenticity. Recall my distaste for people just writing cheques. What Henrique's firm did was born of something that was deeply inspirational for him. It was something that had touched one of their own and many in their community personally. It helped the company understand why they were doing what they were doing. Just as importantly or even more so, the senior leadership of the company was involved intimately in the cause with their own blood, sweat and tears. Those two things together are what make brands with purpose authentic.

In large companies, where giving can become a two-page calligraphic list of charities supported, that connection to the brand and authenticity are often lost. At Allbirds too, one of the co-founders, Joey Zwillinger, is personally the lead for finding new earth-friendly materials to work with and developing new engineering methods to make them suitable for great shoes. How C-suite executives get involved with the charities they support says a lot about the authenticity of brands with purpose.

* * *

*Key Takeaways*

Brands with purpose are a great idea. They work well because they tap into the innate conative energies of consumers, whereby they want to make the world a better place for themselves and others. Thus, many people are drawn to brands with purpose and buy more of them.

However, tick-the-box giving does not create a brand with purpose. Is yours a real brand with purpose? Try this pop quiz:

- Do the activities of the charity fit with what your brand does?
- Does your giving draw on the unique talents and resources of your company?
- Do the company leaders put their heart and soul into the cause?

If you answered 'yes' to all, you've got it!

In the next chapter, I turn my attention to brand execution. Cognitive brands are designed to work the way the brain does. And brand execution, too, must follow the same principles.

Part Three

# How to Execute Cognitive Brands

# 10

# Tales from the Trenches: New Principles for Brand Execution

Brand execution is the fun part of branding, isn't it? This is when you get to go to the island of Kauai to shoot television commercials. This is your chance to pretend play Martin Scorsese. There is the setting sun against the aquamarine waters of the Pacific, beautiful models and actors sunning on the beach, and you pensively downing the requisite mango coconut daiquiri. It's all strictly business; you can expense it. Yeah! Brand execution is the doing part of branding versus the thinking part. Or is it?

Well, consider this: Consumer brains don't see most of what you want them to see in your commercials. They hear a different brand story from the one you are telling. And they don't necessarily pay attention to your ad when it plays; instead, they sleep on it. Say what? Need another daiquiri? Something harder, perhaps?

Traditionally, brand execution or activation has been a straightforward exercise. Write the three things (equities) that your brand is about on the left side of a sheet of paper. Then move over to the right and list all of the places where a customer runs into your brand (customer touchpoints). The latter can include a wide range of places, namely television and magazines, billboards, retail stores, customer service lines, online video channels like YouTube, Instagram, sports sponsorships, T-shirts and hats, streamed audio channels, you name it. Decide what customer touchpoints will display and activate what equities of the brand.

Add it all up and put together: that is how consumers experience your brand. It is your brand experience. Or at least the one you envision. Between that and what consumers actually experience is space, in which sits their prodigious brains. And there's plenty that's lost in translation.

With the latest advances in brain sciences, we are understanding a lot more about how the brain learns and remembers things. For marketers, understanding what the brain latches on to and what it remembers about your brand is very important. To ensure that important stuff is not lost in translation, let's take a look at what brain science tells us about the following four questions:

- What makes for a brand impression? Do all parts of the brand experience matter equally to consumers?
- Which brand experiences are more likely to be noticed by consumers?
- How should a brand experience unfold so that consumers internalize them deeply?

  How much can you say about your brand? Is there such a thing as an information overload?

Let's dig into these questions a bit.

## 1. Brand impressions are based on the climax and conclusion of an experience

Lesson number one is that the brain does not look at everything it is presented. It focuses on a few odds and ends and makes up the rest. This is kind of like hallucinations, which are defined as 'sensations that appear to be real but are created within the mind. Examples include seeing things that are not there, hearing voices or other sounds, experiencing body sensations like crawling feeling on the skin, or smelling odors that are not there'.[1] Paul Fletcher, a professor of neuroscience at Cambridge University, in his lecture entitled 'Psychosis: Bending Reality to See Around the Corners'[2] argues that we, all of us and not just those suffering from mental diseases, routinely hallucinate reality. What is he talking about?

Ever been in a situation when a work colleague was so ponderously explaining an obvious business phenomenon that you jumped up and cut him off with, 'I got it! I got it! Okay?' or, 'You can go faster!'

Well, it turns out our brain does that all of the time. After all, it is flooded with data from the senses every second that we are alive. So, it deals with the barrage by taking short cuts. It picks up a few fragments, connects the dots, jumps up and says, 'I got it!' Well, okay, it does not jump up or anything, but you get the idea.

Here's a fact. When you look out of your window, the only thing that the brain takes in full colour, high definition, is limited to the size of your thumbnail with your arm outstretched in front.[3] All else is peripheral vision with imagined details. All of your senses sort of operate like that, in fragments.

When you step outside in the morning to take your kids to the school bus, your brain takes only rough notes: a large yellow vehicle arrived, and your kids got on it. Other details like the yellow body paint on the bus with the black stripes, Jenny the driver in her blue uniform, the screaming kids ripping each other's heads off are automatically retrieved from prior memories and populated into the experience.[4] This is why witness accounts of the same scene of crime often differ. You would swear that Jenny was driving the bus even when it was Gertie, a substitute.

The consumer's brain focuses only on bits and pieces of your exquisitely crafted brand experience. It does not ignore the rest; it cooks it up with guesses. It does that even when it hasn't quite got it and when what it thinks is happening isn't really. This is also why people may confuse your ad for another brand's! Ouch! Hence, marketers designing brand experiences should note that only selected elements of what they present will register with consumers. Understanding those is key.

Lesson number two follows from the work done by Kahneman, who argues that your recall of an experience is defined by just two things: its peak and ending.[5] So, marketers must pay attention to not only the content of the message but also to its cadence.

Two summers back, I found myself travelling in business class on a flight from Chicago to Zurich on Swiss Air. After trying their selection of wines, I had a French wine with my dinner course and loved it. When the flight attendant came around to ask if I wanted to buy anything from the duty-free catalogue, on an impulse I said, 'No. But I would like to buy a bottle of the wine you served.' Instead of saying 'That's not in the catalogue, dude', she smiled and said, 'Sure.' In a few minutes she came back with a bottle packed nicely in a Swiss Shop duty-free bag. As I handed her my American Express card, she said, 'With our compliments, sir.'

That 'high point' is the only thing I recall about that seven-hour flight. I don't remember anything about how comfortable my lie-flat seat was or how delicious my bircher muesli breakfast was or even the perfectly perked faces of the crew members. When we landed in Zurich, I used the showers in the Senator Lounge, which were drop-dead, drown-in-luxury gorgeous. And that was the 'ending' to my flight experience as I boarded my connection to Vienna. If you ask me, how Swiss Air was, I would say they were fabulous. The high point and finish were the sum total of my brand experience.

At restaurants, servers have figured out that what translates into bigger tips is how well the meal ends. A waitress who leaves a check with a pleasant smile earns better tips than those who quietly slide it across. Waitresses who draw a smiley face on the check and write 'Thank You, Mr Smith (get the last name from the credit card)' earn even bigger tips.[6] And it is not a coincidence that many come and ask you how you like the 'special' or the 'favourite dish you were dying to eat' while you are eating it, as that is the high point of the dinner.

In pharma marketing this can be irksome. All of their advertisements are required by US laws around 'fair balance' to not only speak of the benefits of the drug but also to itemize its risks. The ads usually open with a titillating story about how life with the drug is awesome and ends with a laundry list of heart-stopping side effects of the 'may result in genital warts and suicidal thoughts' variety. The side effects are detailed in a monotone with calming elevator music in the background, in the hope that it won't alarm prospective patients.

Yet, the ending, it turns out, is important. In focus groups, we often hear patients talk about how scary those ad tails are. That may be exactly what the FDA intends, but it makes life not fun for both the marketers and patients. A better strategy is thus to shift the fair balance statements in between the climax and the end, ensuring that the conclusion of an advertisement is sufficiently positive versus merely an obligatory suggestion to talk to the doctor about the drug.

## 2. Doing what customers expect isn't what's noticed; doing the unexpected is

What does the brain gloss over? For one, it is wired to ignore sameness and note differences. For some reason, if the school bus you loaded your kid on was green as opposed to the usual yellow, your brain will stop and take notes.

In a series of experiments, researchers at Johns Hopkins[7] showed that babies learn by focusing their attention on the unexpected. When something unanticipated occurs, they try to learn more about it and resolve the mystery. In one test, when the babies saw a ball apparently pass through a wall, they checked the ball by banging it on a table. When they saw the ball seemingly hover in the air, they tested it by letting it drop. Moral of the story: *If your brand experience is what the consumers expect, they are less likely to notice it! If it is the same old same old, they will gloss over it. If it is new but nothing to write home about, same thing.*

Our client Sagent Pharmaceuticals, which sells generic injectable drugs, found a clever way to differentiate its products. Think about this for a minute. Generic drugs are certified by the FDA to be identical to each other. Propofol is propofol. Ibuprofen is ibuprofen. So how do you differentiate?

Sagent noted that there are 1.4 million medication administration errors annually, where a nurse or doctor accidently injects a patient with the wrong drug or dose. Often that happens because all drug vials sit in a tray and look terribly similar. A tired nurse may only look for a few cues to delineate one drug from another and crucial details may be assumed.

Sagent Pharma thus changed the packaging of its drugs so that each type had a unique carton, bottle label, size and colour under a programme called 'PreventIV Measures'.[8] Different doses were also demarcated by fonts or bottle shapes and sizes. In a market where drugs are sold by their chemical name and not their brand, Sagent made its generics stand out and lowered chances of accidents. The nurses and pharmacists at hospitals just loved it. In retrospect, it seems to make so much sense to do what Sagent has done, but competing marketers continue to produce vials that look like vials have looked for fifty years. Their products disappear into the 'sea of sameness'.

Brands that show their differentiating features in a surprising way do better. John West, which markets canned salmon, wanted to differentiate itself by claiming it uses high-quality fish. Its television commercials[9] start serenely enough at a scenic bend in the river, where a sleuth of bears is shown peacefully catching the salmon springing out from the water. A deep, male, National Geographic voice soothingly murmurs, 'At the river mouth, the bears catch only the most tastiest and tender salmon . . .'

This placid calm is interrupted by a crazed man in an orange jumpsuit who rushes out of the forest, directly at the bear, with an '*aaaaahgh*' war cry. The voiceover continues unperturbed, '. . . and that [fish] is exactly what we at John West want.'

A comical fistfight ensues between the bear and the man, with the latter ultimately nailing the grizzly with a kick to its crotch and making off with its catch. The voiceover concludes the scene with, 'John West endures the worst to bring you the best.' The brilliance of this ad is in communicating a fairly common quality claim in an unexpected and hence memorable manner.

So next time you think about meeting customer expectations, don't. Surprise them instead.

## 3. Brands must tell stories, and not recite lists of benefits

In 1981, an Indian man, Rajan Mahadevan, recalled 31,811 digits of the math constant pi (π) from memory. Eight years later, Japan's Hideaki Tomoyori topped that with 40,000 digits.[10] The current Guinness world record is held by Rajveer Meena of India, who, in 2015, pulled off 70,000 digits over a ten-hour period while wearing a blindfold.[11]

If you think there's room for improvement, that could be something to kick at during your next Easter break. But hold on.

There are thousands of kids, schooling in madrasas around Pakistan, who can recite the Koran by rote, all 77,449 words, consisting of 3,20,015 letters, in the right order, accomplishing a feat nearly five times as great as that of the record-breaking memory savant Meena by sheer volume. How?

The answer lies in stories. The decimals in the constant pi constitute a list. The Koran is a story. The *Learner* subunit in our brain is wired to remember stories better than random lists. It checks for how things relate to each other, and the more they do, the better it remembers them. Stories by their very nature have many associations built into them, in how each part of the story connects to another and perhaps in elements of the story that may relate to the consumers' own experiences.

*Brands, if they are to be remembered, need to become great storytellers.*

Some brands do that quite literally. You have many examples of brands that have built stories around their formation. It's almost obligatory for every winemaker to spin a yarn about how generations of his family carefully tilled the soil and nurtured the grapes. However, storytelling for brands is not just about forcing a story around its origins, though it sometimes works. *It is about letting consumers imagine their own stories around your brands.*

*We, as consumers, not only like to listen to stories but also to tell our own. This creates an opportunity for marketers to create brands that can become a part of the consumers' stories.*

Think about it. Every product that you sell is used by the consumer in their own life, becoming a part of it. When consumers can better visualize how your brand will be a part of their story, they are more inclined to buy it.

So, when you are buying groceries, you may think about the meal you would cook for that special someone and how they might react. When you are buying a bison jerky doggie treat, you may envision how 'Ralph' will toy with it. When you are buying a bottle of wine, you might want to imagine what you will say about how and why you picked that bottle for the occasion. Giving consumers the breadcrumbs around the stories they could tell about your product is a fabulous way to engage them with your brand.

To insert your brand into your customer's stories, you must understand their routines, rituals or even the special moments of their lives. These are already alive and kicking in their memories. All you have to do is to place your brand in those stories.

### Tank Garage Winery: Making Your Brand's Story Their Story

Tank Garage Winery takes this kind of storytelling to heart. Each of their bottles has a story, in which they invite you to see yours. Now, selling wines is not easy. In the US, over 700 million bottles are sold each year by the 9600 or so wineries. You might imagine yourself as an oenophile that mentally savours the terroir, vintage and varietal of each bottle you plan to buy. But truth be told, most people buy wine by just considering its label.

Tank Garage wines are inspired by special moments in the lives of the winemakers, James Harder and Jim Regusci. 'Lords of the Boulevard',[12] their Napa red, recalls the 'nostalgic exuberance and naiveté' of the '50s and '60s era. The label dons a famous Joseph Sterling photograph of two youths in starch white tees leaning casually out of the windows of their car at a drive-in. The winemakers capture that spirit by introducing the wine with the tag line, 'We were young, broke and reckless, but we ruled this town.' It is a story of adolescence that perhaps you too can relate to—reminding you of a more carefree time in your life—and more fondly today, now that you can afford a $65 bottle of wine.

The one brand that wins the grand prize in masterfully executing this strategy is Google in India. With a three-minute-long commercial called 'Reunion' that debuted in 2013 on YouTube,[13] they took the country by storm. The ad fictionalizes what was the true story of many when India and Pakistan were partitioned by the British at the end of the colonial era, leading to many friendships and families being ripped apart overnight as masses of people migrated from one country to the other.

It opens with the elderly Baldev, a Hindu, showing to his granddaughter, Suman, a faded sepia picture of himself and his closest friend, Yusuf, a Muslim, from when they were little kids living as neighbours in Lahore, Pakistan. The picture remains the sole vestige of a happier time and of a bond that at the time must have seemed inseparable. Recalling those fond memories, he tells her of the park that was next to his home. It had an ancient gate, from time immemorial of 'Baba Azam', where he and Yusuf would fly kites and eat jhajariyas from Yusuf's family's confectionary shop.

Suman's brow furrows pensively as a sudden thought crosses her mind. She turns into an amateur sleuth flipping open her computer and cruising to Google search. A quick search of 'park in Lahore with ancient gate' uncovers Mochi Gate. 'What is jhajariya' reveals that it is a local dessert made of caramelized milk. 'Oldest sweet shop near Mochi Gate' lists Fazal Sweet along with their telephone number. One search leads to another, until she finally locates 'Yusuf'. In what follows, and as the story unfolds, she is on her way to pick up the long-lost Yusuf at the Delhi airport, checking flight arrival times along the way on Google search, and a touching reunion takes place between Baldev and Yusuf on the former's birthday.

The ad, which has been viewed nearly 16 million times on YouTube to date and also featured on Indian TV, was simply brilliant on multiple levels. It tells a story that is cleverly woven around what Google is. The search engine is invoked six different times during the vignette, for everything from finding phone numbers to checking India visa requirements for Pakistani tourists. Compare that to having an ad that just lists all the things you can do on Google Search. The story touches us, and we know emotional memories last longer. In Chapter 1, I caution against overly emotional ads in which the brand may be lost. Not in this case, not with six well-placed pieces of the story.

But that's not all. I said earlier that recall will be even stronger if you can associate your brand's story with other knowledge and beliefs that the consumer holds deeply. By building the Google story around the events of Partition, a moment set deeply in the Indian and Pakistani psyches, the brand ensured that it would never be unnoticed or forgotten. Further, the way that the search engine is used in the story portrays use occasions that we as consumers can easily relate to.

Yes, the ad is three minutes long, but it does check every box I can think of in getting cognitive brand execution right. Don't get me wrong. Not all brand executions need to have beautiful stories like this, but they do need something, even if it is simple.

A final technical point on this topic. We now know that stories make your brands easier to recall. Why is that important? *Because things that are easier to recall by the brain, seem more important to it.* In psychology, this phenomenon is called *availability heuristic.*[14] If your brand benefits are easier to recall, those features, the strengths of your brand presumably, will seem more important to the consumer in making their choices. When presented with competing choices, they will assess them against the standard set by your brand.

## 4. Brand stories can be long or short, but must be stories

The good news is that brand stories can be short or long. The real point is to tell a good story. Again, marketers wrestle with this idea a lot in branding. Should your brand have a single compelling idea that hits the customer in as little time as possible? But what if they were inattentive, thinking about something else, when you pitched your one-liner at them? And, what should you do when your brand has three or four great features to talk about? Shouldn't you then turn your brand into a 'mixto' burrito with everything on it?

The answer is that those are the wrong questions. *The number of brand equities you put in your brand positioning is not the problem. The real question is whether you can tie them into a coherent story that connects with your customers.*

Remember what we talked about. Most people cannot memorize even a shopping list with just seven items, but just about everyone can follow the storyline of the 142-minute movie *Forrest Gump*. Length does not matter, stories do. Consumer don't need to commit every word of your brand proposition to memory, but they do need to follow the story. So make sure your brand has one.

And while you are at it, tell a coherent story that consumers can follow. Marketers often trip over this. They show ads with multiple vignettes of consumers relishing their brand. This happens because the market research department tells the marketers that they need to target three different consumer segments of use occasions. So, they say to themselves, 'Why choose? Let's put all of them in?'

So, a commercial may feature a black man slipping a protein bar in his pocket as he rushes off to work, a white mom enjoying it as a snack after the morning zumba class and a grandpa partaking of one during his morning walk in the park.

Those are three different stories. To add to it, all of this is also accompanied by a voiceover detailing the ingredients in the bar and their salient benefits. Guess what? Now, they're lost. Make it easy. Tell one coherent story and you'll thank me.

Here's why. Most people think they can multitask. But research shows they can't, especially when it comes to trying to do two things that require deliberation (System 2). You can do a System 2 task together with a System 1 task. For example, most people can drive and think at the same time. But two System 2 tasks are a no go.

Psychologists Christopher Chabris and Daniel Simons demonstrated people's inability to multitask in a hilarious experiment described in their book *The Invisible Gorilla.*[15] The authors made a film[16] of two teams passing two basketballs. One team is dressed in white shirts and the other in black. They are running around each other, passing the balls. The viewer's task is to count the number of times the white team passes the ball to its own members. This is a little complicated because the players are mixed in together, and thus the task requires the viewer to focus. Somewhere in the middle of this, a woman dressed in a gorilla suit saunters across through the players, pauses to thump her chest and then walks back out of the frame. At the end of the video, the viewer is asked how many times the white team passed the ball. They are then asked if they noticed the gorilla! Of the thousands of people who have taken this test, roughly half don't! When System 2 is busy, it can miss some obvious activities that it is not focused on. If you have too many stories that your brand is trying to tell, all at the same time, they will be missed like the chest-thumping gorilla.

Abbott's recent television spot 'We're Changing Parkinson's Tune' succeeds in relating relatively complicated information about treating Parkinson's disease through a coherent commercial. It opens with a scene showing endless rows of artists performing in a string orchestra. The picture is a bit unusual because instead of the usual sixty-odd performers that you would normally see in an orchestra, this one has millions, so many that they disappear into the horizon. The unexpectedness of the imagery catches your eye. Over the reassuring symphonic notes, the voiceover says, 'In the human brain, [there are] billions of neurons playing in harmony.' As the music builds to a crescendo, the narrator walking down the aisle explains, 'For people with Parkinson's, some neurons change their tune, causing uncontrollable tremors.' On cue, one of the performers goes off track, playing his own tune. The obvious disharmony of this draws in the viewers, who wonder, 'What's going on here?' It compels them to absorb the message around what goes wrong with people who have Parkinson's. At that time, the narrator chimes in with, 'Now Abbott technology can target those exact neurons and restore control and harmony once thought to be lost forever.' This is a well-executed ad where the visual analogue of the string orchestra to Abbott's medical technology relates a coherent story. And that's what the game is all about.

Let's turn our attention now to another important subject. How much brand information can you toss at the consumer? How much can they really absorb in a short amount of time?

Marketers believe that consumers have fleeting attention spans. Hence, they often condense brand messages into terse one-liners in hopes of sneaking them into to the consumer's consciousness. Kind of reminds you of moms who fool their kids into opening their mouths and then quickly slide in a tablespoon of thick distasteful tonic with a 'See that wasn't so bad' assurance.

If your customers are slow to tune into you, then your pithy brand proposition will appear and disappear in the blink of an eye before anyone takes note. But there's good news. The brain does not just process dumbed-down brand storylines. It can and does internalize more complicated stuff over time and marketers can take advantage of those background processes.

In the introductory chapter, I described dreams as a time when the *Learner* subunit in the brain can kick back and ruminate over the events of the day. But dreams are not the only occasion for doing so; rather, our brains are constantly thinking, pondering and ruminating when they are not focused on complex mental tasks. To tap into residual dreams and thoughts, marketers need to find ways to keep consumers thinking about their brands.

One way to do this is by presenting brand messages in an enigmatic manner, using anachronisms, hyperbole, surreal imagery and mental riddles. The brain sleeps over those conundrums to make sense of them; it can't help it. When it encounters the unexpected, it not only notices it but tries to resolve it. I have coined the term 'residual thoughts method' for when a brand strategically embeds its proposition in exactly such an enigmatic message and subconsciously triggers the brain into discovering it.

This is the route the drug Skyrizi took in the eczema market. The AbbVie marketers wanted to communicate the idea that once you use their drug to clear those ugly looking splotches on your skin, you could feel that you have been freed of the disease and enjoy life to the fullest. But the problem was that they were late to party, and other entrants had already devised pretty much the same messaging.

Otezla, from Amgen, had blanketed the airwaves with their campaign 'Your spontaneity is showing!' In the ad, we see a woman swinging from a rope like a monkey and flopping into the lake. Stelara, by Johnson and Johnson, had an ad of a guy running around the beach with his surfboard, in a campaign that said, 'That's 361 days to focus on life . . . and not psoriasis!'

That was a reference to taking the drug just four times a year and the rest of the time being free to do whatever.

Of course, all the ads had to be in swimming gear so you could see lots of clean skin. That was a given. With all these ads already cramming the airwaves, you can see the problem AbbVie had. Free as a monkey swinging from a rope. How much freer and more limitless could you show people being? Fire them off on top of a rocket to the moon in a bikini?

Len Spears,* who was AbbVie's point man for Skyrizi in global markets, was not happy with his options. Rarely sticking to the agenda at any meetings and obsessive about his business, Len was a rare and creative strategist. Those two words, 'creative' and 'strategic', don't generally go together, but in Len's case, they exactly do. He asked his agency to develop eight different brand concepts and they did; except that he didn't like any of them. He sent them back to the drawing board so many times that I thought they might just pack up and leave.

'Look at Skyrizi! It has the best data of any drug in the market! We have almost no side effects. Nothing! Zero!' he exclaimed, drawing a big circle on the nearby whiteboard. 'We get 100 per cent skin clearance for more patients than anyone else,' he said writing a '1' above the original '0' and a second '0' below it, to now show a '100' on the board. 'You see? No more patches! No more blotches! Everything's gone! Zippo! It's perfect!' he went on in a how's-this-happening-to-me tone.

Somewhere in the midst of these inspirational outbursts, something clicked with one of the creative wonks at the agency. Nothing but everything? Say what? And that ultimately led to a dazzling campaign around 'Nothing Is Everything'. The tag

---

* The events described in the following passages have been fictionalized, and the names of individuals disguised to remove any non-public information and preserve the privacy of the mentioned individuals. The narrative is thus designed to be instructive rather than accurately biographical or historical.

line presents a paradox: How can nothing be everything? How does zero equal infinity?

The incongruity of the message, which is laced into a sprightly singalong-worthy ditty in the television commercials, triggers residual thoughts in the audience. The answer to the riddle lies in unravelling the brand message, namely that Skyrizi has virtually no side effects and leaves *nothing* of the psoriasis on the skin. And is that not the whole point for the patient? Isn't that *everything*? Yeah! And he scores!

### Old Spice and the Residual Thoughts Method

The residual thoughts method is used more widely than you might think from markets as diverse as pharma, consumer and retail.

The trend may have been revived by Old Spice. In 2010, Old Spice was a seventy-five-year-old tired brand struggling to be noticed by an entirely new generation of consumers. Seven years back, Old Spice had introduced body washes for men, but the products battled in vain to gain traction in the market. The brand's legacy as 'the aftershave that most reminded you of what your grandpa smelled like', was locked around its ankles like an iron ball and chain.

Old Spice also faced competition from industry goliath Unilever, which was launching its Dove for Men bodywash products on the back of the monumental success of its 'Real Beauty' campaign with women, with heavy investments planned for Super Bowl 2010.

Old Spice came up with a campaign that still mystifies marketing experts as to why it worked. A not particularly original, but eminently forgivable, approach would have been to simply splash images of a beautiful woman fawning over her Old Spice-lathered man. But that was not at all what they did. They did something better—a fantastical campaign that made the viewer stop and go, 'Whoa! What the heck was that?'

The TV commercials[17] featured former NFL wide receiver Isaiah Mustafa as 'the man your man could smell like' in a range of clever vignettes.

In the first one, the super-sexy Isaiah finds himself magically transported to a nice yacht. Then, hard-to-find tickets to an exclusive show prance out from an oyster in his hands and turn into a pile of plump diamonds, after which Old Spice appears in the midst of the heap. Thus, explains the narrator, 'Anything is possible when your man smells like Old Spice.'

To erase any doubts as to the premise, in the next moment Isaiah finds himself bare-chested on a paper white horse, observing 'I'm on a horse' leaving unsaid 'How about you?' The commercial finishes off with the tag line, 'Smell like man, man.' Pretty crazy, huh?

Well, apparently, not crazy enough! A second video features former NFL star Greg Jennings, wide receiver for the Green Bay Packers, scoring a touchdown while defying the conventional wisdom that you shouldn't mix business and pleasure. That could be fine, except for the fact that Jennings is cruising through the field with a king-sized bed affixed to his torso, and his lady is lying next to him drinking tea. On the way to the touchdown, he nonchalantly swats down the opposing team's defenders like flies. For those still unimpressed, Jennings also flips open the cover on the tea tray to serve steaming hot pancakes to his lady even as he breaks the plane at the goal line. The whole scenario is so bizarre that it is hard not to blink twice every second and say, 'What's going on here?'

Despite the fantastical visuals, the brand stays true to the idea that anything is possible when your lady is charmed by the smell of Old Spice on you. The key is not just to show incongruous audio-visuals but also to weave the brand narrative into the ad for latent thought processing. But it does take time to get it. You may have to watch the ad a couple of times before it sinks in.

In the aftermath of the campaign, Old Spice sales doubled. Social media engagement of the ads leapt to 40 million-plus viewers across a range of sites including Facebook, Twitter and YouTube.[18] The best form of flattery, as they say, is mimicry, and many different brands have latched on to the idea of 'Anything is possible', with actors portraying unnatural acts empowered by their brands.

The residual thoughts method does not have to be complicated. It just has to inspire consumers to think. A simple example is an iconic billboard that appears a mile before Exit 24 on Interstate 95 between New York and New Haven. All it says is 'Your Wife is HOT!' with the letters 'HOT' in fiery red, a picture of a swimming pool and a suggestion to take the exit and visit 'Fairfield Pool'. You are at Exit 24 by the time you process this and smile sheepishly to yourself. The play on the word 'HOT' causes the reader to pause and make the connection that putting in a swimming pool in the backyard could be a great way for the wife and kids to cool off in the HOT summer.

I should note here that not everyone living in Fairfield County took a liberating view of the poster. In fact, there was a petition[19] signed by concerned citizens on how the ad inappropriately objectifies women. Would you have said 'Your Husband is HOT?' they asked.

Notwithstanding the intricate gender equivalence issues at play here, the method for latent introspection is what marketers should be after. Thinking taxes the human brain. Thus, having a humorous payoff certainly does not hurt.

The residual thoughts method is a different idea from the notion of surprising customers. The 'bizarreness effect' tells us that wacky images, sounds, language and events stand out more and are remembered by the brain better.[20] This, as we saw, is because our brain is wired to focus on differences or changes from the expected. Unfortunately, these two strategies have prompted some ad agencies to create zany spots that at times make no sense. It is not enough to be weird; the ad has to relate to and unfold the story of your brand.

* * *

*Key Takeaways*

In this chapter, we have learned how to be smart about executing our brand strategies in the way the brain works. The following principles should guide your designs:

- Brand impressions are based on only a small part of the total brand experience, namely the climax and the end.
- Brands that deliver only what the customer expects are noticed less; it is the unexpected experiences that stand out.
- The brain tends to remember your brand better and longer if you relate its benefits in the form of a story rather than as an itemized list.
- Brands need not limit the number of things they are about; but what they are about needs to tie into a coherent storyline.
- Brand stories that connect and associate with the consumer's other experiences and stories can be indelible.
- Brand stories and experiences do not have to be oversimplified or dumbed down; consumers continue to process information long after having seen the ad.

One thing I have said a number of times is that the more associations you create between your brand and the consumer's other experiences, the stronger your brand will be in their minds. One way for some brands to create stronger associations is by commissioning all five senses into the experience. In the next chapter, we take a look at the role of our five senses in designing brands. After all, we see, hear, taste, feel and smell our brands through our senses. Your strategy for designing brand experiences thus needs a plan for each.

# 11

# Brand Sensations: Role of the Five Senses in Selling

'I felt enraged. I felt flabbergasted. I felt confused,' fumed Chinyere Ezie, a staff attorney at the Center for Constitutional Rights, on Twitter.

It wasn't anything that anybody had said to her. It was what she saw in the Prada store window in the SoHo neighbourhood of lower Manhattan that left her shaking to the core in anger. And that was a $550 Pradamalia character, the latest in the line of keychain figurines, that looked like a black monkey with outsized red lips.

She took a picture, posted it on her Twitter feed and Facebook page, and lit up a firestorm. Her post went viral, building a tsunami of outrage as people around the world saw in the fantasy charm an obvious resemblance to 'blackface', an odious image from a racist past. It sent executives at the Prada HQ scurrying for cover and apologizing profusely with:

> The Pradamalia are fantasy charms composed of elements of the Prada oeuvre. They are imaginary creatures not intended to have any reference to the real world and certainly not blackface. Prada Group never had the

intention of offending anyone and we abhor all forms of racism and racist imagery.

To be fair, the entire Pradamalia collection did offer several other characters, most of whom looked nothing like monkeys, and some even resembled aliens and spaceships.[1] But the damage was done.

This unfortunate incident offers an important lesson for cognitive brand marketers. Our senses, comprising vision, hearing, smell, touch and taste, are the gateway to our brain. They consciously and subconsciously awaken past experiences, the good and bad, and intertwine them with the present.

Earlier that week, Chinyere had returned from a visit to the National Museum of African American History and Culture in Washington and been deeply moved by the exhibits. That day in New York, no one had tried to sell her a Pradamalia. Nor did she step into the store. It was only what she saw through the store window that enflamed what were still raw emotions from her visit to the museum in Washington.

Brands, in what they show, tell, feel, smell and taste like, say a lot. When designing and executing brand experiences, it is important to think of a plan for each sense, or at least consider its impact on them, rather than have to make one as a byproduct of an unforeseen crisis.

Most real-world brands have a 'theatre of operations' and 'ambassadors'. They go to market through retail stores and/or a salesforce.

Sergio Zyman was the chief marketing officer of the Coca-Cola Company when they sponsored the Summer Olympics in Atlanta in 1996. Years later, I was Sergio's chief marketing officer in his consulting company. Sergio told me that at the time when he ran the sponsorship for the Olympics, he had his teams build a thick binder called the 'Red Book', which was a detailed playbook for everything that Coke would do at the games. How and where Coke would be seen, who would do and say what and when, what it all meant and how it fit together in a single brand mosaic.

The Olympics would be Coke's theatre of operation. Anyone with the red Coke shirt would be a brand ambassador, and every moment would be choreographed according to the Red Book.

When consumers step into a brand's theatre of operations or interact with its brand ambassadors, there is an opportunity to build immersive experiences for them by engaging their five senses. The strongest brand experiences, as we learnt before, are those that are associated with other prior experiences. They are recalled more easily and better than others, last longer and feel more important to the brain. When marketers weave their brands with the human senses, they create even more associations with the experience, making it easier to recall. That's why immersive sensory brand experiences make deep impressions on our brains.

If you walk down the Magnificent Mile in Chicago, even if you have never done that before, you can recognize the Burberry store with its trademark black-and-brown tartan cross hatches from blocks away with no help at all. The store design itself makes a statement about the brand. As you step inside, you can smell it.

During spring and summer, Zaluti scent machines diffuse the spring crocus scent and during autumn and winter, a special autumn scent.[2] You look around and see that the wall colors are neutral with darker accents and furniture. That is deliberately orchestrated to bring to mind Burberry's classic trench coat or tartan.[3]

The personal shopper who greets you leaves an impression with how they look and sound, and how they gently direct you to where you want to go in the store. Every one of those sensations embody the Burberry brand.

The brand theatre of operations does not end with the store. Burberry also live-streams its runway shows, to share the excitement of decloaking new fashions as they happen with its fans worldwide, and lets them buy select new products online with its 'see now, buy now strategy'.

Even brands like Away, Glossier, Farmer's Dog, Made In Cookware, Lively Intimates and Everlane, which started out as pure online brands, have opened exciting stores on Lafayette Street in New York. They realized that bringing people to a brick-and-mortar store was the best way to create immersive experiences for customers—and that is what many consumers want. Virtual companies like Facebook and Google have opportunities to expand their brand theatre of operations into the real world with events and sponsorships.

In this chapter, I will lightly stray into the topic of how brain sciences can help brand ambassadors and brand theatres of operations engage the human senses. The truth is, cognitive selling can be the subject of a whole different book. We flirt with it here because salespeople are the torchbearers of the brands, and how they come across is how the brand comes across.

First, when we discuss engaging the senses, you should know that the brain can mix up the signals it picks up. This happens because sensory inputs are processed by shared neural circuits in the brain and separated by interpretation considering the context and other cues. Most of the time, this works pretty well, but not always.

In the extreme, people who have synesthesia, mix up their senses routinely because the brain messes up the contextually appropriate interpretation. So, for example, when they hear the sound of a trumpet, they may see the colour orange or smell a lemon tart-like scent. But you need not go to the extremes, or be a synesthete, to experience a bias called the 'misattribution of arousal'.

As the theory goes, there are a number of stimuli that elicit the same physiologic response, e.g. shortness of breath or racing heartbeats, which can confuse the brain into mixing one emotion with another. Exercising can cause your heart to beat faster. Meeting a person that you are attracted to might do the same. Since the physiologic response is the same and triggered by the same parts of the brain, cognitively you can confuse the two to some degree.

In this example, if you were to go jogging with this person you are attracted to, your hearts would race, the endorphins would flow (from the exercising), and you may feel a tad bit more attracted to each other than if you had only met and not run.[4] Yes, really! Use it! Broadly, this means that in truly immersive experiences, when many senses are activated together, it all gets mixed up into a single fantastic feeling and association about the brand. In the future, if even a few of those individual associations are missing, the brain can fill in the blanks on those sensations from its memory.

With that, let's start peeling the onion a bit, one sense at a time, recognizing that every brand has to make its own calls on what senses to play with.

## A Picture Paints a Thousand Words

People believe that 'what you see is what you get'. You trust your own eyes. Yet, many experts advise you against that; from the street magician who made your $20 bill disappear up his sleeve to ancient Indian philosophers who swore that the entire world was a *maya jaal*, a perverse illusion of our senses. But despite these warnings, we trust what we can see.

This gets the gears turning inside the heads of marketers, who ask, 'What do people need to see to believe that my brand is true and quite wonderful?'

Visual selling is a System 1 tactic. As we know, System 2 is 'lazy'. So, if a picture looks good based on familiar patterns from the past or makes the choice seem easier, System 2 may take a pass saying, 'If it looks good to you, System 1, it looks good to me.' No further evaluation is necessary.

That is the direction Prudential Finance decided to take. Retirement planning is complicated, and most people, especially the younger crowd, are not highly motivated to plan for a distant future. Prudential commissioned Harvard psychologist Dan Gilbert to help them find a way to get the message across simply.

Gilbert figured out that the one question that most working professionals worry about is, 'Am I saving enough for retirement?' The challenge is how do you tell them 'probably not' without getting mired in mind-bending spreadsheets? When you overload people with convoluted math models, they can shut down and stop listening to you. So, Gilbert took the 'show-them-a-picture' route.

He helped design a series of commercials with games that end with the 'probably not saving enough' answer in a visually memorable manner.

In the 'Walkways Experiment',[5] the narrator asks several randomly intercepted young couples, 'How much money do you think you will need in retirement?' The couples take a guess at a savings number that seems suitably large to them.

Next, they are lined up against what look like lanes in a bowling alley. The foul line at the end of the approach is day one of retirement, and the back end of the lane is presumably the day they die. I say presumably because they don't spell that out so as not to darken the discussion.

As each couple starts walking down the lane, like a bowling ball hurling slowly towards the pins, the tiles behind them light up blue, signalling the passage of time in years. They can keep walking so long as they have money in the bank. When it turns orange, sorry, they just depleted their savings and have to stop. The camera then pans to show that most couples are only partway down the bowling lanes and have a disconcertingly long way to go till the end of retirement with no money left. Picture shown, message sent.

The point is that most people grossly underestimate the money they would need after retirement and therefore must talk to a Prudential planner immediately. The visual is light but memorable, and it makes you wonder which lane you would be in, without making you feel terrible. After all, there is only one person in the game that makes it all the way to the end. The rest suffer an unspecified but surely disagreeable fate.

But what does all this do for Prudential, the brand? It tells consumers that Prudential can be a brand they can look to for helping them understand their retirement needs in a simple manner. That is not the only thing that Prudential the brand is all about, but yes, that is one of the core brand equities.

In pharma marketing, visualization is a particularly effective way of communicating how drugs work. And that is quite a trick because pharma marketers themselves often don't know how exactly their drug works.

If you read the product label of many leading, multibillion-dollar medication brands, you will see an incomprehensible description of how certain proteins or cytokines work in the body, which then ends with a caveat like, 'However, the relevance of specific JAK combinations (their drug!) to therapeutic effectiveness is not known.' In plain English, that says, 'Our drug does work, but we're not sure how.' So, if you don't exactly know how your own drug works, how do you explain to patients how it does? The answer? With a suggestive picture!

In focus groups with patients suffering from joint diseases, we discovered that there was a strong desire to get a medication that went straight to the root cause of the disease and worked from the inside of the body to fix what was wrong. The ad agencies went to work and came back with mock-ups of X-rayed human bodies showing glowing or flashing joints where patients usually report pain.

The concept boards tested well in research with patients, convincing them that the medication was going to work on the pain where the patients wished it would, namely, deep inside their bones at the root cause. No further explanation was necessary. Communicating how the drug works is a core part of the brand proposition and particularly important in convincing patients that the treatment is the right choice.

While visualizations like these can be incredibly helpful, marketers still need to present impactful images unique to their brands. In the market for drugs addressing joint pain, most leading manufacturers have discovered that the glow-in-the-dark skeleton images test well with patients. So now, most competing drugs feature similar images in their television commercials. Even though the drugs are vastly different in some cases, the skeleton makes them all look like they do the same thing.

Hence, in cognitive selling, it is important to own the visualization, like Burberry's signature tartan stripes, and associate it uniquely with your brand—or else it might help the category grow but not necessarily your brand differentially.

## If I Can Feel It, Touch It, It's Real!

Even as scientists puzzle over the psychological connections between the sense of touch and behaviour, it is not news for waiters and waitresses, the brand ambassadors, in the countless restaurants across the US. They have known that a slight, natural brush of arm with a customer creates an instant personal connect and, wait for this, bigger tips!

To be sure, April Crusco and Christopher Wetzel[6] studied the phenomenon and emerged with some interesting findings. It turns out that a touch on the arm by a waitress increased customer tips anywhere between 10–40 per cent. It could be anywhere on the arm, with customer being male or female, at many different types of restaurant. No touch led to a 12 per cent tip on an average. A touch on the shoulder resulted in a 14 per cent tip, while a touch on the palm a 17 per cent tip. Pretty impressive, isn't it? It happens subconsciously. The customer is not calculating, 'Oh! if she touches my arm, I'm doing a bigger tip.' But they do end up leaving bigger tips.

So, what is it about a human-to-human gentle tap that is so reassuring and rewarding? Professor Jane Gruber[7] of Yale University points out that an interpersonal touch (light handshake, pat on the back or arm) triggers reward centres in the brain of the person who is touched, making them more likely to cooperate (be receptive). Simply speaking, 'touchers' make 'touchees' feel more connected and aligned with them.

If you are a brand ambassador, say, a field sales rep or working with a customer in any way, you can use this information. It will help your cause if you gently touch the person on the arm and increase their confidence in your brand.

Of course, make sure you are not creepy about it. In this instance, the brand ambassador is using the sense of touch as a 'brand connector' to build empathy with the customer so that the following brand proposition is more warmly received.

All of this may leave you wondering what a brand like Coke could do with 'touch', other than serve up a nicely chilled can of the soda. Turns out, a lot!

Fifty years ago, ad agency McCann Erikson designed one of the most iconic brand campaigns of all time for the Coca-Cola Company with the tagline 'I'd like to buy the world a Coke.'

The brand transformed itself to the 'real thing' that stood for uniting people of the world with a refreshing drink, which everybody, no matter from where, could enjoy in a shared moment of happiness.[8]

Fast forward forty years to 2013 and hop over to the other side of the planet, to India. Coke and its ad agency, Leo Burnett, unveiled an ingenious brand event 'aimed at breaking down barriers and creating a simple moment of happiness between two nations at odds—India and Pakistan'.[9]

If you read the Google Search example in the previous chapter, you know that the two countries, which were once a united family, were sheared in two along religious lines by the British when they left India in 1947, and have since fought four wars with each other and been bitter enemies. The clouds of suspicion, often fanned by politicians and religious cults, linger.

Coke, with its initiative called 'Small World Machines', installed vending machines in a mall in India with corresponding and connected ones in Pakistan. The machines were fitted with full-length, touch-sensitive, interactive screens that served as virtual portals between the two countries. If you were on the Indian side, you could walk up to it and put your palm on the screen, and a person in the mall in Pakistan could do the same and put their palm against yours.

Over the three days, thousands across the two countries joined hands virtually and drew out peace signs in unison on both sides of the portal screens. Ten thousand chilled cans of Cokes were dispensed from the machines along with the warmth and happiness of two countries united as one, if just for a moment. Andy DiLallo, the chief creative officer Leo Burnett Sydney said:

> Being on the ground in India during the Small World Machines experience is probably the highlight of my career so far. To be able to take two countries that have been divided and to unite them through the world's most iconic brand, and see the purity of the experience was amazing.

And DiLallo was Australian. Imagine how the Indian and Pakistani consumers would have felt.

Even though the touch was only virtual and momentary, the brain knows what a touch is supposed to feel like and is able to trigger emotions and sensations mentally, without anyone touching anyone. The campaign commercial documenting the event has been seen on YouTube almost four million times.[10]

This was not just a 'feel-good' gimmick with no benefit for the brand. As I mentioned earlier, the phenomenon of misattribution of arousal, where the brain confounds two stimuli with each other when they happen together, is at the root of the ad. The ad leads consumers to merge the elation from the experience of the event with the feeling they derive from drinking out of the dispensed can of Coke. It goes to show that for the determined and creative marketer there is always a way.

In the context of branding, when we think of touch, let me be clear that I am not talking about a consumer feeling a product to test its integrity. You may very well pull a sweater off the shelf in a store and yank it around from side to side to see if it tears and leave it at that. I am talking about touching the consumer in ways that say something more about your brand and builds a greater sense of connectedness and alignment.

Another surprising truth about touching a product is that a touch of one object can trigger the purchase of an unrelated object.[11] There are a number of weird experiments that show this. In one, people who were asked to hold a warm therapeutic pad versus a cold one subsequently invested 43 per cent more money with an investment planner. The feeling of warmth was misattributed by the brain for a sense of overall trust and safety.

Likewise, in another test, people sitting on hard chairs negotiated harder on prices than people sitting on soft cushioned chairs. When I worked with Dexter, a company that manufactured automotive coatings, we found that cheap plastic parts coated with paints formulated to feel soft would communicate a sense of luxury in cars and make people more willing to pay a higher price for them. Touch is felt as texture, temperature, vibrations, pressure, weight and humidity. It is a good idea to think those elements through for your brand and marketing collateral.

## Sound Advice

Hearing is a sense that is 'always on' and is thus associated with every experience that we as humans have. It is always on because it is the first line of defence when we are asleep. For the prehistoric man, the best hope of detecting a threat while asleep, before he saw, felt, tasted or even smelt it, was to *hear* it, wake up and hide. Scientists tell us that even when we are in a deep delta-wave sleep, neurons in the reticular activation system at the base of the brain stay active, listening to everything alertly.[12]

Because the brain is associative, sounds can trigger recall of the experiences and emotions connected to them. We feel fear when we hear a blood-curdling scream and pure joy when we hear a young child cackle with laughter. If you have watched the movie *Jaws*, the music accompanying the arrival of the great white shark is undoubtedly burnt into your brain's circuitry. You only have to play the two-note sequence twice, as in '*thumph-thumph, thumph-thumph*', and people will look around and laugh nervously. Try it at your next party. Without the movie experience, that sound would mean nothing, much less a great white on the prowl.

Music has always been a big part of the brand theatre of operations, in retail stores and in both online and offline commercials. The brain's relationship with music is particularly intimate and mysterious. Music has its own persona. It can make us happy or sad just as another person can. When we hear music, we tap our feet, clap our hands, sway from side to side and bob our heads. Who knows why, but we just do. No one is untouched by music. It is how our brain works.

The key to 'sound selling' lies in the '*Jaws* strategy'. You can use sound to:

(a) heighten brand experiences
(b) create your own brand signature
(c) even influence the pace of activity

As an example of the latter, research[13] shows that supermarket sales can be influenced by the tempo and type of the background music. Sales went up when slower music was piped through in a minor mode (the major scale had no impact). The slower music subconsciously caused customers to relax and slow down, so that they browsed and bought more.

Conversely, in a fast-food restaurant, music with a faster tempo will keep the lines moving along at a good clip and reinforce the brand impression of speed and efficiency. People tend to align their behaviour with the background music.

Aren't you likely to get fewer irate customers in a store with tranquil music? Against the murmur of Beethoven's 'Moonlight Sonata', wouldn't you rather whisper your complaints than blare them out at the top of your lungs?

If you are going to make sounds a part of your core brand experience, make them distinctive, so that they are part of your brand signature. Joel Beckerman, in his book *The Sonic Boom*,[14] gives some great examples of companies that have created iconic sounds wired with their brand experiences. He tells us how Disney spaces out the different fantasy lands within the park with 'fake quiet' sounds that kill extraneous noise. This is done to ensure that your experience of being in the Magic Kingdom is not dissected by planes flying overhead or a passing semi-trailer blasting its horn. Yes, they use sound to kill sound!

The restaurant chain Chili's amped up the sound of sizzling fajitas in its commercials to get the audiences salivating and making them want to jump in their cars and grab one.[15] Since Nokia, every cellphone company has hunted for its own perfect ringtone to demarcate their brand signature to millions of users daily.

Man Made Music, a company founded by Beckerman, has mapped the emotions that connect to the sounds of different instruments, so you know the feelings to work into your brands:

- Strings: warmth, scale or scope; passionate, uplifting
- Horns: power, elegance, impact, importance, strength, honour, bravery and heroism
- Synthesizer: modern, forward-thinking, evolutionary
- Piano/percussion: heartfelt, emotive, personal, driving energy, velocity or anxiety
- Drums: driving, motivating, primal, communal
- Electric guitar: power, youthful energy, rebellion

So, there you have it. Next time, you want to sound off your brand, make it your own, make it add to the experience, and pace it to your desired experience.

## If It Smells

The sense of smell is also another 'always on' sense and thus accompanies every brand experience.

Even while you sleep, the smell of smoke may alert you to a fire in the house. We can't possibly underestimate the power of smell. From scientists to budding Casanovas, there has been a high interest in locating and using pheromones to attract the opposite sex.[16] Unfortunately, no joyous news so far, unless you happen to be a fruit fly.

However, smells can by design or inadvertently become a part of the brand experience; they can turn you on or turn you off.

Singapore Airlines has branded its own curated scent and proudly informs customers that 'Stefan Floridian Waters fragrance is a signature aroma of Singapore Airlines. It is used in the flight attendants' perfume, the airplane interiors, and infused into the hot towels given out on take-off.'[17] It is described as silky, feminine and exotic by those with discerning olfactory apparatus.

The strategy of using smell to enhance your brand is not just for rarefied brands like Singapore Airlines and Burberry. For the longest time, the scent of Procter & Gamble's Tide has been the secret of its seventy-year reign over the laundry detergent market. In 2018, Tide was the number-one liquid laundry detergent in the US, controlling over one-fifth of market sales[18] while commanding one of the highest price points of any brand.

Smell started as a necessity for P&G but became something much more. To begin with, P&G added a fragrance to its detergent to hide the smell of the ingredients, alkyl sulfate and sodium triphosphate. Over time, the Tide scent evolved to a citrus, floral and fruity combination, with hints of lemon, orange, lily, rose and apple. Each scent has been market-tested to trigger specific associations for consumers. The smell of citrus relates to a sense of cleanliness. The sweet, fruity scents result in a feeling of comfort and well-being. The floral scents evoke maternal love and care. The scent of Tide recalls childhood memories of how the clothes smelt spilling out of Mom's laundry basket. It has kept millions of consumers across generations hooked to the brand, with its projected feelings of cleanliness and general happiness.

The brain science behind smells is quite extraordinary. Genes in the olfactory bulb of the brain can process and sense nearly a trillion different smells. Compare that to the 1,70,000 words in the English language; that is, more smells than there are words.

The smell receptors of the brain are connected directly to the emotional centres (amygdala and piriform cortex) in the brain. This simply means two things: one, smells are connected to long-term emotional memories; and two, people can be influenced by smell without being conscious of it.

This is why Singapore Airlines creates a lasting and subconscious brand impression with its Floridian Waters fragrance. If you are a retail store, you have to be thinking about the smell of your brand experience.

## Just for the Taste of It

The senses of smell and taste go together because the processing circuits in the brain are the same. If you hold your nose, you would find it hard to distinguish between the taste of chocolate and vanilla ice cream.

Instinctively, it feels like bringing food into a brand experience is a great idea. The idea of breaking bread with someone to build a relationship and engender cooperation is as old as time.[19] So, finally, let's take a look at the sense of taste.

Foods are associated with different experiences and occasions, and tickle more than just your taste buds. Think about champagne. Comité Champagne of France reminds us that it hits every one of your five senses: 'the soft sigh and hiss' of a correctly popped bottle; 'the spectacle of the bubbles as they rise irrepressibly to the surface, collecting in a jostling ring to form the cordon' in your glass; and the scent of white flowers with a hint of orange peel. And then the taste.

'The palate should be surprisingly but pleasantly sparkling, instantly seductive and velvety. The taste should have an underlying fruitiness, with a lingering fragrance that causes you to meditate silently and at length on the wine's aromatic qualities – long after you put down your glass,' according to Louis Bohre, an early twentieth-century champagne explorer.[20]

For me, the taste of champagne equals an intense celebration in your mouth. It feels like a reward for an accomplishment. No wonder that most airlines will serve you champagne the minute you settle into their business class cabin. Hopefully, that starts you off happy on your long flight.

So, how should you think about food and taste if you are a brand? If you are Chanel, and you invite your best customers to a preview of the fall collection at the Oak Street store in Chicago, what should you serve as hors d'oeuvres? If you are a pharma rep calling on physicians, what is the best food or beverage to bring in for office 'lunch and learns'?

Unfortunately, there is not a lot of research out there to help marketers layer their brand experience with taste. However, the basic rules still apply, namely that the sense of taste is linked to our emotional memories, and taste and emotions can influence each other.

It is hard to know whether specific tastes can put people in certain moods. There are six basic tastes: sweet, sour, salty, bitter, savoury (*umami* in Japanese) and fatty. Generally, sweet, savoury and salty foods will influence moods, emotions and memories positively. Bitter tastes are a signal to the brain of things you should not be eating, like poisons, and are acquired over time. They are obviously riskier to incorporate into your brand experience than chocolates and caramel ice cream. Sweet flavours are generally winners and make people feel rewarded and celebratory.[21] Comfort foods (fats) convey a sense of security and well-being. Coffee improves moods, energy and alertness during the day so long as you don't overdo it.

* * *

## *Key Takeaways*

In this chapter, we learnt that both online and offline brands have an opportunity to create immersive and memorable experiences by engaging the five senses thoughtfully in the brand theatre through their ambassadors.

- All brand experiences involve one or more of our senses.
- These sensory responses are woven into our emotional memories and can last for an awfully long time.
- Marketers must think about a plan for involving each sense to enhance the brand experience.
- Sensory experiences should be unique and act like a brand signature.

For marketers thirsting to learn more about sensory branding, the 'go-to' encyclopedia of these methods is undoubtedly Martin Lindstrom's book *Brand Sense*.[21] It is chock-full of real-world examples and practical advice on making these approaches work.

With knowledge about how the brain works, comes the power to control consumer behaviour. That can tempt marketers to manipulate consumers and steer them to brand choices that are not beneficial for them. In the next chapter, we march on to take a look at the ethics of cognitive branding.

# 12

# Minding Our Manners: Branding with a Conscience

You would think that I would be in love with RXBAR.

It represents the heartwarming story of entrepreneur Peter Rahal, who parlayed a $10,000 investment into inventing a new kind of energy bar and sold that company for $600 million to Kellogg's just four years after its launch. Rahal's success is fascinating for more than one reason. He is a life-long dyslexic, which he says makes him a poor linear thinker but gives him a superpower, that of making out patterns and connections where others see just dirt and muck.[1]

In the hypercompetitive breakfast snack market, Rahal could see a gaping hole, an unmet need for a portable and nutritious energy bar targeted at the on-the-go, health-conscious consumer. His branding for the bars was equally brilliant. Each one typically consists of just five simple ingredients, all boldly spelt out on every pouch he sells: egg whites, dried fruit, nuts and dates. And the fifth ingredient?

It is, 'No B.S.'

That last item was, in fact, the essence of the brand. It leveraged the 'transparency effect' to a T to play up RXBAR's 'clean label' positioning, turning millions of consumers into overnight devotees. So what's wrong with this pretty picture?

## Brand Cues That Make It What It Isn't

My issue with RXBAR is its name. In the US, 'Rx' is a term commonly associated with something that is prescribed or recommended by a physician. Don't take my word for that. Here's what Merriam-Webster says about Rx: 'A doctor's prescription, also, something resembling a doctor's prescription in being an advisable or corrective course of action.'[2]

Is RXBAR prescribed or advised by a doctor? No. Would a doctor advise it? Maybe, given its healthy ingredients. Has a doctor actually advised people to take RXBAR? Nope. Maybe the recipe is created by a doctor? No, Rahal concocted the ingredients in his mother's kitchen.

For an energy bar that promises 'No B.S.' on every label, that is a lot of B.S.

The term 'RX' is a brand cue. The brain associates it with 'doctor recommended' subconsciously, given all of past history and the general use of the term. Thus, RXBAR subconsciously cues its customers to believe that it is physician-endorsed, which it isn't. The association with medical science is triggered in your brain without you being aware of it. Is that okay? On the one hand, you might argue that it is not like anyone is going to die from this. The bar is, after all, healthy and good for people. So, no one is harmed.

However, there is a fine point having to do with ethics here. When you use psychology—in this case, a primed association—to attract consumers to your brand, it is good practice to use it to convey what your brand is and not what it isn't.

Now, consider White Claw, a hard seltzer that has become an overnight sensation with millennials in the US. The delicious alcohol-spiked beverage comes in thin tall cans. The package cues the fact that the brand is low-calorie. This is an example of a good cognitive branding practice, where you use subconscious cues to communicate something that your brand truly is.

On the other hand, Kellogg's is going in the opposite direction. They are now using the 'RX' prefix as a foundation for a broader line of products, starting with, RX.AM breakfast oats.[3] But just because you can, should you?

## Anchoring for More

Let's go to another favourite industry of mine, the credit card world. The best customers are those who borrow a lot at the relatively high interest rates that banks charge (and there are good reasons for that, by the way). They are wonderful because they depend on having access to credit to maintain their lifestyle and use the card for large purchases they could not make otherwise. This could be anything from an unexpected medical expense to a dream cruise to the Bahamas with family.

If you carry a balance with a credit card, you know that you have to make a minimum payment every month on the loan. This is the company's way of testing that you are good for the money and won't run away. You can always pay more than the required minimum, but not less without incurring a penalty. So, here's a question for you. If you are that consumer with a loan balance, how much should you pay? The minimum required payment or something more? Turns out that most (over 50 per cent) balance-carrying customers pay something slightly more than the minimum regularly.

Now, you are thinking, 'Well, that's not surprising. People should pay what they can afford to pay back, right up to their payment capacity. If they can pay more, they should. Why pay more interest than you have to?'

When I was working with some of the largest banks in Mexico, here's what we discovered: People were using the suggested minimum payment as an anchor. In focus group discussions, they told us that if they paid a little more than the minimum required payment, they felt like they were being fiscally more responsible.

Here's the rub, though. If you increased the minimum payment, people would pay a little more than the new threshold. If you decreased the minimum payment, they would pay a little more than that reduced payment, or overall a little less. In other words, people were not paying according to their payment capacity but according to the suggested minimum. That is the good old anchoring bias at play. Changing the minimum-payment anchor can make hundreds of millions of dollars' worth of difference to your profitability if you are a large credit card company.

Unfortunately, over time, many credit card companies lowered their required minimum payment, entrapping consumers in high-rate debt for a lifetime. This meant that if your credit card tagged the minimum payment at 2 per cent of the total money you owe them, and the interest rate was 18 per cent per year or 1.5 per cent per month, you would repay roughly 0.5 per cent of the principal per month. Seventy-five per cent of your payment every month would be interest, and you would repay your debt in twenty years or so. Since most people keep buying more things over time, in practice they never repay their debt.

In the US, where credit card debt now stands at nearly $1 trillion, the government decided that enough was enough. It passed the Credit Card Accountability Responsibility and Disclosure (CARD) Act in 2009, intervening with its own anchoring tactic. It required card issuers to specify, on each monthly statement, how much the consumer had to pay if they wanted to settle their full balance in three years and also how long it would take them to zero it out if they only paid the minimum. These new anchors led consumers to repay their debts slightly faster, but not significantly so.[4] Not all anchors work equally well.

If you were the marketer at a credit card company, what would you do? You could take the stand that no one is forcing anyone to take debt on their credit card or to make only the minimum required payment. You may also worry that you are taking advantage of a known human frailty. Is it a good thing for a society that millions of consumers are burdened in debt for life? Did it have to come down to a government intervention? Again, just because you can, should you?

## More Than Putting Two and Two Together

For my final case study on moral dilemmas for cognitive marketers, let's consider the psychological phenomenon called the 'illusions of causality'.[5] The brain likes to connect the dots even when it should not. People tend to believe that there is a causal connection between two events that are in reality unrelated.

Let me give you two random terms: 'mother-in-law' and 'grand piano'. What do you think of them? At numerous workshops around the world, when I do this same exercise, half my audience believes that I am going to say my mother-in-law resembles a grand piano, and the other half believes that I am plotting to drop one on her. To be clear, and for the record, neither can be further from the truth: I love my mother-in-law. I just picked those two terms randomly, as I explained.

This predisposition for causality leads consumers to make all kinds of conclusions from conveniently provided goal posts. And that gives marketers all kinds of ideas. It's like the 'power of suggestion' but without the actual suggestion and only the hints.

Let me go back to our work on PediaSure. In that case, we were simply building on the moms' own beliefs around nutrition and its effects on their kids. They already believed that their children were not eating well. They were convinced that if their kids did not eat well, they would suffer from ungodly mental and physical dislocations in later life. We simply had to acknowledge these two goal posts and position PediaSure as the solution.

Now, there is in fact no evidence that suggests it would be better for kids to eat the same foods that adults do; nor that if they don't, they would suffer any adverse health effects. Kids may very well eat the way they do because that is how nature wants them to. We simply don't know. We do see anecdotally that even kids who don't gobble up daily buckets of arugula turn out just fine.

But for the moms in Jakarta, the concerns about their children not eating the way they wanted them to were profound and made them feel miserable. For us as marketers, it was easier to go with the flow, acknowledge their fears and position PediaSure as an answer. It made for happier moms and kids, and fewer mealtime battles.

Even so, our client, Abbott, was very conscientious about not making an over-the-top claim, and had invested in clinical studies and produced data to back up their core claim of balanced and complete nutrition. In contrast, many of their competitors in Asian markets were unrestrained and promised unproven benefits, like increased intelligence in the child using the illusion of causality.

In the pharmaceutical industry, drugs are serious business. Any claim you make must be supported by facts. Marketing by the illusion of causality gets the FDA's goat. Drug commercials commonly feature patients taking a medication and then dancing around like fireflies in the summer heat. After all, where is the proof that those specific activities will be possible from that particular drug for every patient? Thus, pharma companies have to qualify their claims and say that 'individual results vary' or that only a certain percentage of patients on the drug achieve those results.

Warning letters from the FDA to drug manufacturers fly fast and furious after every perceived infarction; they are dutifully recorded on a public website and make for some excellent in-between-flights reading,[6] if you are that kind of guy (which I am). You can exploit the illusion of causality to make people draw conclusions about your products without saying the words. But, just because you can, should you?

## The Dark Side of Cognitive Branding

There is a dark side to cognitive branding. We know that our brain processes information subconsciously or with low vigilance 95 per cent of the time. It takes mental short cuts and is susceptible to making some choices that are not the most beneficial for us. That is just how the brain works and there is no getting around it. Armed with the new knowledge of the mechanics of the brain, marketers may be tempted to devise strategies that benefit their brands at the expense of the consumers. But just because they can, should they?

This is becoming a major issue to grapple with in the digital age that we live in, where brand stimulus can be delivered at lightning speed to millions of consumers. A 2019 study[7] by researchers at the University of Chicago found substantial use of 'dark patterns' by a number of online retail brands. Dark patterns are 'user interface design choices that benefit an online service by coercing, steering, or deceiving users into making unintended and potentially harmful decisions'.

### Dark Patterns and the Trump 2020 Campaign

When consumers are messaged by a brand they trust, they tend to do what it says without a lot of vigilance. That is our System 1 at work. Unscrupulous marketers use this fact to exploit their customers. Towards the tail end of the 2020 US presidential election, Donald Trump's campaign, which was running on fumes financially, adopted dark patterns as a mantra for their fund-raising efforts.

It was business as usual for the campaign to create a virtual minefield of psychological traps on its online site to make donors unwittingly give a lot more than they planned to. For example, after you had committed to making a donation of, say, $100, the page would present a box that said in bold black letters 'We need to know we haven't lost you to the Radical Left. If you UNCHECK this box, we will have to tell Trump you're a DEFECTOR and sided with the Dems. CHECK this box and we can win the House and get Trump to run in 2024.' Yes, really!

The box was pre-checked with a tick mark and was followed by this statement in non-bold, smaller type, 'Make this a monthly recurring donation.' In other instances, the same small-type message signed visitors up for weekly donations!

'Confirmshaming' is a dark pattern technique for guilting the user into opting for something they didn't intend to. The option to decline is worded in such a way as to shame the user into compliance. In this case, you would be a 'defector' lost to the Radical Left if you so much as dared to uncheck the box.

'RoachMotel' is a trick that gets you into a situation which is not easy to get out of. For instance, if you did get signed up for weekly recurring donations to the campaign, cancelling them would be a tedious task.

'Misdirection' is when the site design purposefully focuses your attention on one thing in order to distract your attention from another. Here again, the first part of the message, which contains many things a Trump supporter might agree with, was prominent and the part about a monthly commitment was much less so and likely to missed as routine fine print.

I didn't cherry pick the above example. A *New York Times* investigation showed that the Trump campaign used dark patterns systematically and consistently to target their loyalists.[8] When Harry Brignull, a user experience designer, published his original list of dark patterns,[9] it was meant as a guide for marketers of what not to do. Who knew that the Trump campaign would make it their bible for exactly what to do. To be sure, Democrats, too, used some dark pattern techniques in their fundraising, but the Trump campaign mastered it into a fine art.

The same story by the *New York Times* also highlighted the case of one donor, a cancer patient, who gave a generous $500 to the campaign from his monthly income of $1000, only to have $3000 withdrawn from his account over the next thirty days, leading his bank to bounce his scheduled utility and rent payments.

Marketers, no matter their political leanings, would do well to remember that their actions have real consequences in real people's lives. With knowledge comes responsibility.

The researchers revealed that 11 per cent of the roughly 11,000 retail sites analysed used such tactics. Remarkably, there is a whole industry of third-party suppliers that sell dark pattern engines for rapid deployment by any retail website.

The researchers cataloged fifteen different types of dark patterns, some of which use psychological approaches, such as artificial scarcity (loss aversion bias), suspect peer reviews (in-group bias) and 'confirmshaming'. The latter refers to the practice of using negative language to describe actions that the consumer would take to reject a brand, for example, 'No thanks, I don't want to take advantage of this incredible offer.'

Online companies are investing heavily in the use of psychology in their branding and marketing. In 2015, Jeff Bezos, Amazon's CEO, rang many alarm bells when he announced to shareholders that his company used seventy million nudges per week through the company's Selling Coach programme.

One concern is that in the gig economy, marketers have asymmetrically more information than their customers.[10] By choosing what they disclose, marketers can influence consumer behaviour with significant power.

For example, when a website tells you that six people just bought the brand you are looking at, they know but fail to disclose that another 120 took a pass. Uber has come under scrutiny for using its information base to nudge drivers to work longer, which in turn keeps more drivers on the road and the price per ride low.[11] Instagram, WhatsApp, Twitter and virtually all other social networks are under scrutiny for hooking consumers to their devices by offering the brain small emotional rewards in the form of pings, alerts and notifications that can be addictive (they hit the same neural reward centres that drugs of abuse do).[12]

These concerns are not new to marketers. By definition, any brand stimulus is going to subconsciously influence consumers, from the music you play in your store to the shape of your packaging. The harder question is where do you draw the line?

## Three Tests for Ethical Cognitive Branding

Rather than be told by the government how to behave, marketers should regulate their own behaviour themselves. To help determine where to draw the line on what's ethical, in my company, Cerenti, we developed three imperatives for testing whether the brand strategies we were proposing were ethical:

1. **Canonical imperative:** Do to others as you would have them do to you. Ask the question: If someone did this to me, would I be fine with it?
2. **Categorical (Kantian) imperative:**[13] Do to others only that which, if done by everyone else too, would be good for society. Ask the question: If everybody started doing what I am doing, would that be good thing?
3. **Sunshine imperative:** Do only that which, if made public, can be easy to defend and explain. Ask the question: If this story broke on page one of the *New York Times*, am I going to look like scum?

RXBAR fails in the canonical imperative. Would you like it if the brands you buy were subtly embedding cues to make you believe that they offer benefits they actually don't?

Credit card companies that offer high interest rates and disproportionately low minimum payments, entrapping people in debt, failed all three tests. That is why they have earned a bad rap, become the punching bag for aspiring politicians, and been told by the government how to behave.

What about PediaSure implying that children will grow up healthy, physically and mentally, with its balanced and complete nutrition? I feel it clears all three tests fine. It meets the canonical imperative. Remember I told you that Walt, the marketing director, used to give PediaSure to all his kids and drink it himself regularly. No problem with the categorical imperative as well. If all kids started doing what Walt's kids were doing, no harm done. There is certainly plenty of evidence to show that the vitamins and minerals that PediaSure offers are beneficial for the human body. Abbott had also done clinical studies that established that PediaSure offered balanced and complete nutrition as defined by acceptable medical standards. One can reasonably expect those nutrients to contribute to the well-being of kids. It also meets the test of the sunshine imperative, in that if it were published that there is no evidence that healthier eating makes for healthier adult lives, people would understand that those are the normal uncertainties of life.

* * *

*Key Takeaways*

In some ways, this is the most important chapter in the book. Power with restraint is the best kind of strength. Cognitive brands work the way our brain works and for the good of our consumers. Stephen Genco puts it well when he says: 'Covert persuasion is unethical if it disrupts, disregards, or attempts to displace a consumer's existing goals with new goals that benefit the seller but do so by damaging the health, wealth, or happiness of the buyer.'[14]

I provide the three tests any branding program must pass for it to be an ethical cognitive brand:

- Canonical: Would you want somebody to do this to you?
- Categorical: Would it still be a good idea if everybody did this?

- Sunshine: Would you run for cover if everyone saw what you're doing?

In the next and final chapter, we close by taking a look at what lies in the future of cognitive branding.

# 13

# Where Do We Go from Here?

Brain sciences are advancing at a near-breakneck pace. In the future, brand marketers will know more and be able to do more. Yet, life will be harder, not easier. Some of that will be because we, brand marketers, will need to stay abreast of the scientific advances.

But the hardest part of the change will be the necessity of evolving ourselves, and our own minds. Let's take a look at what's coming down the road and at what we have to rewire inside our own heads.

## Read My Mind

What if you could get a computer printout of exactly what the customer is thinking? Wouldn't that make life a lot easier? That's the reason for the current fascination that many marketers have with the new wave of neuromarketing research.

For a long time, market research specialists have known well that customers don't always say what they do, and, in some cases, they may not be aware of what they might do when presented with certain brand choices. This makes it hard to figure out which brands consumers will actually buy through techniques like surveys of and focus group discussions with customers, which are the workhorse of marketing research. So, it is tempting to ask if there is a way to stick a probe through customers' ears and get a true reading of their thoughts and intent, maybe even the subconscious ones that they are not aware of. For marketers, that would be a really nice outcome.

With advances in brain science, there are many different tools for peering into the brain. You can strap consumers to electronic devices, expose them to a brand stimulus and see what lights up. While these techniques are still not completely developed, there is enough underway, and it is worthwhile for marketers to start dabbling in such research and get their feet wet.

One of the more accessible and promising tools to use these days are eye scanners. They can be either mounted at the bottom of a computer screen or in the form of a non-intrusive, eyeglasses-like wearable device. These are available, along with appropriate software, at a relatively low cost. The devices track eye movement and pupil dilation.

If a research subject is watching a brand advertisement on a computer monitor, the marketer can tell what part of the screen the person looked at, how long it took him to get to the desired areas of the picture, what the sequence of eye movements was that got him there and the level of reaction. As we have noted before, humans use relatively few visual cues to create a mental image and thus knowing precisely what parts matter in an advertisement or web page, can be valuable information.

New Balance, the sneakers manufacturer, fine-tuned its television campaign by using eye trackers. They compared two campaigns, one based around the idea of the consumer feeling fiercely independent in their New Balance footwear, and another around a community theme of 'your friends and family rooting for you to do well'. New Balance found that viewers engaged more intensely with the latter.

Marianne McLaughlin, Global Consumer Insights leader at New Balance, said: 'This allowed the company to efficiently zero in on the right campaign. Initially it was a learning curve – but the consistent delivery of highly impactful results (from eye trackers) built a level of trust, to the extent that today we require neuro evaluation of marketing, content, and programming. With a turnaround time of five to eight days, neuroscience compares favorably to more traditional approaches to creative testing. In the world of global fast fashion, we need to respond quickly. It's an absolute necessity[1].'

That sums it up pretty well. You get the idea.

Besides eye tracking, there are a number of other tools available to market researchers. Eye-tracking tools may be used in combination with software for facial expression analyses that can help you infer the type of emotional response and its valence (positive or negative).

Law enforcement agencies have long used lie detectors that measure skin conductance (the rate at which a person sweats) to predict whether a suspect is telling the truth or not. That's galvanic skin response (GSR) measurement and may be used to sense subconscious arousal to a brand stimulus.

Electroencephalography (EEG) measures the brain's electrical activity and can help determine brain engagement, motivation, frustration and cognitive workload. Academic researchers and those with a few million dollars to spare can buy a functional magnetic resonance imaging (fMRI) unit to directly peer into the brain's activity. fMRIs use changes in blood flow to detect areas of the brain that are in use and display them on computer screens in colourful three-dimensional plots.

But despite these technological advances, we are far from reading anybody's mind. And don't hold your breath, because we are not about to get there anytime soon. Even with the most advanced brain scanners, we can see that there is something going on in the brain, but interpreting what exactly it means is a whole different matter.

You may see that a subject is having an emotional reaction to your ad, but you can't tell what the emotion is or even if it is positive or negative. Research shows that the brain does not have hundreds of distinct neural areas dedicated to interpreting the multitude of emotions we feel. Instead, there may be just one 'core effect'[2] that we feel, which is interpreted by the brain in a thousand different ways based on context.

In a sense, your brain is like your cellphone screen. Tapping any part of it activates the same electronic sensor that sits underneath the display, but what the action means depends on what particular application was running at the time. Context can make the same effect mean a million different things. You could try to uncover that meaning by combining the information from multiple devices. But is it any better than just doing a focus group?

In certain limited scenarios, researchers have had phenomenal success with neuromarketing-based methods[3]. Researchers at Emory were able to predict a song's future popularity more accurately by observing fMRI signals within the subjects' brains than by simply asking them how much they liked the music. Similarly, a team led by Professor Moran Cerf at Northwestern was able to predict the future success of movies with 20 per cent greater accuracy by using EEG readings of audience members than by traditional methods[4].

So, there's something there. If you have the budget, it is worthwhile for you to figure out which areas of your marketing research can benefit from neuromarketing. But don't ditch your conventional research anytime soon.

A summary of the most commonly used tools in neuromarketing is provided in the following table:

## Table 1: Neuromarketing Tools[*]

*A variety of tools are being used to understand conscious and subconscious consumer reactions to brand messaging and experiences. These tools should generally be used in combination with other conventional research methods.*

| | BRAIN SCAN | | | BODY SCAN | |
|---|---|---|---|---|---|
| | METABOLIC CHANGES | ELECTRICAL CHANGES | | PHYSICAL CHANGES | |
| **Commonly Used Tool** | **fMRI** (functional magnetic resonance imaging) | **EEG** (electroencephalogram) | **Biometrics** | **Facial coding** | **Eye tracking** |
| **What it tracks** | Which parts of a person's brain are active and how active they are | How stimulated is the brain | How normal is a person's sweating, breathing and heart rate | How a person's facial muscles are reacting and changing | What a person is looking towards and whether the pupils are dilated |
| **What it does in response to a brand stimulus** | Maps oxygen and blood flow in regions of the brain known to be associated with specific functions or emotions | Detects electrical activity (usually ERPs)† caused by neurons firing in the brain at different frequencies and intensity | Uses a galvanometer and electrocardiogram (ECG) to measure changes in skin moisture (skin conductance) and heart activity | Uses cameras and software to detect and classify voluntary and involuntary movements of facial muscles into distinct expressions | Uses cameras and software to map pupil movement, angle and dilation |
| **What it could tell us about people** | • How stimulated is the brain<br>• What senses are being activated (sensory perception)<br>• What is getting coded into memory and can be recalled<br>• What emotions (including trust, craving, preference, loyalty) a person is feeling | • How attentive, engaged or excited is a person<br>• How quickly a person recognizes or recalls a stimulus<br>• Whether the person is reacting positively or negatively (valence) | • How stimulated is the person<br>• What is the level of emotional engagement | • What are the conscious and subconscious emotional responses<br>• Measures core emotions: anger, dislike, envy, fear, sadness, surprise, smile | • What in a visual draws focus, attention, excitement or confusion<br>• What parts of an image people scan for or focus on—and how quickly |

* Monica Diana Bercea, 'Anatomy of Methodologies for Measuring Consumer Behavior in Neuromarketing Research', 2012; D. Ariely and G.S. Berns, 'Neuromarketing: The Hope and Hype of Neuroimaging in Business', Nature Reviews, Neuroscience, 11(4), 2010, 284–92.

† ERP stands for event-related potential which is a specific neuron or neuron group firing as a result of a perceived stimulus.

| | | | | | |
|---|---|---|---|---|---|
| **Common brand research applications** | • Testing emotional and sensory response to new products or campaigns<br>• Rebranding<br>• Predicting choices<br>• Identifying needs | • Testing video advertisements, including identifying key moments<br>• Testing taglines and copy<br>• Testing in-store experiences and website usability | • Testing video advertisements or trailers<br>• Measuring emotional reactions in real-world environments | • Testing subconscious spontaneous emotional reactions to campaigns | • Improving web design<br>• Testing store/shelf layout and customer experience<br>• Testing package design<br>• Establishing hierarchy of perception (what is noticed first/last) |
| **What are the advantages** | • Gold standard for predicting future decision-making and measuring specific emotions | • More portable and less expensive than fMRI<br>• Extreme time-sensitivity allows researchers to pinpoint exact stimuli that cause reactions<br>• Can measure rapidly changing reactions<br>• Less intrusive | • Good portability and ability to detect a range of emotions<br>• Non-intrusive | • Relatively ease in measuring spontaneous and unconscious reactions<br>• Non-intrusive<br>• Less expensive<br>• Easy to use | • Easy portability allows for in-field testing<br>• Non-intrusive<br>• Less expensive<br>• Easy to use |
| **What are the limitations** | • Very expensive; limited to small sample sizes<br>• Requires subject to lie still inside a lab machine, for a long time<br>• Tested tasks can have limited complexity<br>• Less time-sensitive than EEG | • Low spatial resolution means it cannot measure precise emotions, only valence<br>• May be overly sensitive to irrelevant stimuli | • Cannot tell the valence of emotion (excitement and stress look similar)<br>• Physiologic responses lag several seconds behind brain activity, making time-determinations impossible | • Some subjectivity in coding emotions, especially with a large range of facial structures | • Software and equipment can be expensive<br>• Reliant on participant's eye condition<br>• Considered to be less reliable; requires a large sample<br>• Often used in combination with EEG |

So, what are marketers to do until such time as we can read people's minds with a hand-held scope? My view is that good qualitative research is the key to uncovering insights that result in great brands. The supercomputer nesting inside our own skulls is not perfect but pretty darn good when suitably trained in the craft.

Those deep in the art of marketing sciences will immediately point out that methods like focus group discussions are overused and flawed. True, but so are all other methods, including those based on neuromarketing. The real trick is to not rely too much on any one method but to use many different ones.

When you are trying to understand the mind of a consumer, it is akin to understanding personal relationships. To decide how great a work colleague is, you may look at how good they are as an individual contributor when they have to produce a work product without help; as a team member when they have to deliver a result for which they must depend on others; and as a person whom you might be stuck with at an airport for several hours and just have a chilled beer with.

Likewise, to get real insights into consumers, instead of just one method, use a mix of them, including in-depth individual interviews (IDIs), focus group discussions (FGDs), metaphor elicitation techniques (involves approaches like interpretive storytelling and image association) and in-home observational research.[5]

## Making Sense

While the senses are the gateway to our minds, there are more such portals than you think, and, in the future, we may discover even more. As a marketer, you will want to keep an eye on that too.

Senses have been regarded by philosophers as irreducible sensations. That means you cannot explain a sense to anyone who does not know it already. If one your five senses has not worked from the time you were born, it is impossible for anyone to explain that sensation to you in a way that you could understand the experience of that sense.

We have more than five senses, maybe twice that or more.[6] For instance, there are senses in our body to track its balance and velocity. If you have ever walked into a solid wall while checking your Instagram feed and felt the world spin dizzyingly around you, you have experienced what these senses do.

For companies whose brand experiences involve putting you in motion, these hidden senses are important to know and manage. Airlines have to design a flight takeoff and landing experience that does not cause nausea. Thus, they don't have aircraft take off as fast and at as sharp an angle as they are mechanically capable of. Disney Parks, on the other hand, may want you to feel that pit in your stomach on its *Star Wars* 'Rise of the Resistance' ride when the ship jumps into hyperspace.

In the future, scientists may invent devices that generate entirely new human senses. For example, we may wear devices that allow us to sense electric fields, in the way sharks do, or the earth's magnetic field, like bats do. Those would be the technological breakthroughs of a lifetime and would create a whole new dimension of brand experiences.

Already, gaming companies are playing with virtual reality (VR) systems that enhance our perceptions of reality. In the future, augmented senses will be as common as Apple Watches and require marketers to rethink their brand experiences more expansively.

## Fire Yourself!

The hardest challenge for marketers lies not in tracking the technological advances but in evolving their own mindsets. Cognitive branding is like a new religion. You need to activate your System 2 processes to truly get it, but this mental process is lazy and takes a lot of effort to utilize.

When I teach cognitive branding in workshops with companies, I see that people try to reduce it to something that they know already (see Box 1 to check if you do). After all, if it is like something you already know, then there is no need to spend any time and effort on learning it. 'Isn't this just like functional and emotional branding?' they ask. Or, 'This is the same behavioural research we have been doing, right?' chime in others. Nothing could be further from the truth, but that is their System 1 trying to associate the new knowledge of cognitive branding to something familiar and old. It is a natural reaction, but also a reliable formula for not learning.

Cognitive branding is the forte of the marketers who want to think about and constantly question what they see in customers and markets. Several of my clients have established incredibly detailed processes for launching innovative products. Every step in the process gets its own box, with a carefully assigned step number (think something like '3.6.2'), and customer research is churned out mechanically. Unfortunately, the better the process, the worse the outcome.

Process maps feel comfortable in corporate environments because they fit well with project management Gantt charts. They create an illusion of progress. Brand strategies arising from these are often unremarkable, falling deep into the sea of sameness. Cognitive branding does not fit neatly into the current boxes. Accepting that can be difficult but can help create spectacular brands that customers love.

Ravi Dhar, a behavioural sciences professor at the Yale School of Management who has done a lot of work on the psychology of consumer decision-making, notes that change is hard because it creates uncertainty.[7] One of Dhar's executive programme trainees, an insights executive from a bank, said, 'What I learnt after three days (in a class about behavioural sciences) is that I should fire myself, and we should do things totally differently.' So true! For those with that kind of self-awareness, the rewards from cognitive branding are extraordinary.

The brand marketers of the future need to dive a lot deeper into the fields of behavioural psychology and the science of human emotions. These areas are experiencing explosive growth, and marketers need to not only stay on top of the new research but also figure out how to apply it to their brands. They have to think more and strive to connect the dots better between science and consumer psychology.

In the coming years, we will continue to learn more and more about ourselves and how our brain works. What we know already today is game-changing. No matter how that plays out, the future of cognitive branding will remain *Right between Our Ears*.

Cognitive Branding Knowledge Essentials

You may know cognitive branding already if:

- You are reasonably conversant with the following five fields of study and research:
    - Evaluative conditioning and priming (see Chapter 4 on brand vibes)
    - Dual Processing Theory, System 1 process of the brain (see Chapter 5 on instinctive brand sense)
    - Cognitive behaviour therapy principles and System 2 process of the brain (see Chapter 6 on deliberative brand sense)
    - Self-determination theory (see Chapter 7 on brand resolve)
    - Peak-end rule (see Chapter 10 on brand activation)

- You have used the knowledge from these fields to make your brands better
- You have both failed and succeeded on those efforts

# Acknowledgements

In my life, I have been fortunate to have had many teachers. Not just the ones in dusty classrooms, from St Xaviers in Jaipur to Yale University in New Haven, but everywhere around me, from my brilliant peers at Cerenti and discerning clients around the world to my always curious friends and family. I have soaked in what I learnt from them like a wet rag under a water fountain. In this book, I squeeze the rag and let the water drip out, if only to make room for more.

I would especially like to thank some of the early soldiers who slogged through the first draft of the manuscript, which at the time was more of a brain dump than a real book. Bill Dempsey—when he was not in a meeting with the four boards he is on, or biking the fifty miles that he regularly does in the Florida sun, or teaching disadvantaged kids—was reading my notes and sending detailed emails with useful feedback. Alok Sharma, who himself is an in-demand, innovative analytic marketer, helped to take the manuscript to a whole new level. Sam Hill, one of the best writers I know, has given measured counsel throughout my journey as a fledgling writer, from the time we both worked at Booz Allen, to now, when he has no reason to bother. Sam made sure I didn't embarrass myself then with my prose, or now. Dane Tyson, who worked as a partner at Cerenti, warned me that his advice on the book would dwell solely on the negatives. That preamble was followed dutifully by a tightly wound, 3000-word, single-spaced essay, with three levels of bulleted points delivering on the said premise. Steve Genco, who is probably the most serious thinker about the implications of brain sciences for marketing, was generous with his time and provided several thoughtful suggestions on improving the core cognitive branding principles. His own book, *Intuitive Marketing*, is the most rigorous tome on cognitive marketing that readers wishing for deeper technical details on the underlying research would want to reach for.

Those brave souls were not the only ones to endure readings of the early manuscript. Jay Prenta, Shyam Khemani, Atul Mathur, Nikhil Pandit, Allan Weiss, Sharat Mathur and Sharad Bhargava were among the many accomplished marketers who weighed in. In writing this book, I discovered that the publishing industry lives on a planet of its own, with its own unique laws of gravity. Anna Biehn, Michele Wucker and Hank Gilman offered valuable lessons on how to navigate the terrain.

Most of the ideas in the book came from my consulting practice. At Cerenti, we have had a culture of holding ourselves accountable for uncovering the truths in branding through unflinching debate. It eats up a lot of time, but often results in very cool insights for helping our clients build epic brands. So, I thank the many colleagues who worked with me on our many branding engagements, including Sudeep Haldar, Aryaman Sudhama (spent a whole summer on research for the book), Danlei Yan, Rachel Lee, Kathryn Mertes-Egland, Dane Tyson, Lynn Whitman, Mark Grossman, Jim Evans, Dipanjan Chatterjee, Cesare Espinosa (deputized from Mastercard), Erik Leipman (on loan from Pinnacle Biologics), Rima Nair,

Puja Lakhanpal, Constantin Loghinov, Silvana Hernandez, Jonathan SooHoo, Mike Connors and Terioska Gamez. It was work for sure, but it was always amazing fun.

Our best clients at Cerenti were exacting and pushed us to dig deep into the recesses of marketing to unearth the best answers for them. After all, it was their money and brands at risk. I want to particularly thank Matt Fisher, Willy Pardinas, Keli Walbert, Guillermo Herrera, Gustavo Abelenda, Ian Jarrett, Tim Walbert, Mark Silverman, Lutz Schlitz, Todd Smith, Brent Paul, Jorge Alfaro, Jaime Parades (always unafraid to test new ideas), Kezia Zito, Erik Von Borcke, Greg Tatsukawa, John Lane, Andy Leong, Vikram Karnani, Vivek Mohan, Susan Hazelwood, Paul Catenero, Ulises Vergara, John Kody, Aaron Lillybridge, Rafael Arana, Ignacio Lara, Prashant Shah, Alain Delongchamp, Jill Rahman, Joep Wijman and Peter Kaemmerer.

I would also like to thank my agent, Kanishka Gupta of Writer's Side, for his undiminished faith in the book. Judging by the fifteen-minute lapse of time between my sending him the book proposal and his calling back to ask for an exclusive, I can only guess that he read just the first two lines before throwing his full weight behind the project. Radhika Marwah, the commissioning editor at Penguin Random House India, has been an equally confident advocate and steady voice in guiding me through the complexity of publishing a book in India while sitting comfortably in Chicago. Last but not least, not too many things can aspire for greatness if they are brimming with imperfections. I thank Vineet Gill, my copy editor, for ensuring that no reader would be discomfited by a letter or word out of place or sentence searching for coherence.

I also want to give a shout-out here to my good friend Hitendra Wadhwa, who teaches an inspirational course on inner personal leadership at Columbia University in New York.

Two summers ago, he invited me to sit in on some of his classes and ruminate on what, at this stage of my life, my own purpose in life might be. That clarity followed from the team of super-bright students I was paired with, who asked of me, 'Why haven't you written a book?' I didn't have a great answer for them then. But now, here it is. Thank you, guys! You know who you are.

My family encouraged me throughout this project in innumerable ways. My two sons, who are normally a step ahead of me in all matters related to the emerging arts and sciences, and routinely disagree with my theses, were a recurrent test bed for my ideas. Ishaan was among the first to suggest that methods developed in the practice of cognitive behavioural therapy may be a source of inspiration for choice paradigms. Ashwin was helpful in identifying tech brands for my case studies. My wife, Sujata, who has a natural instinct for spotting and buying great brands, helped research case studies on South Asian brands.

Even as I acknowledge many of my teachers above, the two things I can be certain of is that I have neither named them all nor thanked them enough. I hope they will rest content in the knowledge that this book and what I have become would not have been possible without them.

# Notes

## Part One: How Brain Science Is Revolutionizing Branding

### Introduction: Brands That Rock


1. Court, David and Dayal, Sandeep 'Beyond Behavioral Bounds', *Marketing Management*, September–October 2002, p. 28.
2. 'Directory of Academic Experts in Behavioral Science', Harvard.edu, https://cpl.hks.harvard.edu/files/cpl/files/for_website_directory_of_academic_experts.pdf?m=1437146451
3. 'Fact Sheet: BRAIN Initiative', the White House, Office of the Press Secretary, 2 April 2013, https://obamawhitehouse.archives.gov/the-press-office/2013/04/02/fact-sheet-brain-initiative
4. A. Tom Horvath, Kaushik Misra, Amy K. Epner and Galen Morgan Cooper, 'Drug Seeking and Cravings: Addictions' Effect on the Brain's Reward System', Centersite.net, https://www.centersite.net/poc/view_doc.php?type=doc&id=48375&cn=1408


### Chapter 1: Beyond the Illusions of the Past: A Quick View of What's New and Different


1. Elizabeth A. Kensinger, 'Remembering the Details: Effects of Emotion', *Emotion Review: Journal of the International Society for Research on Emotion*, vol. 1, 2, 2009, pp. 99–113.
2. Ellie Parker and Adrian Furnham, 'Does Sex Sell? The Effect of Sexual Programme Content on the Recall of Sexual and Non-Sexual

Advertisements', *Applied Cognitive Psychology*, volume 21, issue 9, December 2007, pp. 1217–1228.

3. Martin Lindstrom, *Buyology: Truth and Lies about Why We Buy* (New York: Currency, 2008), pp. 181–82.
4. The Think-Feel-Act model is also a variation of the classic AIDA (Attention, Interest, Desire and Action) model, which was invented as a sales, not marketing, tool.
5. George Lakoff and Mark Johnson, *Philosophy in the Flesh* (New York: Basic Books, 1999), p. 13, '. . . rule of thumb among cognitive scientists: unconscious thought is 95 percent of all thought.'
   Gerald Zaltman, *How Customers Think: Essential Insights into the Mind of the Market* (Boston: Harvard Business School Publishing, 2003).
6. R.B. Zajonc, 'Feeling and Thinking: Closing the Debate over the Independence of Affect', 2000, in J. P. Forgas (ed.), *Studies in Emotion and Social Interaction*, second series, Cambridge University Press, 'Feeling and Thinking: The Role of Affect in Social Cognition', pp. 31–58.
7. The dual processing theory of thought predates Kahneman's description of it, however he deserves credit for making it come to life more memorably than had been done by those before him.
8. James N. Druckman, 'Evaluating Framing Effects', *Journal of Economic Psychology* 22, 2001, pp. 91–101.
9. Heidi Mitchell, 'Can a Person Learn While Sleeping?' *Wall Street Journal*, 16 March 2019, https://www.wsj.com/articles/can-a-person-learn-while-sleeping-11552744800
   Wilhelm, I. Diekelmann, J. S. Born, 'Sleep in Children Improves Memory Performance on Declarative but not Procedural Tasks', *Learning and Memory*, 25 April 2008, Cold Spring Harbor Laboratory.
10. For a good and accessible discussion on how we learn through processes of 'incubation' and 'percolation', see the book *How We Learn: The Surprising Truth about When, Where, and Why It Happens* by Benedict Carey (Random House, 2014).

## Chapter 2: Right between Your Ears: How the Marketing Brain Works

1. Lama Chahine and Ghassan Kanazi, 'Phantom Limb Syndrome: A Review', M.E.J. Anesth. 19 (2), pp. 345–55, 2007, https://pdfs.semanticscholar.org/0f8d/2b80b5c20ed0e21076de4b5ac48327ca05d2.pdf.

'Phantom limb syndrome is a condition in which patients experience sensations, whether painful or otherwise, in a limb that does not exist. It has been reported to occur in 80–100% of amputees, and typically has a chronic course, often resistant to treatment.'

2. 'Collections and Research made by the Michigan Pioneer and Historical Society', *Historical Collections*, volume 28, Annual Meeting 1898, 1900, p. 436.
3. Robynne Boyd, 'Do People Only Use 10 Percent of Their Brains?', *Scientific American*, 7 February 2008, https://www.scientificamerican.com/article/do-people-only-use-10-percent-of-their-brains
4. Jared A. Nielsen, Brandon A. Zielinski, Michael A. Ferguson, Janet E. Lainhart and Jeffrey S. Anderson, 'An Evaluation of the Left-Brain vs. Right-Brain Hypothesis with Resting State Functional Connectivity Magnetic Resonance Imaging', 14 August 2013, https://journals.plos.org/plosone/article?id=10.1371/journal.pone.0071275
5. K. Roy, A. Jaiswal and P. Panda, 'Towards Spike-Based Machine Intelligence with Neuromorphic Computing', *Nature* 575, pp. 607–617, 2019, https://www.nature.com/articles/s41586-019-1677-2
6. 'Human Brain for Kids: Graphic on Functions of the Different Parts of the Brain', https://k8schoollessons.com/wp-content/uploads/2018/08/functions-of-brain.jpg
7. Mercey Livingston, 'Boost Happy Hormones like Serotonin and Dopamine: Here's What You Can Do', CNET, 18 November 2020, https://www.cnet.com/news/boost-happy-hormones-like-serotonin-and-dopamine-heres-what-you-can-do/
8. Educalingo, https://educalingo.com/en/dic-en/conation
9. Kolby Wisdom™, http://www.kolbe.com/why-kolbe/kolbe-wisdom/
10. Stephen J. Genco, *Intuitive Marketing* (Intuitive Consumer Insights LLC, 2019) p. 357.

## Part Two: How to Design Cognitive Brands

### Chapter 3: Brands That Work the Way the Brain Does: A Four-Part Model for Building Cognitive Brands

1. Kevin L. Rand and Stephen S. Ilardi, 'Toward a Consilient Science of Psychology', *Journal of Clinical Psychology*, vol. 61(1), 2005.
2. Nick McCullum, 'Case Study: How 3G Capital Squeezed More Out of Heinz', Sure Dividend, 4 September 2017, https://www.suredividend.com/3g-capital-heinz

3. David Hume, *A Treatise of Human Nature*, Book 2, Part 3, Section 2 (New York: Oxford University Press, 2007).
4. Allan Chen, 'Peering into the Brain with Chemical Biosensors', *Science and Technology Review*, Lawrence Livermore National Laboratory, October–November 2016.
5. 'Viser': to target, to directly aim at, https://en.wiktionary.org/wiki/viser#French

## Chapter 4: Brand Vibes: Tugging at the Heartstrings

1. W. Hofmann, J. De Houwer, M. Perugini, F. Baeyens, G. Crombez, 'Evaluative Conditioning in Humans: A Meta-Analysis', *Psychological Bulletin* 136 (3), 2010, pp. 390–421.
2. More precisely, in psychology, priming is a specific and different phenomenon whereby one stimulus is thought to subconsciously influence another that follows. This means that when certain thoughts are seeded in your mind, other related ones will be activated with greater ease in a process that psychologists refer to as 'spreading activation'. See also, Daniel Reisberg, *Cognition: Exploring the Science of the Mind* (2007), pp. 255, 517.
3. Dior J'Adore Absolu TV commercial, 'The New Absolu: The Film', featuring Charlize Theron, song by Kanye West, 2018, https://www.ispot.tv/ad/davv/dior-jadore-absolu-the-new-absolu-the-film-featuring-charlize-theron-song-by-kanye-west
4. Sneha Yadav, '#Brand Saga Strong Women & Memorable Ads: The Tanishq Advertising Journey', Social Samosa, 26 September 2019, http://www.socialsamosa.com/2019/09/brand-saga-tanishq-advertising-journey/
5. 'Tanishq Breaks New Ground, Celebrates Remarriage with New-Age Collection', YouTube, https://www.youtube.com/watch?v=jqggcpL79qw
6. 'Mia - #BestAtWork', YouTube, https://youtu.be/qymYx4EhTbc
7. 'WEBFILM - Our Blades Are F***ing Great', YouTube, https://www.youtube.com/watch?v=0YwMwTZw12k
8. For a fabulous in-depth case study on the Dollar Shave Club, read the book *Billion Dollar Brand Club* by Lawrence Ingrassia, pp. 1–22.
9. Robert Cialdini, *Influence: The Psychology of Persuasion* (New York: Harper Business, 2006).
10. Celebrex TV commercial, 'Body in Motion', iSpot.tv, https://www.ispot.tv/ad/7V7z/celebrex-body-in-motion

11. Jelani Cobb, 'Behind Nike's Decision to Stand by Colin Kaepernick', *New Yorker*, 4 September 2018, https://www.newyorker.com/news/daily-comment/behind-nikes-decision-to-stand-by-colin-kaepernick
12. Soo Youn, 'Nike Sales Booming After Colin Kaepernick Ad, Invalidating Critics', ABC News, 21 December 2018, https://abcnews.go.com/Business/nike-sales-booming-kaepernick-ad-invalidating-critics/story?id=59957137
13. Mary Hanbury, 'The Rise and Fall of Victoria's Secret, America's Biggest Lingerie Retailer', Business Insider, 20 February 2020, https://www.businessinsider.com/victorias-secret-rise-and-fall-history-2019-5

## Chapter 5: Brand Sense: Using System 1 Easers to Go with the Flow

1. Sadahiko Nakajima, Mariko Yamamoto and Natsumi Yoshimoto, 'Dogs Look Like Their Owners: Replications with Racially Homogenous Owner Portraits', *Anthrozoos*, vol. 22, issue 2, June 2009, https://go.gale.com/ps/anonymous?id=GALE%7CA207324088&sid=googleScholar&v=2.1&it=r&linkaccess=abs&issn=08927936&p=AONE&sw=w
2. T.L. Chartrand and J.A. Bargh, 'The Chameleon Effect: The Perception–Behavior Link and Social Interaction', *Journal of Personality and Social Psychology*, 76(6), 1999, pp. 893–910, https://psycnet.apa.org/doiLanding?doi=10.1037%2F0022-3514.76.6.893
3. Eric Jaffe, 'Mirror Neurons: How We Reflect on Behavior', Association for Psychological Science, 1 May 2007, https://www.psychologicalscience.org/observer/mirror-neurons-how-we-reflect-on-behavior
4. Interestingly, one possible short cut to opening your mind and rewiring your System 1 circuits is through the use of psychedelic drugs. Recent research suggests that psychedelics, like MDMA, LSD and psilocybin (magic mushrooms), may alter the biochemical bonds in the brain's neural network. Research from Johns Hopkins University showed that adult mice that had stopped learning certain new social skills by a certain age could be rewired with MDMA to learn those skills, just like younger mice. Now, because System 1 is capable of borrowing its knowledge from the System 2 of others, you might be tempted to try psychedelic drugs. After all, if researchers at Hopkins, with their prodigious System 2 brains, think there is something to it, does not your System 1 tell you this is a possibility? Before you proceed, you may want to remember that the subjects in this research were dispensable, 'we'll-make-more' rodents. On a more serious note, research with psychedelics

is expanding with human subjects and is showing promise in a number of common mental diseases.

5. Tim Henderson, 'Too Many Pedestrians Injured by Looking at Their Phones', Governing.com, 11 December 2014, https://www.governing.com/topics/transportation-infrastructure/too-many-pedestrians-injured-by-looking-at-their-phones.html
6. S.J. Maglio and T. Reich, 'Choice Protection for Feeling-Focused Decisions', *Journal of Experimental Psychology*, 16 January 2020, https://www.researchgate.net/publication/338635749_Choice_protection_for_feeling-focused_decisions
7. Daniel Kahneman, *Thinking Fast and Slow* (New York: Farrar, Straus and Giroux, 2013), chapter 5, 'Cognitive Ease'.
8. Tatiana Homonoff (NYU Robert F. Wagner School of Public Service), Lee-Sien Kao (ideas42), Doug Palmer (ideas42), Christina Seybolt (University of Chicago Energy and Environment Lab), 'Skipping the Bag, Assessing the impact of Chicago's Tax on Disposable Bags', ideas42, September 2018, https://www.ideas42.org/wp-content/uploads/2018/09/Bag_Tax_Paper_final.pdf. In their study, they say that while '82% of customers used disposable bags prior to the tax, this fraction declined to 40% after the tax was implemented. In contrast to the overwhelming impact of the tax, a five-cent bonus for reusable bag use had almost no impact on disposable bag use, evidence consistent with a model of loss aversion'.
9. Andrew K. Przybylski, Kou Murayama, Cody R. DeHaan and Valerie Gladwell, 'Motivational, Emotional, and Behavioral Correlates of Fear of Missing Out', *Computers in Human Behavior*, 29 (4).
10. 'Announcing the Fyre Festival', YouTube, 12 January 2017, https://youtu.be/mz5kY3RsmKo
11. Sandeep Dayal, Helene Landesberg, and Michael Zeisser, 'How to Build Trust Online', *McKinsey Quarterly*, 2003.
12. Michael I. Norton, Daniel Mochon and Dan Ariely, 'The IKEA Effect: When Labor Leads to Love', *Journal of Consumer Psychology*, 22 (3), July 2012, https://dash.harvard.edu/bitstream/handle/1/12136084/norton%20mochon%20ariely%20third%20round%5b1%5d.pdf?sequence=3&isAllowed=y
13. Tang TV advertisement in Pakistan, YouTube, 2018, https://youtu.be/yfpEQn9XNDM
14. Lizzie Widdicombe, 'How Everlane Hacked Your Wardrobe', *New Yorker*, 25 September 2017, https://www.newyorker.com/culture/on-and-off-the-avenue/how-everlane-hacked-your-wardrobe

15. Laura Stevens, 'On Amazon, Fake Products Plague Smaller Brands', *Wall Street Journal*, 19 July 2018, https://www.wsj.com/articles/on-amazon-fake-products-plague-smaller-brands-1532001601
16. Sascha Topolinski and Fritz Strack, 'Scanning the "Fringe" of Consciousness: What Is Felt and What Is Not Felt in Intuitions about Semantic Coherence', *Consciousness and Cognition*, volume 18, issue 3, September 2009, pp. 608–618, Department of Psychology II, Social Psychology, University of Wuerzburg, Germany.
17. Guinness TV commercial, 'Wheelchair Basketball', iSpot.tv, https://www.ispot.tv/ad/7bSd/guinness-wheelchair-basketball
18. Guinness reveals 'Made of More' advertising campaign created by AMV BBDO, TheDrum.com, 1 October 2012, https://www.thedrum.com/news/2012/10/01/guinness-reveals-made-more-advertising-campaign-created-amv-bbdo
19. Stephen J. Genco, *Intuitive Marketing*, chapter 7, pp. 115–130.
20. As a side note, I would add that rheumatologists have had the last laugh over their peers. When Remicade, a cutting-edge biologic drug, was launched, it was a 'buy-and-bill' medication, meaning that the physician would buy the drug and earn a mark up on it each time it was used. Also, the drug was one of the most expensive ($20,000–$30,000 per year) at the time, and infused in the physician's office only, which meant there was a ton of money to be made. Rheumatology was overnight transformed from being one of the lowest compensated medical professions to one of the highest—certainly leaving primary care physicians in the dust.
21. 'Who Sharpened Occam's Razor?', IrishPhilosophy.com, http://www.irishphilosophy.com/2014/05/27/who-sharpened-occams-razor/
22. Aristotle, *Analytica Posteriora*.

## Chapter 6: Brand Sense: Using System 2 Deliberators to Give New Religion

1. https://www.businesstoday.in/magazine/lbs-case-study/how-kraft-foods-won-over-customers-in-china-and-india/story/193162.html, Koellmann, Benjamin, Smart Cookie, Business Today, March 31, 2013
2. S.G. Hofmann, A. Asnaani, I.J. Vonk, A.T. Sawyer and A. Fang, 'The Efficacy of Cognitive Behavioral Therapy: A Review of Meta-analyses', *Cognitive Therapy and Research*, 36 (5), 2012, pp. 427–40, https://www.ncbi.nlm.nih.gov/pmc/articles/PMC3584580/table/T1/?report=objectonly. In several clinical trials, cognitive behavioural

therapy (CBT) has been shown to be superior to medicines like SSRIs in the case of a number of common psychological disorders.
3. David D. Burns, *Feeling Good: The New Mood Therapy* (New York: Harper, 1999).
4. Evan Mayo-Wilson, Sofia Dias, Ifigeneia Mavranezouli, Kayleigh Kew, David M. Clark, A.E. Ades and Stephen Pilling, 'Psychological and Pharmacological Interventions for Social Anxiety Disorder in Adults: A Systematic Review and Network Meta-analysis, *Lancet Psychiatry*, 2014, 1, pp. 368–76, published online 26 September 2014, https://www.thelancet.com/journals/lanpsy/article/PIIS2215-0366(14)70329-3/fulltext
5. These experiments are described in detail in Chapter 3 of Ariely's book *Predictably Irrational* (New York: Harper Perennial, 2010).
6. https://www.youtube.com/watch?v=3iIkOi3srLo, Follow the Frog, YouTube
7. Opdivo TV commercial, iSpot.tv, 'A Chance to Live Longer', https://www.ispot.tv/ad/wIsF/opdivo-a-chance-to-live-longer
8. In fact, the cost of the treatment can exceed $250,000 as many patients require a combination of expensive drugs. Deena Beasley, 'The Cost of Cancer: New Drugs Show Success at a Steep Price', Reuters, 3 April 2017, https://www.reuters.com/article/us-usa-healthcare-cancer-costs/the-cost-of-cancer-new-drugs-show-success-at-a-steep-price-idUSKBN1750FU
9. K. Witte and M. Allen, 'A Meta-Analysis of Fear Appeals: Implications for Effective Public Health Programs', *Health Education and Behavior*, 27 (5), 591–615, 2000. G. Hastings, M. Stead and J. Webb, 'Fear Appeals in Social Marketing: Strategic and Ethical Reasons for Concern', *Psychology and Marketing*, 21 (11), 2004, pp. 961–86.
10. 'CDC: Tips from Former Smokers – Terrie's Tip Ad', YouTube, 15 March 2012, https://www.youtube.com/watch?v=5zWB4dLYChM. Terrie unfortunately died in 2013. The CDC released the following statement: 'The Centers for Disease Control and Prevention (CDC) mourns the passing of Terrie Hall, one of the people featured in CDC's Tips From Former Smokers® (Tips®) national tobacco education campaign. Terrie, 53, died Monday, September 16, 2013, from the cancer she fought so bravely during the final 13 years of her life. "The passing of this public health hero is a loss for us all, and a reminder to heed her warning about the dangers of smoking," said Tim McAfee, MD, MPH, director, Office on Smoking and Health.' (https://www.cdc.gov/tobacco/campaign/tips/stories/anti-smoking-champion-

terrie-hall-dies.html#:~:text=The%20Centers%20for%20Disease%20Control%20and%20Prevention%20(CDC),during%20the%20final%2013%20years%20of%20her%20life)

11. 'The Facts about Scare Tactics', Regional Center for Health Communities, Metrowest, Education Development Center, http://masstapp.edc.org/sites/masstapp.edc.org/files/Talking%20points%20about%20scare%20tactics_0.pdf
12. Enbrel TV commercial, 'My Mom's Pain', iSpot.tv, https://www.ispot.tv/ad/w1X2/enbrel-my-moms-pain
13. Xarelto TV commercial, 'Not Today', iSpot.tv, https://www.ispot.tv/ad/Z5DV/xarelto-not-today
14. https://en.wikipedia.org/wiki/Dumb_Ways_to_Die
15. https://www.youtube.com/watch?v=IJNR2EpS0jw, Dumb Ways to Die, Nov 15, 2012, YouTube, 187 million views
16. 'The Warby Parker Marketing Strategy Decoded', TapJoy, 19 September 2019, https://www.tapjoy.com/resources/warby-parker-marketing-strategy/
17. Danny Parisi, 'They Have One Goal, Take Over the World', Glossy, 16 May 2019, https://www.glossy.co/fashion/they-have-one-goal-take-over-the-world-how-independent-eyewear-brands-compete-with-the-behemoth-of-essilorluxottica
18. Carey K. Morewedge and Colleen E. Giblin, 'Explanations of the Endowment Effect: An Integrative Review', *Trends in Cognitive Sciences*, 19 (6), 2015, pp. 339–348, https://s3.amazonaws.com/academia.edu.documents/37850808/EndowmentReview.pdf?response-content-disposition=inline%3B%20filename%3DExplanations_of_the_endowment_effect_an.pdf&X-Amz-Algorithm=AWS4-HMAC-SHA256&X-Amz-Credential=AKIAIWOWYYGZ2Y53UL3A%2F20200316%2Fus-east-1%2Fs3%2Faws4_request&X-Amz-Date=20200316T200922Z&X-Amz-Expires=3600&X-Amz-SignedHeaders=host&X-Amz-Signature=d7c3b1e40f72673b65f6e728df2e363eac63ce8d5005cce4137d9b55accfbeb3
19. https://www.ispot.tv/ad/7Jim/prudential-the-prudential-magnets-experiment
20. Stephen Pulvirent, 'The Untold Story Of Watchmaking's Most Iconic Advertising Campaign: The "Generations" Campaign Of Patek Philippe', Hodinkee, 27 December 2016, https://www.hodinkee.com/articles/untold-story-patek-philippe-generations-advertising-campaign
21. Slavoj Žižek, *Less Than Nothing: Hegel and the Shadow of Dialectical Materialism* (London: Verso, 2012).

22. Edward Jay Epstein, 'Have You Ever Tried to Sell a Diamond?', *Atlantic*, February 1982, https://www.theatlantic.com/magazine/archive/1982/02/have-you-ever-tried-to-sell-a-diamond/304575/
23. Actually, wurtzite boron nitride and lonsdaleite are harder and rarer in nature. Lonsdaleite is sometimes formed when graphite meteorites slam into Earth, while wurtzite boron nitride is created under extremely high temperatures and pressures in volcanic eruptions. Jessica Griggs, 'Diamond No Longer Nature's Hardest Material', *New Scientist*, 16 February 2009, https://www.newscientist.com/article/dn16610-diamond-no-longer-natures-hardest-material/#ixzz68b0Laio9

## Chapter 7: Brand Resolve: A Mantra for Happiness

1. Steve Genco provides a great overview of such research in his book *Intuitive Marketing*, in Chapter 11, 'Consumer Goal in Action', pp. 197–223. As I mentioned earlier, he elegantly simplifies the problem of inaction by suggesting two *universal* motivations that drive behaviour. The first is the desire to be happier and better off tomorrow than today; and the second is the need to feel good about ourselves and others.
2. M. Milyavskaya, and K.M. Werner, 'Goal Pursuit: Current State of Affairs and Directions for Future Research', *Canadian Psychology/Psychologie canadienne*, 59 (2), pp. 163–175, 2018.
3. B.S. Wiese, 'Successful Pursuit of Personal Goals and Subjective Well-Being', in B.R. Little, K. Salmela-Aro and S.D. Phillips (eds.), '*Personal Project Pursuit: Goals, Action, and Human Flourishing*, pp. 301–28, Lawrence Erlbaum Associates Publishers, 2007, https://psycnet.apa.org/record/2006-11798-011
4. Juliano Laran, Chris Janiszewski and Anthony Salerno, 'Exploring the Differences Between Conscious and Unconscious Goal Pursuit', *Journal of Marketing Research*, 1 June 2016.
5. K.C. Berridge, M.L. Kringelbach, 'Pleasure Systems in the Brain', *Neuron*, 2015, https://www.ncbi.nlm.nih.gov/pmc/articles/PMC4425246/,
6. Clark Buckner, 'Four Chemicals That Activate Happiness, and How to Gamify Them', Technology Advice, 30 October 2017, https://technologyadvice.com/blog/information-technology/activate-chemicals-gamify-happiness-nicole-lazzaro/. Dopamine is involved more with anticipation and striving than the actual 'happiness' feeling. Oxytocin makes us feel empathy with and closeness to others. Serotonin puts you in a good mood. Endorphins mask pain or discomfort and help

with the 'fight or flight' response. The exact role of each chemical is under debate and study. The general idea that specific neurochemicals contribute to a sensation of happiness is well established. See, 'How Brain Chemicals Influence Mood and Health', UPMC, *Neurosurgery and Brain Health*, 4 September 2016, https://share.upmc.com/2016/09/about-brain-chemicals/

7. This is real enough that people whose reward systems are compromised can suffer from serious disorders like anhedonia (lack of pleasure) or dysphoria (negative affect or emotions).
8. Gregory P. Strauss, et al., 'Anticipatory vs Consummatory Pleasure: What Is the Nature of Hedonic Deficits in Schizophrenia?', *Psychiatry Research*, vol. 187, 1-2 (2011), https://www.sciencedirect.com/science/article/abs/pii/S0165178111000461?via%3Dihub
9. Richard M. Ryan and Edward L. Deci, 'Self-Determination Theory and the Facilitation of Intrinsic Motivation, Social Development, and Well-Being', *American Psychologist*, January 2000, https://selfdeterminationtheory.org/SDT/documents/2000_RyanDeci_SDT.pdf

   Ryan and Deci, 'Self-Determination Theory: Basic Psychological Needs in Motivation, Development, and Wellness', Guilford Publishing, New York, 2017.
10. Japan Dentures Recycling Association, https://disposalknowhow.com/dentures/
11. Steve Genco captures these concepts simply but in much greater detail in his book *Intuitive Marketing*, pp. 208–10.
12. National Car Rental TV commercial, iSpot.tv, https://www.ispot.tv/ad/7EJ5/national-car-rental-control-enthusiast-feat-patrick-warburton
13. Tanya Gazdik, 'National Car Rental Extends "Go Like A Pro"', MediaPost, 12 September 2016, https://www.mediapost.com/publications/article/284369/national-car-rental-extends-go-like-a-pro.html,
14. Mastercard baseball commercial, YouTube, https://youtu.be/71KAO_bmc2o

   'MasterCard, McCann-Erickson and a Campaign That Never Got Old? Priceless', AAAA.org, 1997, https://www.aaaa.org/timeline-event/mastercard-mccann-erickson-campaign-never-got-old-priceless/
15. Ancient Indian philosophers were so unhinged by the idea that material pleasures (derived from *prakriti* or creation) could never deliver eternal happiness that they posited that real happiness could only be achieved by relieving the mind of all desires. Patanjali, in the

Yoga Sutra, regards the mind as an unwelcome appendage to the soul (*purusha*). By stilling the mind (ceasing thought, cognition, ideas and images—or, together, the *vrittis*) through meditation, one can liberate the soul to return to the eternal reality (Brahma). This, by the way, was a huge leap of faith by Hindu philosophers, who chose not to dwell on the possibility that vacuuming the mind of all might lead merely to an empty mind rather than any broader reconciliation with the universal soul (moksha). If everyone did this, we would not need brands, as no one would be wanting or buying anything. Luckily, even most Indians treat these ideas as only a compartmentalized thought experiment, and most yoga enthusiasts worldwide are not clued into its actual purpose and treat yoga (a dumbed-down adaptation of Lord Shiva's dance, *tandav nritya*) as a stretching exercise. For a good discussion on the Hindu philosophy of yoga, read *The Yoga Sutra of Patanjali* by Edwin F. Bryant.

16. Esteban Ortiz-Ospina and Max Roser, 'Happiness and Life Satisfaction', Our World in Data, 2017, https://ourworldindata.org/happiness-and-life-satisfaction. It is noted that an average happiness score of 7 is likely to be seen in more developed countries like the US. In countries like Burkina Faso, where there is political turmoil and the basic needs of the population are not met, the score is lower, at around 4.5. Also to be noted is the 'Easterlin Paradox', named after Richard Easterlin. At the heart of the paradox is the fact that richer countries tend to have higher self-reported happiness, yet in some countries for which repeated surveys were available over the course of the 1970s, happiness was not increasing with rising national incomes.
17. Paul Bloom, 'The Good Life: Happiness', Open Yale Courses, https://youtu.be/7dep9KPWp3g?t=1200. Paul Bloom, of Yale, who has a phenomenal lecture on this topic, does point out that there are exceptions to the rule of regression to the mean for happiness. For example, breast enhancement and reduction surgeries do make women sustainably happier.

## Chapter 9: Brands with Purpose: Branding to Make a Difference

1. 'A Brand New World', *The Economist*, 25 January 2020, https://www.economist.com/business/2020/01/23/it-has-never-been-easier-to-launch-a-new-brand
2. Zelle is a way to easily send small sums of money to anyone with a bank account from a mobile phone. See zellepay.com.

3. Allison Gauss, '6 Socially Responsible Companies to Applaud', Classy, https://www.classy.org/blog/6-socially-responsible-companies-applaud/
4. Pfizer UK, https://www.pfizer.co.uk/tackling-rise-antimicrobial-resistance
5. Tom Huddleston Jr., 'How Allbirds Went from Silicon Valley Fashion Staple to a $1.4 Billion Sneaker Start-up', CNBC, 18 December 2018, https://www.cnbc.com/2018/12/14/allbirds-went-from-silicon-valley-staple-to-billion-sneaker-startup.html

## Part Three: How to Execute Cognitive Brands

### Chapter 10: Tales from the Trenches: New Principles for Brand Execution

1. 'Hallucinations: Symptoms & Signs', MedicineNet, https://www.medicinenet.com/hallucinations/symptoms.htm
2. Paul Fletcher, 'Psychosis: Bending Reality to See Around the Corners', TEDx Cambridge University, YouTube, 3 December 2016, https://youtu.be/tV2RLLtOgL4?t=312
3. Daniel Kahneman, 'Objective Happiness', in Daniel Kahneman, Edward Diener, Norbert Schwarz (eds), *Well-Being: Foundations of Hedonic Psychology*, Russell Sage Foundation, pp. 3–25, 1999.
   Dr Karl Kruszelnicki, *Curious and Curiouser*, Macmillan, 2010.
4. This connecting of the dots is sometimes referred to as a Bayesian inference model of the brain.
5. D. Kahneman, 'Evaluation by Moments: Past and Future', in D. Kahneman and A. Tversky (eds), *Choices, Values and Frames*, pp. 693–708 (New York: Cambridge University Press and the Russell Sage Foundation, 2000).
6. Steve Gillman, 'The Science of Tipping: 16 Proven Ways to Increase Your Tip Income', Penny Hoarder, 26 March 2015, https://www.thepennyhoarder.com/make-money/side-gigs/how-to-get-more-tips/
7. Jill Rosen, 'Element of Surprise Helps Babies Learn Best, Johns Hopkins Researchers Say', Johns Hopkins Magazine, 2 April 2015, https://hub.jhu.edu/2015/04/02/surprise-babies-learning/
8. https://www.preventivmeasures.com/
9. https://www.youtube.com/watch?v=gP92j-uEnps
10. Tanya Lewis, 'Pi, Anyone? The Secret to Memorizing Tens of Thousands of Digits', LiveScience, 13 March 2015, https://www.livescience.com/50134-pi-day-memory-experts.html

11. 'Most Pi Places Memorised', Guiness World Records, https://www.guinnessworldrecords.com/world-records/most-pi-places-memorised?fb_comment_id=752963494793308_901656546590668
12. '2016 Lords of the Boulevard, Red Wine, Napa Valley', Tank Garage Winery, https://www.tankgaragewinery.com/product/2016-Lords-of-the-Boulevard-Red-Wine-Napa-Valley?pageID=F1B68FC6-0646-3105-39E7-367771BBB06A&sortBy=DisplayOrder&maxRows=100&&productListName=Current%20Releases&position=17
13. 'Google Search: Reunion', YouTube, https://www.youtube.com/watch?v=gHGDN9-oFJE
14. Norbert Schwarz, Herbert Bless, Fritz Strack, Gisela Klumpp, Helga Rittenauer-Schatka, Annette Simons, 'Ease of Retrieval as Information: Another Look at the Availability Heuristic', *Journal of Personality and Social Psychology*, 1991, https://psycnet.apa.org/doiLanding?doi=10.1037%2F0022-3514.61.2.195
15. Christopher Chabris and Daniel Simons, *The Invisible Gorilla: How Our Intuitions Deceive Us* (New York: Harmony Books, 2011).
16. Selective Attention Test, YouTube, https://www.youtube.com/watch?v=vJG698U2Mvo
17. Old Spice commercials, YouTube, https://youtu.be/VrdqqTvyiV8
18. https://www.inc.com/articles/201108/5-marketing-lessons-from-old-spice.html
19. 'Demand Removal of Sexist Billboard!!!', Change.org, https://www.change.org/p/fairfield-pool-278-meadow-street-fairfield-ct-demand-removal-of-sexist-billboard
20. Lisa Geraci, Mark A. McDaniel, Tyler M. Miller, Matthew L. Hughes, 'The Bizarreness Effect: Evidence for the Critical Influence of Retrieval Processes', National Library of Medicine, https://www.ncbi.nlm.nih.gov/pubmed/23737359
21. Martin Lindstrom, *Brand Sense: Sensory Secrets behind the Stuff We Buy* (New York: Free Press, 2005).

## Chapter 11: Brand Sensations: Role of the Five Senses in Selling

1. Robin Givhan, 'Seriously, Prada, What Were You Thinking?: Why the Fashion Industry Keeps Bumbling into Racist Imagery', *Washington Post*, 15 December 2018, https://www.washingtonpost.com/arts-entertainment/2018/12/15/seriously-prada-what-were-you-thinking-why-fashion-industry-keeps-bumbling-into-racist-imagery/

2. ‘Scent Marketing in Flagship Store Burberry Regent Street’, Zaluti, 30 January 2017, https://www.zaluti.com/blog/scent-marketing-in-flagship-store-burberry-regent-street
3. Cate Trotter, ‘Inside the Retail Strategy of Burberry’, Insider Trends, 16 January 2018, https://www.insider-trends.com/inside-retail-strategy-burberry/#ixzz6NT422F3i
4. G. White, S. Fishbein, J. Rutsein, ‘Passionate Love and the Misattribution of Arousal’, *Journal of Personality and Social Psychology*, 41(1), pp. 56–62, 1981, https://psycnet.apa.org/record/1982-05734-001
5. Prudential TV commercial, ‘The Prudential Walkways Experiment’, iSpot.tv, https://www.ispot.tv/ad/wBUg/prudential-the-prudential-walkways-experiment#
6. April H. Crusco and Christopher G. Wetzel, ‘The Midas Touch: The Effects of Interpersonal Touch on Restaurant Tipping’, *Personality and Social Psychology Bulletin*, 1 December 1984, https://doi.org/10.1177/0146167284104003
7. ‘Human Emotion 6.3: Emotion Behavior III (Touch)’, YouTube, https://youtu.be/HqEG2USh-J4
8. ‘Creating “I’d Like to Buy the World a Coke”’, Coca-Cola Company, https://www.coca-colacompany.com/news/id-like-to-buy-the-world-a-coke
9. Ricki Green, ‘Coca-Cola Connects Indians and Pakistanis Together through a Live Communications Portal Via Leo Burnett Chicago and Leo Burnett Sydney’, Campaign Brief, 20 May 2013, https://campaignbrief.com/coke-connects-indians-and-paki/
10. ‘Coca-Cola Small World Machines - Bringing India & Pakistan Together’, YouTube, 19 May 2013, https://www.youtube.com/watch?v=ts_4vOUDImE&feature=youtu.be
11. Lawrence Williams and Joshua Ackerman, ‘Please Touch the Merchandise’, *Harvard Business Review*, 15 December 2011, https://hbr.org/2011/12/please-touch-the-merchandise
12. ‘The Psychology of Sound’, CBC, 24 May 2019, https://www.cbc.ca/natureofthings/m_features/the-psychology-of-sound
13. Klemens M. Knoferle, Eric R. Spangenberg, Andreas Herrmann and Jan R. Landwehr, ‘It Is All in the Mix: The Interactive Effect of Music Tempo and Mode on In-Store Sales’, *Marketing Letters*, 2012.
14. Joel Beckerman, *The Sonic Boom: How Sound Transforms the Way We Think, Feel, and Buy* (Boston: Mariner Books, 2014), p. 53.
15. Houghton Mifflin Harcourt, ‘The Fajita Effect’, Medium, 21 October 2014, https://medium.com/galleys/the-fajita-effect-504838a5f2f0

16. Carolina Gomez-Diaz and Richard Benton, 'The Joy of Sex Pheromones', EMBO Press, 13 September 2013, https://www.ncbi.nlm.nih.gov/pmc/articles/PMC3807217/
17. 'From Signature Fragrances to Curated Background Music', Equal Strategy https://www.equalstrategy.com/portfolio/media-scent-marketing-music-styling/
18. 'Sales of the Leading Liquid Laundry Detergent Brands of the United States in 2018', Statista, https://www.statista.com/statistics/188716/top-liquid-laundry-detergent-brands-in-the-united-states/
19. A.V. Jaeggi and C.P. Van Schaik, 'The Evolution of Food Sharing in Primates', *Behavioral Ecology and Sociobiology*, 65, 2125, 2011.
20. 'The Champagne Tasting Experience', Champagne.fr, https://www.champagne.fr/en/tasting-and-appreciation/champagne-tasting-experience/language-of-the-senses
21. Julie Beck, 'Our Moods, Our Foods', *Atlantic*, 6 March 2014, https://www.theatlantic.com/health/archive/2014/03/our-moods-our-foods/284238/

## Chapter 12: Minding Our Manners: Branding with a Conscience

1. Alejandro Cremades, 'How This Entrepreneur Turned a $10,000 Startup Investment into a $600 Million Acquisition', *Forbes*, 26 March 2019, https://www.forbes.com/sites/alejandrocremades/2019/03/26/how-this-entrepreneur-turned-a-10000-startup-investment-into-a-600-million-acquisition/#4eec4642b7e1
2. https://www.merriam-webster.com/dictionary/Rx
3. Cathy Siegner, 'RXBAR's Prescription for the Future: New Name, New Products, Changes in Leadership', FoodDive, 7 March 2019, https://www.fooddive.com/news/rxbars-prescription-for-the-future-new-name-new-products-changes-in-lea/549696/
4. Jialan Wang and Benjamin J. Keys, 'Perverse Nudges: Minimum Payments and Debt Paydown in Consumer Credit Cards', *Penn Wharton Public Policy Initiative*, Book 25, 2014, http://repository.upenn.edu/pennwhartonppi/25
5. H. Matute, F. Blanco, I. Yarritu, M. Díaz-Lago, M.A. Vadillo, I. Barberia, 'Illusions of Causality: How They Bias Our Everyday Thinking and How They Could Be Reduced', *Frontiers in Psychology*, 2 July 2015.
6. https://www.fda.gov/drugs/warning-letters-and-notice-violation-letters-pharmaceutical-companies/warning-letters-2019

7. Arunesh Mathur et al., 'Dark Patterns at Scale: Findings from a Crawl of 11K Shopping Websites', *Proc. ACM Hum.-Comput. Interact*, vol. 3, No. CSCW, article 81, November 2019, https://arxiv.org/pdf/1907.07032.pdf
8. Shane Goldmacher, 'How Trump Steered Supporters into Unwitting Donations', *New York Times*, 3 April 2021, https://www.nytimes.com/2021/04/03/us/politics/trump-donations.html
9. https://www.darkpatterns.org/types-of-dark-pattern
10. Alex Rosenblat and Luke Stark, 'Algorithmic Labor and Information Asymmetries: A Case Study of Uber's Drivers', *International Journal of Communication*, 30 July 2016, https://papers.ssrn.com/sol3/papers.cfm?abstract_id=2686227
11. Noam Scheiber, 'How Uber Uses Psychological Tricks to Push Its Drivers' Buttons', *New York Times*, 2 April 2017, https://www.nytimes.com/interactive/2017/04/02/technology/uber-drivers-psychological-tricks.html
12. D.J. Kuss and M.D. Griffiths, 'Social Networking Sites and Addiction: Ten Lessons Learned', *International Journal of Environmental Research and Public Health*, 2017, https://www.mdpi.com/1660-4601/14/3/311
13. This comes from the great German philosopher Immanuel Kant, from his 1785 work *Groundwork of the Metaphysics of Morals*, which states, 'Act only according to that maxim whereby you can, at the same time, will that it should become a universal law.'
14. Stephen J. Genco, *Intuitive Marketing*, p. 350.

## Chapter 13: Where Do We Go from Here?

1. Saga Briggs, 'Neuromarketing: 10 Lessons About the Brain from a Growing Field', informED, 19 March 2019, https://www.opencolleges.edu.au/informed/
2. L.F. Barrett, 'Solving the Emotion Paradox: Categorization and the Experience of Emotion', *Personality and Social Psychology Review*, 10 (1), 2006, pp. 20–46.
3. Gregory Berns and Sara E. Moore, 'A Neural Predictor of Cultural Popularity', SSRNm 17 December 2010, https://ssrn.com/abstract=1742971
4. Samuel B. Barnett, Moran Cerf, 'A Ticket for Your Thoughts: Method for Predicting Content Recall and Sales Using Neural Similarity of Moviegoers', *Journal of Consumer Research*, volume 44, issue 1, June 2017, pp. 160–81, https://doi.org/10.1093/jcr/ucw083

5. Robin Higie Coulter and Gerald Zaltman, 'Using the Zaltman Metaphor Elicitation Technique to Understand Brand Images', *NA - Advances in Consumer Research*, volume 21, 1994, ed. Chris T. Allen and Deborah Roedder John, Provo, UT: Association for Consumer Research, pp. 501–507, https://www.acrwebsite.org/volumes/7644
6. Philip Perry, 'Think You Have Only 5 Senses? You've Actually Got About 14 to 20', Big Think, 2 May 2018, https://bigthink.com/philip-perry/think-you-have-only-5-senses-its-actually-a-lot-more-than-that
7. Hal Conick, 'Read This Story to Learn How Behavioral Economics Can Improve Marketing', American Marketing Association, 12 January 2018, https://www.ama.org/marketing-news/read-this-story-to-learn-how-behavioral-economics-can-improve-marketing/